The Becoming of Time

The Becoming of Time

Integrating Physical and Religious Time

Lawrence W. Fagg

DUKE UNIVERSITY PRESS

Durham & London 2003

© 2003 Duke University Press

All rights reserved

First edition 1995

Published by Scholars Press

Printed in the United States of

America on acid-free paper ∞

Library of Congress Cataloging-

in-Publication Data appear on the

last printed page of this book.

To a man of love and courage,
my nephew, Alfred Watson Shea

TABLE OF CONTENTS

PREFACE

The simple question, "What is time?" has challenged the imagination and intellectual capacity of the world's greatest thinkers since the dawn of recorded history. Their contemplations about time and relevant temporal phenomena have followed every conceivable avenue of reason and logic, and unfolded a myriad of vistas provided by intuition, imagination, and spiritual insight. The consequent accumulation of literature is vast, awesome, and bewildering.

Given this formidable body of thought, I would never have attempted to write my first, much less my second, book about time were it not for a rather pivotal event when I was well into my middle years. Following a growing interest in world religions, I gradually became involved in a graduate program in religion at George Washington University, to which I devoted my efforts whenever I could spare time from nuclear physics. Toward the end of this period my advisor suggested writing a thesis comparing the time views of two men well-versed in physical sciences and also possessed of unique religious orientations, Erwin Schrödinger and Alfred North Whitehead.

This work suggested a way to approach the very general problem of understanding subjective, humanly experienced time and objectively observed or measured time as well as their interrelation. I did this by confining the study of this duality to an examination of time concepts from modern physics and the major world religions. While these subjects have remained my primary emphasis, I have unavoidably had to assimilate considerable amounts of information from the fields of philosophy, psychology, biology, chemistry, history, and literature. Nevertheless, to the best of my knowledge this basically two-pronged, physics-religion approach to the problem of time is relatively unique.

Often I have heard lectures on a subject directly or indirectly involving the consideration of time in which speakers have attempted to add color and meaning to their words by concluding with the quotation of some time-related passage of religious scripture. With this book I take religion seriously by bringing the religious time concepts that such passages represent into intimate juxtaposition with time concepts of modern physics. I do this with the hope and intent of providing a basis for deeper insights into the problem of time.

In writing this book I have tried to thread the dangerous and narrow line between academic rigor on the one hand and readability for the interested lay person on the other. Accordingly, except for $E = mc^2$, I have avoided using any mathematical equations in the main text. Also, in order to give additional thrust to the theme of the book, I have restricted the choice of words in my writing for two reasons. First, I have insisted on conveying the importance of speaking of time on, and in, its own terms by refusing to use patently spatial words such as "arrow," "direction," or "linear." Admittedly even the words I have used are by no means purged of spatial connotations. Nevertheless I by no means regret the effort, for it at least gives emphasis to the depth of the problem of time. Even with access to a full vocabulary it seems impossible to adequately express the irreversible, holistic becoming of time.

My second constraint in selection of words comes in expressing the concept of God when treating the religious views of time. There is a glaring deficiency in the English language in that there is no genderless pronoun for God. Try as I may, I have not been able to suggest an appropriate one; "It" hardly expresses the necessary reverence. So except in using quotations of others, I have refused to use the usual male pronouns at all. This is far more than a perfunctory courtesy to women. It touches on a significant theological issue, because giving God a gender directly impairs our access to a more realistic and valid sense of God. The anthropomorphic aspect of God can still be apprehended without the obfuscation of gender.

Modern physics, especially astronomy, cosmology, and elementary particle physics, are rapidly progressing fields. I have tried to base my interpretations concerning time on the very latest published results. Accordingly, what is written in this book is based on results available as of April, 2002.

With the foregoing constraints and limitations in mind I have pursued this treatment of time by dividing the book into five parts. Part I introduces the subject in terms of the subjective and objective duality as expressed in science and religion in Chapter 1, and in philosophy in Chapter 2. A survey of time concepts from modern physics and world religions is presented in Part II, where the modern physics discussion is approached from the viewpoint of our being enveloped in a kind of "cosmic cocoon," whose limits are realized in terms of the relativity and quantum theories as well as electromagnetic theory. In Part III I examine the nature of time from the viewpoints of the question of whether time began, its relation to motion and space, its irreversible character, the uniqueness of the moment, and the notion of timelessness. I discuss time in Part IV in the context of the possible future of humankind and the universe, present some interpretations of the relevance of time and death, and treat the question of the reality of the future. I conclude with Part V by first considering arguments for time being described as a two-fold concept as well as a unified concept, and finally by addressing the age-old , unyielding question: "What is time?".

I am sincerely grateful to Prof. Joe Rosen, Fr. Christopher Corbally, S.J., Dr. Eugene Mallove, Mr. John Lewis, and my wife, Mary Skipp, for prereading the manuscript. I also greatly appreciate helpful discussions with Prof. Joe Rosen, Prof. David Park, Dr. Anindita Balslev, Prof. Harry Yeide, Prof. Robert G. Jones, Prof. Alf Hiltebeitel, Dr. J. T. Fraser, Prof. Jack Leibowitz, Fr. Christopher Corbally, S.J., Prof. Marjorie Suchocki, Dr. Timothy Eastman, Prof. Sonya Quitsland, and Dr. Francoise Macar. The excellent work of Nancy Monacelli on the figures is greatly appreciated. I particularly wish to express my gratitude to Prof. Harry Yeide for having guided me into such an intriguing field during my graduate study in religion. The patience, support, and forbearance of Mary Kathryn Winner in the typing and word processing of the manuscript were absolutely invaluable in the writing of this book.

Lawrence Fagg
Stephens City, Virginia

Part I   THINKING ABOUT TIME

"Ah, time is a riddling thing, and hard it is to expound its essence!"
—Thomas Mann

Some concept of time vitalizes the core of virtually every category of human intellectual and spiritual endeavor. Like the translucent facets of a diamond, perceptions of time from the viewpoint of one cultural source can complement and illumine those from another. These temporal perceptions and their implications in the quest for meaning have haunted the imagination of thinkers and scholars for millennia. The possibility of some kind of synthesis of time concepts from different sources continues to this day to challenge the ingenuity and thinking of modern scientists and humanists alike.

Given the vast heritage of thought and writing about the problem of time, what is the most propitious starting point for the journey into time we pursue in this book? How do we start thinking about time? Certainly one starting point is provided by the basic realization of how we experience life. There is our inner, subjective world of sensations, feelings, and thoughts, and the outer world of nature, creatures, and other humans that evoke from us a continued and varied chain of reactions. These fundamental facts by their very nature impose on us a two–fold approach in our living. We tend to objectify the outer world and tend to intuit and feel our inner world. Thus it seems natural that subjective and objective components might comprise our view of time.

In the next two chapters different aspects of this subjective–objective duality will be discussed. The duality is introduced in the first chapter in terms of the science and religion dichotomy in general, and later in terms of an approach to the problem of time that is primarily confined to the joint consideration of concepts from modern physics and the major world religions. Possibilities for finding a unified view of time are also outlined. A distillation of the philosophical thought that expresses objective and subjective temporal concepts, and helps complete our initial thinking about time, is then given in Chapter 2.

1   TIME: A TWO–FOLD MYSTERY?

"Time is the One Essential Mystery."

—Jorg Luis Borges

TIME AS A DUALITY

Despite oppressively hot summers, messy winters, and a frenetic life-style, Washington, D.C. has its moments. At least it has for me. It was a soothing spring morning some years ago. I had just missed the Metro; it would be a five or ten minute wait for the next train. I put aside the reading material with which I usually reinforce myself, and simply sat.

Letting myself drift to this and that, I happened to look down at my watch with its second hand spastically jerking ahead in one second increments. Somehow it reminded me of a Caribbean breakdancer. But at the same time as this precise ticking was going on, I became aware of my presence within the enfolding presence of the budding trees surrounding the station. My living moment, as I felt it, was different. It was smoothly, gently, indistinguishably succeeded by the next moment, and the next. I could only diffusely record a given moment, then in the gliding procession of succeeding moments it drifted into the past.

This dual experience of objectively observing the measured precision of a timepiece and subjectively sensing the living moments with no clear markers to separate them, capsulizes one of the apparent paradoxes characterizing contemplation about time. It serves as a doorway, opening to awareness of the essential mystery of time.

Aspects of this dual view of time in one form or another have occupied the thought of philosophers, scientists, and religious scholars for centuries. It has profoundly challenged these thinkers, generating a resultant accumulation of a massive body of literature on the subject. Relatively recent work addressing this challenge involving an essentially two–pronged approach to the study of time are not hard to find. For example, some authors (e.g., Park 80, Denbigh 81) clearly support the separation of the time of human consciousness and subjective experience from that of physical theory and objective measurement. Undoubtedly investigation of the validity of this position, so rich in dimension and subtlety, will continue for years to come.

SCIENCE AND RELIGION

However, the fundamental subjective–objective, or the intimately related intuitive–rational, dichotomy comes into play on an even larger and more inclusive stage than that concerned strictly with time. For example, in one way or another, it has been a central ingredient in the discourse of philosophers since the time of the Greeks. In particular it is obviously at the very heart of the dialogue between science and religion that has been going on with varying intensity for centuries. It is certainly in the comparative consideration of these two areas of human culture that the objective–subjective polarity comes into sharpest focus and reaches its richest development. This being the case, a joint science–religion approach to the problem of time and its apparent duality suggests itself as a fruitful general area in which to search for an inviting path of inquiry.

To lay the groundwork for this general approach, it will be helpful to outline very briefly selected aspects of the historical background of the science–religion interchange in order to better appreciate the subsequent discussion of their relation in modern times. This discussion in turn will provide a useful basis for ultimately justifying the more specific physics–modern religions inquiry adopted in this book.

Let us start with the discovery of Copernicus that the Earth is not at the center of the universe. In these early years the science and religion dialogue sometimes had life–threatening consequences. The story of Galileo's conflicts with the church is well–known. After great tribulation and moral wrenching, he managed at least to emerge from the fray with all of his organs in tact. However, Giordano Bruno was not so lucky. He eagerly embraced Copernicus' discovery and further postulated that the universe is a life–impregnated cosmos, a totally unified and animated system with other inhabited worlds. This was among the views for which he was burned at the stake in 1600.

Bruno lived just a little too early, because his death launched the century of what could be termed the "First Scientific Revolution," highlighted by the monumental work of Kepler and Newton in understanding the force of gravity. This period in turn served as a grounding for the 18th Century Enlightenment (or Age of Reason) which was characterized by a wealth of rational and humanitarian thought as well as further scientific discovery.

Meanwhile Western religion was being racked with internal problems starting with the schisms of the Reformation inspired by Martin Luther and John Calvin. However, internal reform was also developing within the Catholic Church itself, the seeds of which were planted as early as the time of St. Catherine of Sienna in the 14th Century. This reform more fully developed with the founding of the Jesuits by St. Ignatius of Loyola and with the work of other saints, including St. Theresa of Avila. The Jesuits were especially effective in eliminating corruption, improving church administration, and insisting on educational standards for the clergy. It was undoubtedly this latter program which helped originally to bring the Church into closer contact with the world of science and ultimately had some effect on the theology of the Church, although resistance to science continued in the Church into the 19th Century.

The Church was especially challenged in the latter half of the 19th Century with what could be termed the "Second Scientific Revolution." Darwin's study of evolution profoundly altered our idea of who we are. Freud and Marx produced blueprints for the fields of psychology and politics, which were undoubtedly among the early justifications for ultimately calling them sciences. Maxwell unified electricity and magnetism in a theory of elegant beauty and symmetry.

However, the final and climactic phase of this revolution came at the beginning of this century when the relativity and quantum theories burst onto the scene. These two pillars of modern physical thought matured in a short span of 30 years with an incredibly productive intellectual interchange involving, for example, the now–classic argument between Einstein and Bohr over the completeness of quantum theory. Bohr won, and his interpretation of quantum theory is still considered today to be that of the mainstream in physics; but other interpretations continue to contend. In any case the reverberations of the quantum and relativity theories in terms of their philosophic ramifications and their meaning in our lives and future are still being cogently felt today.

In the presence of this mind–shattering explosion of scientific understanding and the attendant technology, religion in effect could only helplessly stand by in awe, and in some cases dismay. The scientific eruption was seen by some as a devastating blow to existing religiously based ideas and a threat to the integrity of long–standing theological structures, especially among the Western religions.

However, there were many religious leaders, Western and Eastern, who made sincere attempts to reconcile their theology with the results of this burgeoning scientific cornucopia. Groundwork for present–day science–religion dialogue was also laid by the religious and philosophic interpretation of relativity and quantum theory provided by several of the contributors to these theories, especially Schrödinger, Heisenberg, and Eddington. (Schrödinger 47, Schrödinger 51, Schrödinger 58, Schrödinger 64, Heisenberg 71, Heisenberg 74, Eddington 29, Eddington 35).[1]

Since World War II there has been a more intense, self–conscious, and deliberate effort to bring the scientific and religious communities into dialogue. A number of universities and colleges have unfrozen the traditional demarcations of the scholastic disciplines embodied in their academic departments and have been offering interdisciplinary programs and courses, including many in science and religion. A growing array of books treating various aspects of the subject are now available, including several for popular consumption (e.g., Capra 77, Jastrow 80, Davies 83) as well as books at a more rigorous and scholarly level (e.g., Barbour 97, Peacocke 81, Jones 86, Russell et al. 88, Polkinghorne 98, Barbour 90, Peacocke 90, Russell et al. 93). In the last few decades several active organizations whose specific mission is the search for meaningful relationships between science and religion have come into being.[2]

Among these I have been primarily involved in the Institute on Religion in an Age of Science (IRAS) which holds week–long summer conferences on Star Island, ten miles off the coast of Portsmouth, NH. The conference theme each year varies. A spectrum of subjects from genetics and cosmology to the meaning of God have been addressed by speakers from such diverse fields as physics, biology, psychology, philosophy, literature, and religion. Somehow the haunting beauty of this small rocky island seems to play a role, serve as a catalyst, in

---

[1]For a selected collection of the mystical thought of these physicists and others see Wilbur 84.

[2]For example, the Institute on Religion in an Age of Science, which sponsors "Zygon," a journal of science and religion; the Center for Theology and Natural Sciences in Berkeley, CA; the Zygon Center for Religion and Science; the Center for Process Studies in Claremont, CA; and the European Society for the Study of Science and Theology, Weil am Rhein, Germany.

promoting dialogue among such a divergent group. In between conference sessions when I can sit out on the rocks, watch the churning surf, and listen to the seagulls laughing, my contemplation somehow becomes more integrated and more deeply anchored. The spiritual magnetism of this little gift of the sea, with the quaint 19th Century stone chapel crowning its highest point, has drawn me and many of my colleagues back year after year.

The dialogue that takes place at such conferences as well as other conferences and scholarly interchanges throughout the science–religion community are made possible in part because there has developed a clearer mutual understanding of the bases for knowledge and truth in each of the two fields. The religious scholars on the one hand see that science attempts to understand the predictable and reproducible features of nature. They realize that truth in science is based on the experimental method. Logical and rational interpretation of experiments suggest a theory, which to be successful must, with the simplest, most reduced model, describe and predict the behavior of a large class of phenomena. It must be amenable to further unrelenting, ever more refined experimental scrutiny; that is, it must continually submit to the test of falsifiability. They also understand that while a formulated theory may have an applicability to a considerable range of natural phenomena, this range is nevertheless limited. And although a given theory may someday be subsumed by another encompassing an even larger domain of nature, during the period that it is experimentally supported it generally enjoys universal acceptance. This is because anyone anywhere can test the theory using the appropriate techniques and equipment.

On the other hand the scientists in this interdisciplinary community realize that truth in a religion arises from the spiritual insight and revelation of its leaders, and that the truth's verification comes from the common spiritual experience of the religion's adherents. They understand that, in contrast to a scientific theory, the range of applicability of the religion is in principle universal in the sense that the religion will generally have a world–view that includes all mankind and nature.

In general it seems clear that if science and religion are to become more completely reconciled and their relation to become more fully understood, theologians of whatever religion must come to grips with the impressive accomplishments of modern science. However, scientists may also come to appreciate more deeply that religious traditions, particularly as expressed by their literature, constitute a rich repository of ancient, abiding insight and of the accumulated wisdom of centuries of thought and spiritual contemplation. It is there, a treasured heritage, waiting to be understood and interpreted for use today.

History can certainly provide us with inspiring examples of people who have realized fulfillment and productivity by engaging in both scientific and religious thought and pursuit. St. Augustine's analysis of time is impressively rigorous and objective; the Austrian monk, Gregor Johann Mendel, provided us with some of the basic tenets of genetics. As counterparts in science, Newton was strongly influenced by some distinctly Christian religious viewpoints; and in modern times, Erwin Schrödinger, one of the originators of quantum mechanics, was deeply affected by Vedantic Hindu thought.

What can we distill from these remarks concerning the relation of science and religion? I believe that religion needs to utilize the knowledge gained from science to revitalize its theological structure and to refine its moral and spiritual values for more effective meaning and use in the 21st Century. However, science needs religion for more enlightened and altruistic motivation, for deeper intuitive insights into nature's essence and its relation to mankind, and for enrichment of its meaning in the mosaic of human culture.

Einstein once said, "science without religion is lame, religion without science is blind" (Einstein 54, p. 55). Although he always rejected the idea of an anthropomorphic god, he was strongly influenced by the philosophy of Spinoza and maintained that "the cosmic religious feeling is the strongest and noblest motive for scientific research" (Einstein 54, p. 49). Eddington observed that it is "somewhat of an anomaly that among the many extraphysical aspects of experience, religion alone should be singled out as specially in need of reconciliation with the knowledge contained in science" (Eddington 29).

I extract from these reflections that science is far from a monitor of religion. However, science with its characteristic of universal acceptance can have at least an indirect ecumenical influence on religion. On the other hand religion can inspire, guide, and support the faith which science has that nature can be understood in terms of rational quantifiable models. Faith and reason are not incompatible. They are exchanging brothers. Science and religion must both be considered as growing, evolving, but interacting, pursuits.

Pursuits in science and religion based on these or similar principles are going on today with increasing vigor. Indeed there seems to be an underlying restlessness in both the scientific and religious communities. They each seem engaged in an inarticulable groping for sweeping and fundamental reformulations of the scientific and spiritual conceptions of the universe, its operation and meaning.

Theoretical physicist John Wheeler, has on occasion speculated that the next great breakthrough in physics may have a quality of meaning in its foundation. It is as if a "third scientific revolution" may be fermenting and ready to erupt at any time. However, attendant with it may also be a revolution in the relation between science and religion.

Why have I expended the last few pages in discourse about the science–religion dialogue? It is because generally our most sharply focused objective views about time come from the sciences, more precisely the physical sciences, while some of our most penetrating subjective views about time are drawn from the religions. Of the physical sciences, physics has presented us in this century with the greatest changes in our objective and rational notions about time and space. These changes have arisen not only from the relativity and quantum theories, but also from great advances in the fields of thermodynamics, astronomy, cosmology, and elementary particles. On the other hand it is from the religious traditions of this world that we can derive our deepest awareness about our subjective and intuitive sense of time.

In many respects physics and religion lie at opposite ends of what might be considered the spectrum of scholastic disciplines. That is, the spectrum would range from the study of the most irreducible elements of nature, physics ("the hardest of the sciences"), to the most holistic of studies embracing the largest syntheses of human concern, religion ("the softest of the humanities"). However, in bringing together these two extremes in our examination of time, any concerted intent to merge the two disciplines or subordinate one to the other must be avoided. They are separate enterprises, but ones which are in need of dialogue.

TIME AS A UNITY

Whether or not the approach is primarily via physics and religion, underlying one's attempts to elucidate the objective and subjective ideas of time is the almost primal apprehension that they might be somehow reconciled, and perhaps be simply aspects of a more fundamental unified perception of time itself.

One approach occasionally used by many scholars to help reconcile dual views about something is to invoke a generalization of what is known as Bohr's Complementarity Principle. Among other arguments, Niels Bohr used this principle in his discussions with Einstein and others to reconcile the wave and particle characteristics of electrons, photons, and other inhabitants of the microscopic world.

As I will point out in Chapter 16, perhaps some case may be made for regarding the two views of time as complementary and constituting two mutually exclusive yet equally valid expressions of time, both of which are necessary for a complete picture. The Chinese have a more gracious, holistic, and intimately interactive means of expressing such complementarity in terms of the Yin–Yang Principle, the yin being feminine and intuitive, the yang, masculine and rational.

On the other hand perhaps under more penetrating investigation, one of the two modes may ultimately be revealed as dominant, as somehow reducible to the other. Or, perhaps both modes may be subsumed by an integrating concept other than complementarity.

Whether the subjective and objective descriptions of time can be integrated or not, it clearly behooves us to understand as extensively as possible the relation between the two if we are to comprehend more fully the nature of time. I believe that a significant problem encumbering us in sensing its true nature, as well as the possibility of its fundamental unity, is our almost universal habit of spatializing it. Numerous books have been written about the "direction" or "arrow" of time; both are spatial terms. While it is true that it is probably impossible to measure time or record its measure without using or referring to something spatial (e.g. the minute hand on a clock dial), by becoming so entrenched in the spatial representation of time we tend to submerge our sensitivity to its unique nature and especially to its subjective aspects.

We created the clock and now it is our master. Thousands of years ago when some of the major world religions were developing, priests, prophets, and religious thinkers had only the sun, moon, and stars. What these individuals lacked in modern scientific precision, they more than made up for in a rich capacity for intuition and spiritual insight. This realization reinforces my intent in this book to draw largely from religious traditions along with philosophy in treating the subjective aspects of time. More especially it motivates me to use as much as possible strictly temporal (non–spatial) terms in my discussion of time.

One of the simplest ways to understand the scope of the daunting problem in such a search for some way either to elucidate or to unify the two views of time is to look up the definition of time in a dictionary. For example, in Webster's Twentieth Century unabridged dictionary there are twenty–seven different meanings assigned to the word "time." The problem becomes compounded by the realization that whenever we chose a word for a concept, in this case "time," the word seems to assume a reality of its own by either embracing a host of meanings or by limiting and rigidifying the concept to the exclusion of subtle nuances inherent in the concept that somehow are not fully expressed by the word.

In addition to the problem of manifold definitions and language, the task of seeking a more simplified coherent conception of time is still further complicated by the fundamental age–old question of its reality. Mathematician Gerald Whitrow points out in his definitive work "The Natural Philosophy of Time" that the basic philosophical dispute about time has for centuries been between those who would "eliminate" time altogether as a reality, and those who believe "it is fundamental and irreducible" (Whitrow 80, p. 1, 370). He further explains that "The central point of dispute concerns the role of time in the relation of man to the external world," which somehow brings us back to me sitting in the subway station wondering about what I see as an apparent duality in viewpoints of time.

So in this state of mind, despite the formidable background of manifold fragmenting considerations that characterize any attempt to understand time, in this book I will still attempt a simplification of the problem by pursuing the dual approach of using modern physics, primarily but not entirely, for my "objective" source, and major religious traditions, primarily but not entirely, for my "subjective" source.

Astrophysicist Sir Arthur Eddington once observed: "In any attempt to bridge the domains of experience belonging to the spiritual and physical sides of our nature, time occupies the key position" (Eddington 28, p. 91). If this is true, then perhaps it may be valid and productive to turn the statement around and use the spiritual and physical sides of our nature to learn something about time.

Summary

Time seems to exhibit two general aspects: that of subjective, intuitive experience and that of rational, measurable observation. Though this duality plays a role to varying degrees in the study of many subjects other than time, it is obviously central in any investigation of the interrelation of science and religion. While this in turn suggests that one way to pursue the study of time would be to examine it jointly from the viewpoint of science and religion generally, in this book we use a more focused version of such an approach by primarily limiting our comparative study to modern physics and relevant features of the major world religions.

One of the underlying motivations in proceeding with this plan is to test its usefulness in seeking ultimately a unified view of time. Among the possible means of achieving unification, a generalization of Bohr's Complementarity Principle, or the Chinese Yin–Yang Principle, suggest themselves as ways to explore the possibility of holistically embracing the subjective and objective aspects of time. However, I believe that the search for unity may be significantly aided by abandoning as much as possible the ubiquitous habit of spatializing time.

Sir Arthur Stanley Eddington
1882-1944

By permission of Niels Bohr Library, American Institute of Physics

2 Philosophers Thinking About Time

"Time will reveal everything. It is a babbler and speaks even when not asked."

—Euripides

Many scholars have maintained that philosophy, in particular metaphysics, serves as a link between science and religion. Some case can be made for this supposition, not only because philosophy indeed addresses the entire spectrum of human concern, but also because, more specifically, the subfields of philosophy of science and philosophy of religion have been vigorously pursued for centuries. Whether the approach has been religious or scientific, philosophers, in their attempts to provide a coherent, rational understanding of mankind, nature, and their relationship, have found the problem of time to be one of central importance in their deliberations since the time of the Greeks.

Greek Objective Time

This importance was clearly being expressed at the birth of Western philosophy, which is considered by many to have occurred roughly around 500 B.C. in the days before Socrates. In contrast to the basic biblical view of time, which we will see reveals time as a sequence of events, the early Greeks essentially looked upon time in one way or another as a cycle, as if there were movement around a circle. However, beyond this area of consensus the pre–Socratic Greeks were generally divided into two clearly opposing schools of thought. One school primarily lead by Heraclitus maintained that the all–pervasive feature of the world is change; and since change is real, time in some form is real. This dynamic, immanent viewpoint contrasted with the more transcendent position of the other school represented by Parmenides and Zeno, which held that only the static and permanent are real, change and motion are illusory. To demonstrate this Zeno proposed his famous paradoxes, which are to this day subjects of heated discussion. In the "paradox of the arrow," assuming the existence of instants in time and points in space, Zeno argues in essence that if at a given instant the arrow is in a given position, how can it be distinguished from an arrow that was resting in that position all the time? Therefore motion is an illusion.

These notions of cyclicity, change, and permanence strongly influenced Plato and Aristotle. For Plato, many of whose works were written as dialogues between Socrates and his followers, anything we experience possesses two aspects. The first is the form or the ideal essence of the thing. The second is the individual everyday manifestation of the thing which we experience via any of our five senses, e.g., the idea of a tree is independent of a particular tree that we can touch. The domain of forms is timeless and never changing, while that of sensible objects undergoes temporal changes. In his Timaeus, Plato follows Parmenides in seeing the world as subject to a changeless pattern. The universe is viewed as an imperfect reproduction of a perfect pattern embodied by an eternal Living Being, who made the universe a moving image of the pattern. Along with this the Living Being made time "a moving image of eternity." Thus Plato divided the cosmos into the temporal domain of the natural world and the nontemporal realm of an eternal Ideal.

While Aristotle followed much of Plato's thought, he placed a stronger emphasis on an extensive and comprehensive study of the phenomena of the natural world. In particular he was concerned with a meticulous analysis of the measure of time and the relation of time and motion. In the impressive analytical discourse in his work "The Physics," he arrives at the conclusion that time is the means we use to "measure motion;" it is the "number" of motion with respect to before and after (Aristotle 83, p. 45). So Aristotle partially, not totally, identified time with motion, perhaps more precisely he identified time with becoming (Roque 90).

TIME AND THE PERSON

Contemporary philosopher Charles Sherover maintains that the classic Greek approach of examining the temporality of the external world was changed by Plotinus, who lived some 600 years after Aristotle and is considered to be the founder of neo–Platonism. Plotinus began a new era in the study of time by shifting the focus into the center of personal experience (Sherover 89). Although he was born in Egypt and spent his earlier adult years pursuing philosophy in Alexandria, at age forty he moved to Rome where his school attracted many followers.

In developing his thought Plotinus drew not only upon Plato and other Greek philosophers, but also on Persian and Indian religious philosophy, which undoubtedly informed his strong mystical inclinations and his subjective view of time. Despite the fact that he was a pagan, his compelling mystical thought was to be a strong influence on the Christian, St. Augustine. Plotinus' subjective perception of time as well as his mysticism is apparent in his definition of time: "Time is the Life of the Soul in movement as it passes from one stage or act of experience to another." He disagreed with Aristotle that time was the measure of motion, and effected a fundamental reversal of Aristotle's thought by elevating time to a higher order of reality and claiming that things were just the reverse: motion or change is the measure of time (Sherover 89).

The personalization of time was continued by St. Augustine who, although strongly influenced by Plotinus, was a convert to Christianity. An intellectual giant as well as a profound mystic, rising from moral degradation to spiritual heights, he was a powerful mainstay of the Church during the perilous times of gradual disintegration of the Roman Empire. Most of Augustine's thought on time is found in Book XI of his "Confessions," which is one of the most well–known and incisive discourses on the nature of time in Western literature. His prime motivation was theological in that he wished to examine and contrast time in the inconstant created world with that of God's eternity.

Augustine clearly rejects the Greek cyclical view of time and extensively develops the biblical heritage of progressive historical time in two fundamental ways. First, he establishes that there was an unrepeatable beginning of time. In his cogent interpretation of the Genesis account he states that although God preceded and caused the world, it was not in time that it was done, for God created time along with everything else in the world. Thus antecedent to God's creative act, there was no time (Augustine 61, p. 263).

Second, he takes a major step beyond the idea of historical chronology evident in the Old Testament by giving us a lucid analysis of progressing time. He carefully examines the characteristics of the three general divisions of time: past, present, and future, and demonstrates that only the present exists:

> How can...the past and future be when the past no longer is and the future is not yet. As for the present, if it were always present and never moved on to become the past, it would not be time but eternity (Augustine 61, p. 264).

Augustine applies this view of the past, present, and future in a meticulous analysis of the measurement of time. In measuring some period of time," it was gaining extent in time by which it could be measured, but not in present time, for the present has no extent (Augustine 61, p. 274)."

After a considerable intellectual struggle, he finally concludes that he really measures time in his mind. What transpired in the measurement makes an impression on the mind, which remains after the time of measurement ceases to be. So that when Augustine measures the time between two events, the present moment that existed at the first event is a recorded memory when the second event occurs, which in its turn becomes a recorded event. The measurement is then the difference between these two memory records of time.

In probing the human experience of time in terms of the constant decisions, however trivial, that must be made in shaping one's course through the day, Augustine tended to see time as flowing the reverse of what is usually accepted, i.e. he saw it moving from future, through the present, to the past (Sherover 89). That is, when we observe the objects around us we see a progression from past, to present, to future. However, our subjective life involves a continuous chain of decisions, large and small (even doing nothing is a decision), which shape the anticipated future and bring it to a present reality, after which it slips into the past. We are swimming upstream as the flow of time comes at us from the future. So that "the time of the objective external world and of human decisions proceed in opposite directions: within the human outlook they come together in what we call the living present" (Sherover 89).

Aspects of this "reverse flow" of time, as we will see, were much later examined by Husserl and subsequently refined by Merleau–Ponty (Merleau–Ponty 62, p. 410ff). Merleau–Ponty sees us subjectively dealing with the passage of time with an anticipatory outlook characterized by "lines of intentionality which trace out in advance at least the style of what is to come" (Merleau–Ponty 62, p. 410ff). This "two–way street" of future to past and past to future will be discussed further in Chapter 15.

THE CLOCK AND TECHNOLOGY

Another extremely important influence on the philosophical heritage that has profoundly affected modern thought came not from philosophy, but from technology, i.e., the invention and development of the mechanical clock, starting in the 13th century. According to Sherover "no invention since that of the wheel provided such a pervasive impact on all subsequent history" (Sherover 89).

In Renaissance Europe no self respecting village was without its clock on the tower of the church or town hall, proudly providing the heartbeat of the community. The clock ultimately helped lay the foundation for the industrial revolution and all of the technology that has evolved to this day. It affected commerce and economics not only by rendering navigation more precise, but also by its monitoring of labor and the prompt delivery of goods: "time is money." It has thus engendered an irresistible cohesive force on the world, equaled only in modern times by satellite transmission, radio, and television.

As a consequence, the clock exerted a powerful influence on philosophy by revitalizing the objective aspect of time and providing a renewed focus on the temporal behavior of the physical world around us. By separating mankind from direct dependence on solar time and gearing our lives to days divided into twenty–four equal hours, each in turn divided into sixty equal minutes, the clock has irrevocably entrained the course of our lives (Sherover 89).

Descartes among others abandoned the gracious cycles of the sun and moon for "tick–tock" time. This time, which could now be expressed in mathematically equal units, was soon geometrized and represented by a line drawn in space and divided into equal segments (Sherover 89). Objective time was on its way to becoming the fourth spatial dimension. Newton, whom we will discuss later, made a crucial step by endowing objective time with an ultimate transcendence that was to last for two centuries. He held that time flowed externally and independently of nature and the world. Thus nature was imbedded in time and not time in nature.

The intellectual gravitas of Newton and his supporters in expressing the universality of objective time clearly "polarized the philosophic issue" (Sherover 89). The stage was set for the controversy about how to reconcile the external time of observed physical objects with the internal time that was personally experienced. The controversy

18th Century Tower Clock Mechanism

By permission of National Museum of American History,
Smithsonian Institution

continues to this day. Among the early leaders in the battle were Leibniz and Kant, the intellectual giants of German Enlightenment.

Leibniz rejected the spatialization of external time, holding that it cannot be reduced to an infinite series of instants represented by points on a line, as originally maintained by Descartes (Sherover 89). For him the fundamental character of time is succession, a processive development of nature and mankind (Benjamin 81, p. 20). For Kant time as well as space are not empirical concepts derived from experience, but pure forms or patterns arising from our intuition. Space and time are not what we perceive but part of how we perceive.

BERGSON, HEIDEGGER, AND WHITEHEAD

However, the importance of the subjective aspect of time and the challenge to the mathematization and spatialization of time has been taken up forcefully in modern times by, among others, Bergson, Heidegger, and Whitehead. Each approached the problem from distinctly different viewpoints.

French philosopher Henri Bergson was especially critical of the way science spatializes time. For all its precision in objective measuring, science cannot measure subjectively experienced time. Thus Bergson clearly distinguishes between the qualitative experience of duration as a succession of immeasurable conscious moments and the measurement of time which he maintains ultimately involves its spatialization (Bergson 10, p. 100ff; Bergson 65, p. 44ff).

Pure duration personally experienced, a central theme in his thought, is a transition made possible by one's immediate memory which prolongs the "before" into the "after." It is an "uninterrupted transition," a "succession without separation" (Bergson 65, p. 44).

Furthermore, our experience of duration extends beyond us to include the outside world:

> To each moment of our inner life there thus corresponds a moment of our body and of all environing matter that is "simultaneous" with it; this matter then seems to participate in our conscious duration. Gradually we extend this duration to the whole physical world...(Bergson 65, p. 45).

In relating time to space Bergson uses the example of a shooting star. Its fiery trajectory can be precisely incremented and measured because it is spatial, but it is obviously distinguishable from the mobility that caused it; "it is this mobility that is pure duration" (Bergson 65,

p. 49). With examples such as this in mind, he grants that we are unable to measure time without somehow converting it to space.

He posits that time is connected to space and measured via simultaneities (Bergson 65, p. 51–57). For example, there is simultaneity between the alighting of a bluebird on the fence post we happen to be looking at and the tick of a clock. The bluebird's period of respite on the post is marked by a second simultaneity between his departure and a later tick of the clock. But each of these simultaneities is in turn simultaneous with a given moment of our conscious awareness. So that in each case a triple simultaneity is involved between the bluebird's action, the tick of the clock, and the relevant moment of our consciousness. These two sets of simultaneities delimit a period of duration.

The exploration of human temporal experience as well as the attendant challenge to the spatialization of time was also undertaken by Martin Heidegger, a student of Husserl. A profound thinker, he developed impressive insights on subjective temporality. Heidegger in effect spent a major part of his adult life contemplating the underlying meaning of being. For him it is unavoidable that this probing is done in the context and perspective of time, for it is in terms of temporality that human experience is structured (Sherover 75, p. 519). His approach to the problem of living experience was one of holistic synthesis, wherein there were no clear cut demarcations between intellect and emotion, between one's self and one's world, or between successive moments. The living present is seen as including features of the past and future in a temporal unity (Sherover 75, p. 455–6).

His attack on time's spatialization is eloquently expressed in a brief discourse on time measurement with a watch:

> ...we pick up a watch..., look at the hands, and say: 'Now it is eight–fifty (o'clock).' We say 'now' and mean time. But time cannot be found anywhere in the watch that indicates time, neither on the dial nor in the mechanism, nor can it be found in modern technological chronometers. The assertion forces itself upon us: the more technological—the more exact and informative—the chronometer, the less occasion to give thought first of all to time's peculiar character (Heidegger 77, p. 11).

Indeed he goes on to further claim (which I find somewhat debatable) that "the dimensionality of time, thought as the succession of the sequence of nows, is borrowed from the representation of three–dimensional space" (Heidegger 77, p. 14).

However, at the core of his thought are penetrating insights into the nature of being and its intimate relation to time. For Heidegger being is much more than a sense of the present: being means *presencing*, that is, letting the present come to be, or "unconcealing" the present. In other words it involves allowing the present to come to fully revealed fruition. He introduces a term not too familiar in philosophy: *appropriation*. He uses the term in explaining that the potentialities of the immediate future are *appropriated* in the process of presencing to create what we know as the present. In this sense then being is the event of appropriation (Heidegger 77, p. 21), and time can be said to be the way that appropriation appropriates (Heidegger 77, p. xi). This intimate relation of being and time is evident in Heidegger's thesis that time and being determine each other reciprocally.

Although there are some manifest differences, the notions of appropriation and presencing, as we will see, bear some underlying similarity to the thought of Alfred North Whitehead. After realizing a very successful career as a mathematician and educationist in Great Britain, Whitehead turned to philosophy and moved to the United States. He developed one of the most comprehensive formulations of metaphysics to be offered in this century, encompassing a spectrum of religious and scientific insight. His thought continues to engage the assiduous interest of philosophers and has engendered an entire area of religious study known as process theology.

The central notion of Whitehead's philosophy is that the world can be described as a process involving "quanta or atoms of experience," called "actual occasions," which are the ultimate things of which the world is made (Whitehead 29, p. 32). They constitute a basis for a concept of time and space (Wassermann 92). The becoming of an actual occasion defines and atomizes a particular region of space and time, and each occasion mirrors a world of occasions from its perspective. In this manner everything in nature "experiences"—from humans to rocks—so that all of reality is interrelated and processive in character (Mellert 75, p. 22).

A fundamental and complementary concept in Whitehead's scheme is that of "eternal objects," which are pure ideas, ideal potentialities, or possibilities for realization.[1] There are all varieties of "eternal objects":

---

[1]The concept of eternal objects derives from Plato's teaching that true reality does not consist of observable objects like houses and dogs, but the idea or "universal prototype" of the object. That is, the idea of a house exists independently of whether a particular house exists. Thus Whitehead in his

shapes, colors, numbers, sounds, feelings, etc. Eternal objects are the abstract pure idealic elements in terms of which actual occasions develop their identity and realize their novelty (Whitehead 29, p. 32ff).

Another important aspect of Whitehead's system is that of "prehension," which connotes grasping, feeling, apprehending, or appropriating (Whitehead 29, p. 335ff). Thus an actual occasion prehends or acquisitionally "feels" a certain pattern of eternal objects in its process of maturation. In brief, an actual occasion is a prehensive, processive unification of a given pattern of eternal objects that is *unique* and peculiar to that occasion; and this occasion atomizes space–time (Thompson 71, p. 23).

Actual occasions can integrate to become an interrelated complex or "nexus" of actual occasions. A human being is a nexus or society of actual occasions as well as a series of actual occasions that make up personal experience. It is at this point that we can note some underlying similarity of Whitehead's idea of prehension to Heidegger's concept of appropriation, bringing about presencing.

Among the ways in which religion plays a role in his philosophical system is Whitehead's view of how God affects the maturation of an actual occasion. He does not see God as omnipotent, because otherwise God would be responsible for the evil as well as the good in the world. Accordingly in Whitehead's words "The limitation of God is His goodness" (Whitehead 26, p. 153). It is as the source and provider of the ideal direction that the strength of God is manifested: "The power by which God sustains the world is the power of Himself as the ideal" (Whitehead 26, p. 156). So that God provides the flawless conceptual ordering of the eternal objects that might potentially be prehended by actual occasions (Thompson 71, p. 58). This ideal ordering may not be actually achieved by the actual occasion; in general it falls short of this ideal. Thus God lures, not determines, the world of actual occasions towards the ideals and values ultimately possible for it (Whitehead 26, p. 158; Thompson 71, p. 59).

Time is regarded by Whitehead as an intrinsic expression of reality, which for him is creative process in nature. He therefore is convinced that time is in, or a part of, nature, and not nature imbedded in time as held by Newton. Time being in nature is consistent with his concept of "actual occasions," wherein he holds that events are atomic and

---

unique and comprehensive analysis of time is in effect integrating Platonic concepts with those of the meticulous study of time in the tangible world given by Aristotle.

manifest a finite temporal interval in acquiring their pattern of eternal objects and in achieving completion. Therefore Whitehead does not believe in instants of time (i.e., points in time) or points in space. He maintains that the mathematical concept of a continuum of points and instants is given a role beyond its theoretical one; it is asserted to be a facsimile of the real spatiotemporal continuum in nature where no points or instants are actually perceived (Whitehead 19, p. 7). Thus Whitehead, with his insistence on direct personal observation of nature as it is, places challenging qualifications on the conventional scientific view of time in his encompassing metaphysics.

I have focused attention on the thought of Bergson, Heidegger, and Whitehead because as modern philosophers I believe they represent most cogently the present day dialectic between the subjective and objective aspects of time. Each of them has provided us with unique and incisive thought about time from a more personally experienced point of view. In so doing each has not only had to develop his own interpretation of the awesome heritage of past philosophers, but also has had to come to grips with the objective revelations of modern science, especially the relativity and quantum theories. Their struggle to find an integration or reconciliation of subjectively sensed and externally observed time is now being continued by others. The hope for a clearer view will never die:

> A dwarf standing on the shoulders of a giant may see farther than the giant himself.
>
> —Didacus Stella
> 1st Century A.D.

SUMMARY

In the context of two opposing philosophies: one that only change is irreducibly real, the other that permanence represents ultimate reality, the Greeks began to submit time and related concepts to comprehensive rational examination. Plato saw time and the natural world as imperfect dynamic reflections of a static eternal Ideal, while Aristotle placed more emphasis on temporality in the natural world with his exhaustive analysis of motion and saw time as the measure, or "number," of motion.

In contrast to such objective, rational thought, Plotinus brought the human experience of time into consideration and held that time was a higher order of reality than motion. Influenced by Plotinus, St. Augustine in his meticulous study of time concluded that it is the immediate memory that plays the key role in its measurement. Augustine's work raised the possibility that time could be considered as flowing from future to past as well as the reverse, the two flows meeting in the present. In his interpretation of the Genesis creation account, he maintains the God, outside of time, created the world and time along with it.

Emphasis began to shift back to an objective view of time with the development of the mechanical clock and the attendant technology. The objectivity of time found powerful support from the work of Newton and his followers, thus setting the stage for the controversy continuing to the present as to the primacy of objective, or subjective, time.

Among the leading modern philosophers who most comprehensively discuss this objective–subjective controversy are Bergson, Heidegger, and Whitehead. In particular Bergson and Heidegger are especially compelling in their observations concerning the spatialization of time. The impressive metaphysical structure of Whitehead embracing both scientific and religious concepts provides, through his concept of "actual occasions," an unique and ingenious approach in considering the subjective and objective aspects of time.

Part II TIME IN OUR COSMIC COCOON

"The awakening of human consciousness carries with it an awareness of Man's limitations which entails, at the same time, an almost irresistible desire to peer over at the 'other shore.'"
—Raimundo Panikkar

The contemporary religious philosopher, Raimundo Panikkar, suggests that all of our human limitations can essentially be reduced to a primal three: knowledge, space, and time. Of these he maintains it is the last that is the most discomforting. The three limitations, as far as our view of the natural world is concerned, depend largely on three fundamental physical quantities, described below, which help define a kind of cosmic cocoon in which we are encapsulated. It is a cocoon of somewhat diffuse, ill–defined boundaries.

In one form or another these boundaries are evident at all three levels of the physical world that we probe and try to understand: *microscopic*, the realm of the very small; *macroscopic* or intermediate, the realm of everyday living; and *cosmic*, the realm of the astronomically large.

Our cosmic view, where the theory of general relativity comes into play, is fundamentally limited by the first of the three physical quantities, the speed of light. The boundary encountered in probing the microscopic world, where the quantum theory holds sway, is described by the Heisenberg Uncertainty Principle, whose measure is the second physical quantity, known as Planck's constant, to be discussed in Chapter 4. We are limited macroscopically in the sense that we observe the world primarily via the electromagnetic force, whose strength is essentially determined by the third physical quantity, the elementary unit of electric charge, which happens to be the magnitude of charge on the electron and the proton. These three quantities—the speed of light,[1] Planck's

---

[1]The speed of light, usually denoted by c, is a very large quantity equal to 186,000 miles per second.

constant,[2] and the unit electric charge[3]—are constants of nature, that is, they stay the same regardless of the vicissitudes of nature and the phenomena it experiences. The constants are at the very core of the constraints with which we are encumbered in pressing the physical limits of space, time, and knowledge.[4]

How do these three unchangeable numbers, and the theories in which they are imbedded, color, constrain, and delimit our world view? How do they show us that we are indeed in a cosmic cocoon with nebulous boundaries? Let us briefly examine each of the relevant theories (relativity, quantum, electromagnetic) to see how they and their associated constants circumscribe our access to the reality of nature, and thus to our concepts of time. Let us also see how our cosmic cocoon is seen from the holistic perspective and world view of selected religious traditions. These traditions provide intuitive and spiritual views of our cocoon's temporality which will complement the concepts of time based on modern physics.

---

[2]Planck's constant, usually denoted by h, is a very small quantity equal to 6.6 x 10^{-27} erg-seconds. 10^{-27} is a fraction: one billion, billion, billionth. An erg is a small unit of energy such that an erg per second is one ten millionth of a watt.

[3]The unit electric charge is that possessed by the proton (positive) and the electron (negative).

[4]There are, of course, other physical constants, particularly G, the gravitational constant (which gives the strength of the gravitational attraction), that significantly affect these limits, but for the time–relevant purpose of this discussion I consider the three that I have cited to be primal.

3   Einstein, Time, and the Speed of Light

"The law of the constant velocity of light in empty space,...and the equal legitimacy of all inertial systems..., between them made it necessary, to begin with, that the concept of time should be made relative, each inertial system being given its own special time."

—Albert Einstein

I live on a farm in the Shenandoah Valley. When I first bought the place in the spring of 1968, I drove over to the neighboring farm owned by Mrs. Einstein, an adorable, gutsy old lady who lived alone. As soon as I walked in, I noticed a picture of Albert Einstein on the living room wall. Not quite believing there would be any familial connection, I made some slightly flippant remark about the picture's presence. She kindly informed me that her deceased husband's grandfather and Einstein's father were brothers. That was one among many things I was to learn from this amiable, wise woman. I think what I admired most about her was her insistence on trying to maintain her farm alone well into her eighties, despite the pleadings of her sons to come and live in the city with them.

Einstein and 19th Century Physics

This perseverance made me think of Einstein himself. How, to the end of his life, he never gave up trying to find a theory that would unify gravity and electromagnetism. Actually this persistence, this disposition to consummate uniqueness, characterized Einstein from his earliest years. In school he was in many respects a maverick, who often aroused the displeasure of his professors because of his independent interests and thinking. As a result, on graduation he could not find a satisfactory academic position and finally took a job in the Swiss patent office in Bern.

Although this may at first seem to be an unlikely atmosphere for the generation of anything like a theory of relativity, it proved to be a most auspicious environment. This was in part because the job itself in a fundamental way helped train him and complemented his after–hours efforts in developing relativity theory. His boss was a kind and wise man, but a strict one. He taught Einstein to see through to the core concept in any patent he was examining and to express succinctly why it would or would not work.

Einstein turned these seven years of work and training to good use by, among other things, questioning the generally accepted Newtonian view of time. Newton considered time as a totally separate entity, flowing independently and completely divorced from space and the rest of the universe. This transcendent view of time is expressed in Newton's famous statement in his "Principia" (Newton 1686):

> Absolute, true, and mathematical time of itself and from its own
> nature...flows equably without relation to anything external.[5]

It was Einstein's insight that time and the physical world were interdependent and interactive that was a major step in devising his new theory. In particular he realized that time had to be interrelated with space in a way that qualified and softened the rigid independence of the two. For there had also grown a firm belief in absolute space. By the 19th century this belief developed into the conviction that there existed some kind of stationary and pervasive medium with respect to which all motion could be referred.

Specifically, physicists of the late 19th century generally were convinced that there existed an "ether" which essentially embodied absolute space. Since early in the century it had been experimentally well established that light exhibited a wavelike character, it was naturally supposed that a universal, stationary medium, the ether, must exist in which these waves propagated. The common experience of pressure waves propagated in water and sound waves in air were undoubtedly among the analogies upon which the supposition was based.

It was also experimentally well–known since the time of Galileo that the laws of mechanics governing the motion of material bodies were the same for any observer moving at some fixed speed in a fixed

---

[5]It should be noted that this view was subject to considerable controversy at the time, but with the growing universality and accuracy of clocks it gradually gained general acceptance.

direction relative to the ether or to another observer with a different speed and direction. For example, if you throw a ball vertically in the air, it returns along the same path, and you catch it. The ball's motion is experienced to be the same, and is described in the same way by the laws of mechanics whether you are standing on the ground or in a train moving at constant velocity (you, the ball, and the train are all moving together).[6] So that you can still throw the ball up and then catch it the same way.

However, while the laws describing mechanical motion, (e.g., the ball's), were considered independent of the velocity of the reference frame, such as the ground or the train, this was not considered to be the case for light. Here the word "light" does not mean just visible light but electromagnetic radiation of any frequency in the spectrum from very low frequency radio waves to very high frequency gamma rays. That is, assuming the absolute ether exists, measurements of the speed of light were expected to vary depending on the velocity of the frame of reference in which the measurement was made. For example, a spaceship observer measuring the speed of solar light would record a different value depending on whether the ship was moving toward, or away from, the sun. But the true speed of light should only be observable relative to the absolute and stationary ether. So that in general it would appear to have one speed if measured on earth, which is itself moving with respect to the ether, and another speed if measured on a space shuttle.

This essential inconsistency of mechanical measurements being independent of the observer's velocity and light measurements not being so, brought into question the reality of the absolute ether. Michelson and Morley settled the question in an experiment which compared the speed of light measured along the direction of the earth's motion to that measured perpendicular to the motion. If the ether existed the measurements should be different. They were not (Michelson and Morley 1887). Thus nature either does not possess an ether, or it does not have one that is detectable.

---

[6]Constant velocity by definition means constant direction as well as constant speed.

EINSTEIN'S FIRST STEP: SPECIAL RELATIVITY

In 1905 Einstein in effect used this negative result[7] to develop a theory which no longer depended on the assumption of an absolute frame of reference. So that not only for the measurement of mechanical motion but also for light, all frames are on an equal footing, none are sacrosanct, they are all relative. Indeed there is no way of ultimately distinguishing rest from constant velocity. In particular all measurements of the speed of light give the same result regardless of the velocity of the frame of reference.

By thus totally "democratizing" the principle that frames of reference are relative, Einstein in effect shifted the notion of absoluteness from the existence of an absolute frame of reference to an absolute maximum velocity, the velocity of light (Fraser 81, p. 473; Harrison 85, p. 144). If we think about it for a moment, we may be impressed with the reasonableness of this "democratization." It would be a strange, anarchic, and complicated universe indeed if the results of a measurement, e.g. the speed of light, depended on whether it was made on the moon or the earth. Einstein's relativity theory shows how all observers regardless of their relative velocities (the relative velocity of course always being less than the maximum velocity, that of light) see their world in the same way in their own frame of reference.

Nevertheless it is reasonable to question how this can be so, and to wonder how the speed of light can possibly be measured to be the same regardless of the observer's direction and speed. Einstein resolved this apparent contradiction of common sense by realizing that the time and space scales of one frame of reference had to be flexible with respect to another. The nature of this flexibility can be seen by considering the example of two observers, Willie and Lucy. Willie, an observer on earth, looking at the measuring devices of Lucy, an astronaut flying by on a very fast spaceship, would see her yardstick contract and her clock to slow down, compared to his measuring devices. But since there is nothing sacrosanct about the earth and its velocity, Lucy, looking at Willie's instruments, would see exactly the same effect. Furthermore, the greater their relative velocities, the greater is the effect.

These phenomena of time dilation and space contraction are not just optical illusions of some kind. Time dilation has been confirmed by

---

[7]Some historians of science maintain that Einstein never knew of the Michelson-Morley result. Here I am assuming that he was at least aware of the physical effects consistent with the result.

comparing a stationary clock on Earth with one flown around the world. The latter registered less elapsed time by a small but measurable amount. This effect is also the basis for the famous "twin paradox," which is not really a paradox. If one twin sister stays on earth and the other takes a long, fast space journey, when she returns she will be younger than her earthbound twin.

This unfamiliar behavior arises from the fact that there is an interflexibility of all time and space scales. They vary in just the right proportions to render the measurement of the speed of light to be the same for all relatively moving systems. Another result of the interdependence of the time and space scales can be seen by considering the spacetime interval between two events. That is, we regard not only the spatial interval but also the temporal interval as jointly comprising a composite interval in four–dimensional spacetime. Considered from the four–dimensional standpoint, the spacetime interval between two events turns out to be the same for all observers regardless of their relative velocity. Again, it is the mutual flexibility of the time and space scales that intercompensate so that, just as for the speed of light, the spacetime interval can remain constant (Taylor and Wheeler 66). Thus the "title" of absolute and unvarying is conferred not only on the speed of light, as mentioned earlier, but also on the four–dimensional spacetime interval between events.

The concept of four dimensional spacetime has been very useful in making mathematical calculations in relativity theory, but for this very reason has been in part responsible for the tendency to spatialize time. It has been so convenient in such calculations to treat time as if it were just another spatial dimension, that time for the theoretical physicist has tended to lose its unique nature. Therefore it must be stressed that though relativity has shown time and space to be intimately interrelated, time is not a form of space. Relativity has broken down the isolation of time and space but not their distinction (Denbigh 81, p. 46).

Another time–related effect of relativity is that our familiar ideas of simultaneity are seriously challenged. That is, two events that are seen as simultaneous by an observer in one frame of reference can in general be observed as one occurring after the other by an observer in another frame moving at an appropriate relative velocity.[8]

---

[8]This is a general statement, and does not contradict the earlier remark that everyone sees nature to be the same in their local frame of reference. For if the two events took place in your reference frame and were seen as simultaneous, they would also be seen that way in another frame if you and the events were

For example, two widely separated lightning flashes observed as having occurred simultaneously by Willie in his laboratory, can be considered as having occurred one after the other by Lucy moving in her spaceship. These results and the fact that each observer can nevertheless measure the velocity of light to be the same is again only reconciled by realizing that there are differences between his and her time and space scales of just such magnitude as to make this reconciliation possible. Thus the idea that simultaneity is relative, which this example illustrates, is inextricably related to the interdependence of time and space.

However, in considering whether or not two events are simultaneous it is important to emphasize that relativity does not say that the causal order of two events can be changed or reversed, only that the observed time interval (not spacetime interval) between them can vary depending on the reference frame[9]. Indeed it is important to keep in mind that the fundamental approach in developing the concepts of relativity was from the viewpoint of relating events. It was by carefully analyzing the connection and timing of events that the effects described thus far in this chapter can be seen to occur. Since only a qualitative description of relativistic effects is appropriate here, a detailed demonstration of this analysis is not given.[10]

Although not as apparently time–related as the phenomena discussed thus far, perhaps the most popular relativistic effect is one that is implicit in Einstein's famous equation $E = mc^2$. This equation says that the energy E is equal the mass m multiplied by the square of the speed of light, c^2 (again, c is the velocity of light). It is the formula used particularly in subatomic interactions, where often mass actually does convert to energy and vice versa. The relativistic effect implied in Einstein's formula is that m is in general not the mass as we might see it at rest, but is what is known as the relativistic mass. This mass is in general larger than the rest mass because of the additional energy furnished it by virtue of its velocity. We here on earth will observe a spaceship to have a slightly smaller mass (in fact its minimum) when it is at rest on the launching pad than when it is in flight to the moon. The

---

transferred to that frame. The difference appears when people in different frames look at the same two events regardless of where the events are located.

[9]Remember it is the four–dimensional interval that is invariant; the separate time and space intervals can vary reciprocally.

[10]The number of books presenting this analysis is manifold. Among them are the following references: Einstein 20, Feynman *et al* 65; French 68; Resnick 68.

designers of high energy particle accelerators must take this effect into account in synchronizing the accelerator components that boost the energy of the particles which move at speeds close to the speed of light. These are but two examples of the empirical fact that mass is but a form of energy.

It is again important to understand that the relativistic effects discussed thus far, e.g., the time dilation, length contraction, and mass increase, are all characterized by their extreme smallness in terms of our everyday experience. This is why they had eluded notice for so many ages. They only become apparent in phenomena involving very high velocities, approaching that of light. Such velocities are not easily detectable in ordinary life, but are easily observed both in the world of the "very large" (cosmological) and the "very small" (microscopic). As an example, even at a velocity of one–tenth that of light (that is 18,600 miles per second), the above three effects concerning time, space, and mass involve changes of about one–half of one percent. So that, the time will dilate, the length contract, and the mass increase by that percentage. If we care to go to extremes and consider what would happen as the velocity of light is approached, the time would approach cessation, the length would shrink toward zero, and the mass would approach infinity.

EINSTEIN'S COMPLETE THEORY: GENERAL RELATIVITY

Thus far, we have limited our examination to the special theory of relativity, which gives the relationship of observations made on frames of reference moving relative to each other with some constant velocity. Although relative accelerations can also be handled by the special theory, a full conceptual understanding of the meaning of acceleration is furnished by the general theory reported by Einstein in 1915. Thus the general theory, true to its name, not only describes phenomena covered by the special theory, but also deals with relative accelerations in terms of gravitational effects and curved space–time geometry. This essentially means that special relativity by itself is only valid when gravitational effects are zero, or as is the case here on earth, relatively small compared to such effects seen by astronomers observing very large and massive bodies, e.g. stars, galaxies, and clusters of galaxies.

Basic to the general relativity theory is the insight that the effects of gravity and acceleration are equivalent; in fact Einstein called this the Principle of Equivalence. For example, if you were sitting in a large, completely sealed box which is resting on the earth, you would not be able to tell whether you were being held to the bottom of the box by gravity or being accelerated upwards by one "g," the bottom of the box pushing you in that direction. If the box were freely falling in the earth's gravitational field, you would experience weightlessness because your acceleration is then the same as that of the box; you would be "floating" in the box.

More specifically, Einstein was able to correlate the physical properties of gravity with geometrical concepts of curved space first devised by the mathematician G. F. B. Riemann. One can get some notion of what curved three–dimensional space might be like by thinking of a two–dimensional analogy, i.e. how a surface might curve under appropriate stress. A good example is a bowling ball resting on a trampoline net. The curvature of the mesh of the netting is greatest closest to the ball.

In this curved–geometry context, a spaceship orbiting about the earth is thought of as following its curved path, not because the earth's gravity is continually pulling on it, but because it is naturally and freely drifting in curved space. Thus in the words of physicist John Wheeler: "Space tells mass how to move, and mass tells space how to curve" (Wheeler 82, p. 65). Indeed the whole structure of space and its curvature depends on the distribution of matter in the universe.

The principal time–related effect in general relativity is that clocks run slower near larger masses or when subject to larger accelerations. Using some imaginative intuition you may almost be able to "feel" that if, for example, the earth were ten times more massive, you as well as your bedroom clock would slow down by the encumbering drag of the additional "g's." In any case given the intimate interrelation of time, space, and mass, perhaps physicists may someday be using the compound word "space–time–mass" instead of simply "space–time."

SOME ASTROPHYSICAL EFFECTS OF RELATIVITY

There are a number of attendant phenomena involving the speed of light that astrophysicists see and ponder on when studying the heavens. Among the most dramatic are black holes. After burning their nuclear fuel, stars with cores twice or more massive than the sun are predicted ultimately to collapse and experience this fate (Pagels 85, pgs. 55–6). These objects are currently thought to occur mostly in two or three places. The first is as a partner in some binary stars, i.e. two massive objects rotating around each other. They also are believed to occur at the center of some galaxies. In fact there is growing evidence that a black hole may exist at the center of our galaxy, the Milky Way.

Black holes are thought to be the driving force of the colossal engines of matter and radiation called Active Galactic Nuclei (AGN) at the center of some especially energetic galaxies. Quasars, extremely concentrated, very distant and brilliant objects are one kind of AGN. Some of the more dramatic AGNs are surrounded by mammoth doughnut–shaped dust clouds inside of which are circular accretion disks, gathering and serving "food" to a voracious central hole. Perpendicular to the disks are tremendous jets of radiation, so that the whole churning engine looks somewhat like a gigantic wheel spinning on an axle as depicted in Figure 1.

Black holes possess such enormous mass densities that not even light can escape them, hence the label black hole. Thus mass can affect light. Indeed one of the astronomical effects that served as an early confirmation of Einstein's general relativity was the observation that the path of light was curved as it passed by massive objects, such as stars and galaxies.[11] Although photons, particles or quanta of light (to be discussed in Chapter 4), have no rest mass, they do have relativistic mass by virtue of their energy of motion and thus can be subject to gravitational attraction and, when near a black hole, to being swallowed up.

For many years now continuing theoretical study has been devoted to black holes in an effort to predict their properties and behavior. Such calculations indicate that space–time inside a black hole does not behave as it does in our ordinary experience; space is in a sense turned "inside–out" (Pagels 85, p. 55). Indeed it can be shown that close to a black hole centrifugal force, that is usually understood as being directed outward, reverses so that its direction is inward (Abramowicz 93). Some of these theoretical predictions may someday be compared with astronomical measurements, for already the renovated Hubble Space Telescope has found convincing evidence that a giant black hole lurks at the cores of a number of galaxies.

With black holes some form of limit of time being slowed, space being contracted, and mass being concentrated has been reached, so

---

[11]This effect is the basis for what is called gravitational lensing. For example, a large mass in the line of sight between an observer and an observed star can serve as a lens and focus more light to the observer than without the mass. The effect has recently been useful in detecting the presence of dead stars in our galaxy which chance across the astronomer's line of sight.

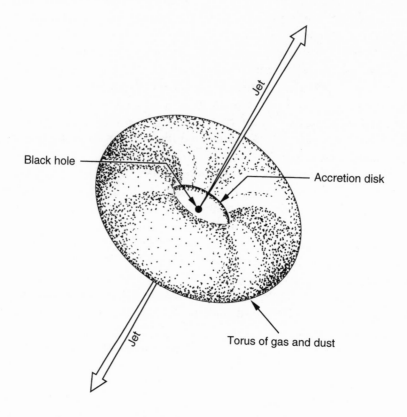

Black hole

Accretion disk

Torus of gas and dust

Jet

Jet

FIG. 1 Schematic view of the center of a galaxy
with an "active galactic nucleus" (AGN)

much so that even light is not fast enough to escape. Thus black holes may be isolated reminders scattered throughout the universe of the limitations placed on our perception by the speed of light. However, it is the universe as a whole and its continuing expansion that furnishes us with the most powerful illustration of the constraints imposed by this speed.

Since the occurrence of the big bang the universe has been expanding at a prodigious rate. The farther a galaxy is from us the faster it is moving. While this behavior is a characteristic of an ordinary explosion that we see here on earth, the universe's expansion is different. An ordinary explosion starts from a center, but for the universe there is no center.

That this is the case can perhaps be understood by thinking about the well–known analogy of an expanding spherical balloon with ink spots (representing galaxies) distributed randomly on the balloon's surface. So that we imagine that we live in a universe of only two spatial dimensions, those on the balloon's surface; the radial dimension is not known or available to us. As we move about this surface we find no center, every place on the balloon is just as good a starting or ending point as any other. If we stay at one of the spots, as the balloon expands, we notice that the farther away any of the other ink spots is, the faster it is moving away from us.

How fast can the farthest move away from us? Or, coming back to our universe of three spatial dimensions, how fast can the farthest massive body move away from us? The answer is that we may not be asking quite the right question. The central point to realize is that the universe is not expanding in space, but that the space which envelops the universe is itself expanding—the universe consists of expanding space (Harrison 85, p. 179). The "edge" of the observable universe is where the expansion velocity equals the velocity of light. This being the case, it may seem that the galaxies contained in the space beyond this limit are violating special relativity's speed limit (the speed of light), but they are not. They are moving at some acceptable speed within their own local space. From a cosmic standpoint special relativity with its speed limit is actually applicable "locally" and in relatively gravity-free regions, not "globally" when considering major sections of the universe (Harrison 85, p. 183).

The *observable* universe is enlarging at the speed of light. We cannot see that part of the universe the light from which has not yet reached us. However, sooner or later it will; thus as time goes on more and more galaxies or quasars come into our purview. In any case it is the speed of light which places a limit on the observable universe and encloses us in what I have called a cosmic cocoon, however vast.

In recent years astronomers have been able to observe extremely distant and incredibly concentrated, brilliant quasars, which are receding from us at very great speeds. From what we have learned, the greater the recession speed, the greater the distance the quasar is away from us. In turn the greater the distance from us, the longer elapsed time it takes for the light from the observed object to reach the astronomer's telescope.

In the case of some quasars the time elapsed is great indeed, about 13 billion years. Their distance away measured in light years (a light year being the distance covered by light in one year) is of course 13 billion light years. Because of the present imprecision of many astronomical measurements, especially distance measurements, the age of the universe is not accurately known. Current estimates (which could change) put it at between 13 and 15 billion years. Therefore quasars are very ancient objects and may have been around when the universe was as young as 15% of its age today.

In any case the deeper into space that astronomers probe, the further back in time they are able to see. So astronomers peering progressively farther into space are watching time and natural history go backwards. How far back they can look, and the stage of evolution of the galaxy or other cosmic body they see, is essentially limited and controlled by the speed of light. This speed of electromagnetic radiation, being a speed, is a link between space and time. It makes it possible to convert the expanding space of our universe into a history book, a history of cosmic time.

On the other hand speculating in terms of the present, perhaps on a stellar planet in some galaxy 3 billion light years away, unimaginably bizarre creatures of awesome intelligence are building and expanding their civilization, but we will never know it. Only in 3 billion years might the characteristics of the electromagnetic radiation emitted from this planet and received on earth give our progeny (if any have survived) a clue.

The speed of light also has a powerful influence in the more "local" arena of our own galaxy in placing limitations on our knowledge and in realizing our constraints in attempting to deal with cosmic time scales. In no endeavor are these limits more evident than in the search for extraterrestrial intelligence (SETI) that has been conducted with increasing sophistication and intensity since about 1960. So far no conclusive evidence for extraterrestrial intelligence (ETI) has been found.

If we think on it, it is not difficult to understand why. As we will see in Chapter 13, the number of stellar planets with just the right ecological conditions, say comparable to earth, and also that are within the purview allowed us by astronomical instruments, is very small. However, an equally restricting effect is what might be called the "time overlap."

Let us consider for a moment the lifetime of our sun, an average star, which has now lived for about 4.5 billion years and is estimated to live for about another 6 billion before it consumes all of its primary source of nuclear fuel. Perhaps another star, maybe in our galaxy, was born a billion years earlier (or later) and hosted a planetary civilization. Suppose that after this civilization reached the technological competence we have today it lived another 300 years before it blew itself up in a nuclear holocaust, became exterminated by disease, suffocated itself by over–population and consequent over–consumption, or was obliterated by a collision with an asteroid. If we compare the time scale of a billion years to 300 years, it is like comparing a year to 10 seconds.

We have only been looking with any technological competency for roughly 30 years, making the comparison a year to 1 second. Thus a "time–overlap" constraint is basically imposed by the velocity of light, for if it were not 186,000 miles per second but much greater, or essentially infinite, among the some 100 billion stars of our galaxy, not to mention the some 100 billion galaxies in the observable universe, we might possibly observe some ETI. Furthermore, if on the other hand we have any hope that we might receive any response to the electromagnetic signals sent out by us, it will probably be a long time before they are realized. For example, if an ETI 500 light years away (a mere pinch in space on a cosmic scale) were someday to receive our TV signals and start enjoying "I Love Lucy," we would not hear their "rave notices" for 1,000 years.

We will examine more about SETI as well as other aspects of relativity in Chapter 13, but it must now be apparent how the speed of light influences our sense of time on the cosmic scale. It not only limits how much we can know about our universe and its past, but also how much we can know even about possible intragalactic neighbors in our life time. Although on a cosmic scale the size of our cocoon is almost unimaginably large and getting larger very fast, there is still, in effect, a nebulous "edge of the universe," a limit to its temporal history, whose measure is basically the speed of light.

Summary

Relativity and the attendant limitations imposed by the speed of light reveal a number of thought–provoking time–related effects in our cosmic cocoon. A central effect in special relativity is the time dilation and space contraction that appears when comparing observations in reference frames moving at a constant velocity relative to one another. Furthermore from the viewpoints of different frames our concept of simultaneity also must be revised, because two events observed as simultaneous in one frame will in general not be so in another.

With the theory of general relativity an essential temporal effect is the slowing of time in the proximity of mass or the gravitationally equivalent action of acceleration. By virtue of its relativistic mass, light passing near a star or other large mass can be deflected by the gravitational attraction. In the case of black holes this attraction is so great that light is captured and cannot escape. The speed of light severely limits the number of ETI we might possibly observe in our lifetime. Moreover the speed of light delineates the "edge of the universe," since this is where this speed equals the expansion rate of space. We cannot see those regions beyond the "edge" whose light has yet to reach us. Thus the speed of light encloses us in a "cosmic cocoon," however vast.

4 TIME AND THE QUANTUM

> "The elementary quantum phenomenon is the strangest thing in this strange world."
>
> —John Archibald Wheeler

For over 30 years now I have been working in a sub–field of nuclear physics in which the nucleus is studied by shooting a beam of high energy electrons at it, thereby exciting it to a higher energy state. By examining how the electrons are affected in their direction and energy when scattered from the excited nucleus, we can infer a lot about the characteristics of these energy states of the nucleus. The international community of physicists that has been doing this work, initially close knit and on a first name basis, has grown tremendously, especially in the last decade. Throughout this growth one of the outstanding physicists and leaders in the community has been Jochen Heisenberg, one of Werner Heisenberg's many children.

The primary thing that struck me about Jochen whenever I talked with him at nuclear physics meetings was the clarity, perception, and completeness of his response when I asked him about his work. It was a conversation that was invariably edifying and that I always appreciated.

I am sure it was similar intensity and perception that served the senior Heisenberg when he retreated to the sand dunes of Helgoland (a German island in the North Sea) to recover from a bout of hay fever and to ponder the quantum. Here he found the insight to devise his version of quantum mechanics, that was to later help him arrive at his famous Uncertainty Principle, which is at the core of the quantum theory. With Heisenberg's principle and the quantum theory we are pressing the limits of the "other end" of our cosmic cocoon, probing the boundaries of the microscopic realm of the very small.

How small is small? To grasp some feeling for the sizes involved in the microscopic world, the diameter of an atom is roughly one hundred millionth of a centimeter; that is, if the atom were the size of a pea, then the centimeter would be the distance from New York City to Pittsburgh. The nucleus in turn is more than ten thousand times smaller than the atom; so that if the nucleus were now the pea, the diameter of the atom would be roughly the height of the Sears Tower in Chicago.

It was because of the extremely small sizes characterizing the microscopic world that explanations of unfamiliar quantum effects went undiscovered for so long. Recall this situation is entirely analogous to that of relativity where relativistic effects went undetected in the work-a-day world for so long because they become most apparent at speeds approaching that of light. This illustrates why the advent of these two cornerstones of modern physics, the quantum and relativity theories, constituted such a dramatic upheaval of classical 19th century Newtonian thought.

The Development of the Quantum Theory

But what are some of these quantum effects? Undoubtedly the most famous historically was discovered by Max Planck in 1900. His discovery opened the 20th century with the first breakthrough into the quantum world. Planck was struggling to find a mathematical equation which properly predicted the spectrum of light emitted by a certain kind of light source that emits a continuous range of wave lengths.[1]

True to the accepted 19th century theory that light exists only as a wave phenomenon, he tried to find this equation in terms of the wave theory. After much painstaking analysis, he was forced to conclude that light could also exist as indivisible quanta or particles of electromagnetic energy, called photons. In particular Planck showed that the energy of the light was quantized and equal to the frequency of the light times what is now known as Planck's constant, which was cited at the beginning of this Part of the book. Thus, in the quantum theory a beam of light is not a continuous stream, but consists of individual photons, increments of energy, the magnitude of the energy being directly proportional to the frequency of the light.

It was Einstein who gave the quantum theory its next major impetus by exploiting Planck's discovery in explaining what is known as the photoelectric effect. This occurs when light shines on a flat piece of

---

[1] This source has the perhaps confusing name of "black body radiator." Examples of rather good black body radiators are lampblack and charcoal; when they are heated to high enough temperatures, a continuous spectrum of wavelengths is easily observed.

metal, for example; it can cause electrons to be emitted from the surface. Again the explanation of the details of the process came only in terms of light as photons or quanta of energy.[2] It was specifically Einstein's work on the photoelectric effect that was cited in his Nobel Prize award (surprisingly he received no award for his work on relativity).

After almost a century of wave theory dominance, the revelation by Planck and Einstein that light could also behave as a particle started the 20th century with a revolution in the natural sciences. However, on hindsight this perhaps should not have been too much of a surprise, at least in a sense. This is because physicists had been able to observe essentially only two possible modes of transporting energy, i.e., via particles or waves (Weidner and Sells 65, p. 142ff).

In fact many physical phenomena at the macroscopic level of everyday living exhibit a form of what is popularly termed a wave–particle duality. For example, in understanding sound propagation in air, a wave theory is needed, but in describing the temperature and pressure of the air, a particle theory is used. However, it was a surprise when, at the microscopic level, electromagnetic radiation or light was found to be characterized by this kind of a duality. Depending on what aspect of light was being studied, that is, depending on the measuring device and the conditions under which the measurements are made, either a wavelike or a particle–like behavior is observed, but not both simultaneously.

But the duality did not stop with light. In 1924 Prince Louis de Broglie furnished the key insight that not only photons, which only have mass by virtue of their energy of motion, but also microscopic particles which have mass when at rest, such as electrons and protons, also can exhibit a wave–particle duality. Specifically, he showed that the momentum (which is velocity times mass) in the particle mode is inversely proportional to its wave length in the wave mode, i.e., the greater the momentum the shorter the wave length.

One can see a certain symmetry in the fact that light or electromagnetic radiation, initially thought to be only wavelike, turned out to be also particle–like, while microscopic matter such as electrons, protons, etc., initially thought to be only particles, also exhibited

---

[2]It should be remembered that the existence of quantization in nature was not new in 1900. For example, atoms were known to have discrete masses, not just any mass; the standing waves in a child's skipping rope are maintained only at certain discrete wavelengths.

wavelike properties. Undoubtedly it was this sense of symmetry that influenced de Broglie in reaching his insight.

It was Niels Bohr who played the leading role in attempts to reconcile and bring coherence to the wave–particle duality. This resulted in his famous Principle of Complementarity, which essentially states that the wave and particle modes are mutually exclusive but complementary. If a given individual measurement reveals the wave character of the phenomenon, then it is impossible to observe the particle character in the same measurement, and vice versa. That is, which one of the two modes is observed when a given individual measurement is performed is always quite definite, and the two can never be seen simultaneously. Since the modes are mutually exclusive and one cannot be reduced to the other, for the most complete and coherent picture possible both modes are needed.

Bohr's Complementarity Principle has been applied in a generalized form to all kinds of dichotomies, many quite nonphysical and philosophical. For example, there have been many attempts to apply a generalization of the principle to the apparent dualism between science and religion with the hope of better understanding the relationship between the two fields.[3]

Heisenberg's Uncertainty Principle

The Complementarity Principle, as we shall soon see, can actually be deduced from the famous and more quantitatively precise Heisenberg Uncertainty Principle which remains the essence of the quantum theory. Briefly stated in its most well–known form, it says that the uncertainty in the observation of the position of a particle multiplied by the uncertainty in its momentum can never be less than Planck's constant h,[4] the measure of the "lower" extreme of our cosmic cocoon.

The principle tells us that infinite exactness in simultaneous momentum and position measurements is impossible since the product

---

[3]The description of several such attempts can be found in "Zygon, Journal of Religion and Science" (Blackwell Publishers, Cambridge, MA, 1966-present).

[4]Mathematically the principle includes a factor of 4π, so that if a particle with momentum p moving in a given direction has a position, denoted by s, as measured along that direction from some established origin, we then have:

$$\Delta s \, \Delta p \geq h/4\pi,$$

where Δ is the symbol for the quantitative range of uncertainty in the value of a quantity. So that Δs is the range of uncertainty in the measurement of the position s, and Δp is the range of uncertainty in the measurement of the momentum p. The symbol $\geq$ means "greater than or equal to."

Werner Karl Heisenberg
1901-1976

By permission of Niels Bohr Library, American Institute of Physics

of the two measurement uncertainties can never be reduced to nothing. There is a clear limit then as to how precisely a given pair of such physical measurements can be made at the same time, for, although h is a very small quantity, it is not zero. This physical reality has nothing to do with imperfections in the measuring equipment but is an intrinsic fact of nature.

Thus if one wishes to measure the position of the particle with ultimate exactness, this is in principle possible, but only at the expense of simultaneously knowing nothing as to its momentum, and vice versa. If, on the other hand, we are content with partial or imprecise knowledge of the particle's position, then a complementary partial knowledge of its momentum is available to us.

One of the principal reasons often given for this is that one cannot perform a measurement on an object as small as an atom or an electron without interfering with its motion to some extent. That is, how else can one learn about the position of such a particle, for example, unless a photon of light is scattered from it. The scattered light will indicate the particle's position, but not any more accurately than the distance between adjacent crests in the wave oscillations of the photon. If, for more accuracy, we use a higher frequency photon with a shorter crest–to–crest distance, the attendant higher energy of the photon will cause a greater change and uncertainty in the particle's momentum (Hawking 88, p. 54).[5]

With some understanding of the Uncertainty Principle, the connection with complementarity can now perhaps be clarified. When the position of the object of observation, whether matter or radiation, is accurately known, then since it is so closely localized spatially, it assumes a particle form. On the other hand, if the momentum of the object is precisely known, which means (because of de Broglie's relation between momentum and wavelength mentioned above) that the wavelength is known, then it assumes a wave form. Thus the Complementarity Principle, dealing with the role of particles and waves in a duality, can be seen as evident in the extremes, i.e. position or momentum exactness, of Heisenberg's Uncertainty Principle.

However, of more direct interest with respect to the subject of time is a version of Heisenberg's principle which places similar restrictions on

---

[5] There are equivalent and complementary ways of explaining and understanding the Heisenberg Uncertainty Principle.

the simultaneous measurement of time and energy.[6] In fact the principle can be applied to any such pair of physical quantities which in physics are known as conjugate,[7] such as position and momentum or time and energy. In essence for time and energy, the principle says again that the uncertainty in the measurement of the energy of a particle times the uncertainty in the time it exists with that energy can never be less than Planck's constant.

This energy–time relationship has a direct application, for example, in determining the average lifetime of a nucleus that is subject to radioactive decay. Suppose the energy state of the nucleus is rather precisely known, then the Uncertainty Principle tells us that the period of time the nucleus remains in that state is less accurately known. In effect, this means that the average lifetime of the state is longer. So, although it is true that the nucleus can decay at any instant, the period of time over which this instant can occur is of greater duration than if its energy were less precisely known. This relation between energy and time is an important time–related feature of the quantum theory, and leads us to another equally important feature.

The uncertainty relation involving time and energy can be converted, using Einstein's $E = mc^2$ equation, into an uncertainty relation between time and mass. This relation is very useful in elementary particle physics in the detection and study of short–lived subnuclear particles. The larger the uncertainty in the mass of the particle, the shorter will be its average lifetime.

The mass–time relation can also tell us something very important about the nature of space–time. Consider a hypothetical very small, very short–lived particle. If the uncertainty in its mass times the uncertainty in its life time is *less than* Planck's constant, h, the principle tells us that it is indeed unobservable. However, this does not mean that it cannot exist for its very short life time, only that we cannot directly detect it. For example, the greater the uncertainty in its mass is, the greater its actual mass can be within the range of that uncertainty. But for the particle to remain undetected, then by similar reasoning the

---

[6]As with the momentum-position uncertainty relation, this one takes the mathematical form: $\Delta E \, \Delta t \geq h/4\pi$ where ΔE represents the uncertainty in the measurement of the energy, and Δt is the similar quantity for the time.

[7]A given set of conjugate quantities (generally called conjugate variables in physics) provides a particular mode of describing the dynamic behavior of a physical system. Often a given physical system is more easily described by one pair of conjugates than by another.

shorter its lifetime must be, as long as the product of the two uncertainties does not exceed h.

Such particles are known as virtual particles, and generally arise out of bare space, the vacuum, in oppositely charged pairs. A well–known example, is the very brief emergence of an electron (negative electric charge) and its opposite, a positron (positive electric charge). During this very short time even the great Law of Conservation of Energy can be violated, but only if Heisenberg's Principle is obeyed.

The assumption of the spontaneous creation of such unobservable short–lived electron–positron pairs has been vital to the success of the theory of quantum electrodynamics (Q. E. D.), which, as will be discussed in the next chapter, reconciles the theory of electromagnetism with the quantum and relativity theories. Although Q. E. D. is applicable only to electromagnetic phenomena it is incredibly precise, the most precise of all physical theories, but without the effect of these fleeting particle pairs the theory could not yield the right answer when compared to experimental measurements.

Thus the uncertainty principle and the success of the Q. E. D. theory tells us indirectly that empty space–time, the vacuum, is not really empty. It is a vibrant and dynamic complex of evanescent pairs of particles, not directly observable. They emerge and vanish, always with a mass and lifetime such that the product of the two is less than Planck's constant thus allowing the Heisenberg Uncertainty Principle to hide them from our view.

In fact the Heisenberg Uncertainty Principle itself implies the existence of such an active vacuum. Let us see how. In the thus far successful elementary particle theories, every such microscopic particle is associated with a field. For example, for the photon there is the electromagnetic field, which can, in a sense, be thought of as the influence of the particle being extended over a domain, similar to the influence of a magnet being spread out over a region. The higher the energy of the photon, the more intense or stronger is the field. A particle with rest mass, such as an electron, can also have an associated field.

Although a field can be extremely small in strength, it cannot be exactly zero, for then the conjugate quantity,[8] which is the rate of change of the field, would also be exactly zero. This would be similar to saying the position and the momentum of a particle can simultaneously

---

[8]We have already seen examples of conjugate quantities: position and momentum as well as time and energy.

be determined to have an exact value, zero, which is in clear violation of the uncertainty principle (Hawking 88, p. 105). So it is impossible for the field and its rate of change to simultaneously have an exact value, in this case zero; hence the vitality of the vacuum.

QUANTUM MECHANICS

After de Broglie's insight that matter could also behave as waves, Schrödinger and Heisenberg soon developed separate but equivalent mathematical formalisms of quantum mechanics capable of describing the behavior of microscopic phenomena. Schrödinger's formulation was known as wave mechanics, and Heisenberg's as matrix mechanics.

In terms of Schrödinger's wave viewpoint, which is more descriptively amenable, knowledge of the position of a particle is given by what is often called a wave packet (but physicists usually call them wave functions), the amplitude or magnitude of which at any point in space is directly related to the probability that the particle is there. Specifically the probability is equal to the square of the amplitude. A typical wave packet for a particle localized in the general vicinity of a point in space can be visualized in one dimension as having the bell shape shown in Figure 2a. Thus, according to the theory, the most probable position of the particle is at the point corresponding to the maximum of the curve (point A in Figure 2a). The farther away from that point we look, the less probable it is that the particle will be observed there.

If the position of the particle is more precisely known, then the wave function will be more closely collected or peaked, as in Figure 2b, and its particle nature will be emphasized. If it is less well known, then the function will be more spread out. As it continues to become even less precisely known, the particle begins gradually to develop a wavelike character, as in Figure 2c. By approaching a clearly defined wave length, (recalling the de Broglie relation between wavelength to momentum), the momentum of the particle is becoming more precisely known in accordance with the Heisenberg Uncertainty Principle. In describing the probabilistic state of a microscopic system the wave function then can cover the full range of possibilities from a particle–like, position–focused mode to a wave–like, momentum–focused mode. In this role, the wave function links and subsumes the wave and particle

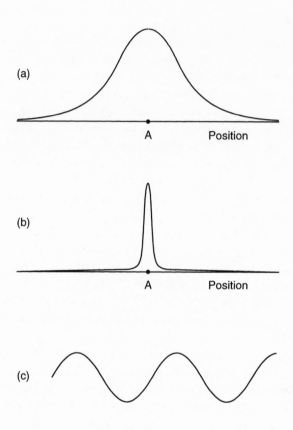

FIG. 2–Wave functions

modes, and serves as a coherent embodiment of Bohr's Complementarity Principle.[9]

OVERLAPPING WAVE FUNCTIONS

As you may notice in the curve in Figure 2a, the amplitude slowly dies away at the extremes of the wave packet, but a very important feature is that it never dies to precisely zero. This is true of essentially all wave packets or wave functions describing natural microscopic phenomena.

Therefore quantum mechanics tells us that the wave function describing each entity in the universe, at least to some infinitesimal degree, overlaps with that describing any other. The wave function of a macroscopic object such as an apple for all practical purpose dies out within a distance of a few times 10^{-8} centimeters[10] from what is macroscopically taken to be the apple's surface. Such a distance is quite unobservable to the naked eye. Nevertheless, according to the theory there is an extremely minute remainder that stretches out, continually diminishing, to the far reaches of the universe.

One must exercise care here about inferring conclusively that by this means we are somehow linked to everyone in the world and everything in the universe. The prevailing body of physical opinion is that such wave functions are only a mathematical representation of a set of statistically related probabilities. That is, the wave function in Figure 2a can be mapped out by an experiment, in which the position of the particle whose probability the wave function is describing would be measured many, many times. If the number of measurements yielding each given value of the position is plotted against the position itself, then the statistical accumulation of these data would result in a curve gradually assuming something like the shape given in Figure 2a as more and more measurements are recorded. In gathering these data it is clear that any given position measurement will in general not be reproduced on the succeeding measurement, but the accumulated ensemble of measurements yielding the probability pattern in Figure 2a is reproducible. It is often said that quantum mechanics because of this probabilistic character is "fuzzy," inexact, or unpredictable, but actually the wave functions and associated probabilities can be calculated quite exactly and give very accurate predictions of many physical quantities.

---

[9]Some argue that the existence of the wave function renders the Complementarity Principle unnecessary or redundant.

[10]10^{-8} is a fraction: one hundred millionth, or one divided by a number which is one with eight zeroes behind it.

Erwin Schrödinger
1887–1961

By permission of Niels Bohr Library, American Institute of Physics

Despite the well–established probabilistic nature of the quantum theory, it is difficult to escape the haunting thought that there may be some metaphysical meaning to the quantum mechanical prediction that there is a finite probability, however incredibly small, that you, or some part of you, could be found in Tahiti in the winter instead of shivering on a street corner in Montreal. Although this is a fascinating thought, in expressing it we must again realize that this probability is so small that in practical life experience it is effectively zero.

THE OBSERVER AND THE OBSERVED

The mathematical formalism based on the quantum theory has been enormously successful in predicting the behavior of microscopic systems. The accumulation of confirmatory experimental results in the study of molecules, atoms, nuclei, and elementary particles over a period of some sixty–five years has been extremely impressive. However, though the mathematical framework yields reliable results, some of the conceptual and metaphysical aspects of the quantum theory are still under considerable controversy (Herbert 85; Bohm 80; Wheeler 76).

Perhaps the most extensively discussed of such aspects has been the problem of observer theory. As we learned earlier, in contrast to the macroscopic measurements of our daily lives which can be made with minuscule effect on the object measured, a microscopic system cannot escape being affected by an observation. This is because generally the only measuring mechanism available is an interaction with something comparable in size to the object being measured. Thus the observer is no longer objectively detached from the observed as seems to be the case in the macroscopic world: observation is now an interactive process. In this process whether one can draw the line between observer and observed is unclear. It is because of the nature of this interaction between the two that John Wheeler in his provocative discourses on the subject substitutes the word "participator" for "observer" (Wheeler 76). But regardless of such labels, when is the interactive process of observation or participation complete?

Of the early formulators of the quantum theory, it was Niels Bohr who probably gave the most extensive thought to this question. According to Bohr, no "elementary phenomenon is a phenomenon until it is a registered [observed] phenomenon." Wheeler's version of this is perhaps more specific: "No phenomenon is a phenomenon until brought to a close by an irrevocable act of amplification" (Wheeler 94, p. 120). The act of amplification is of course the act of our measurement with some macroscopic instrument, which is used to amplify the interaction between some particle (or particles) we use as a microscopic probe and the particle under study so that we can register or record it. On the other hand, Bohr went so far as to claim that no phenomenon was valid until it had not only been recorded but also reported to someone else. We can therefore see that where to draw the line between observer and observed, or even whether an attempt should be made to make such a demarcation, might be a matter for considerable discussion.

The irrevocable act of amplification in an observation has clear implications with respect to the irreversible character of time. Why is this so? Before we measure, say, the position of a particle, all we know is that the probability that the measurement will yield a certain result is given by some wave function or "pattern," an example of which was given in Figure 2a. But once we have made the measurement on the phenomenon and have a fixed, specific, numerical result, we have by the measurement process irreversibly determined the outcome of the phenomenon. The process of measurement is often called "collapsing the wave function," compressing it to one result out of all the other possible results of varying probability. The performance of the measurement with its resultant irrevocable effect on the phenomenon is a temporally irreversible event; we and the phenomenon have participated in the irreversible nature of time (Davies 88, p. 106).

The problem of the observed phenomenon being affected abruptly and irreversibly by a measurement is extremely profound. The depth of the problem is demonstrated in a number of now–classic "thought" experiments, as well as a number of actual experiments very ingeniously designed to test the quantum theory. Probably the most famous of the experiments is known as the Einstein–Podolsky–Rosen (EPR) experiment (Einstein *et al.* 1935). It was first devised as a thought experiment by Einstein and his collaborators to demonstrate the incompleteness of the quantum theory. This came about because, after contributing to the development of the quantum theory by his explanation of the photoelectric effect, he never believed the theory to be a fully adequate description of the microscopic world. The strength of this belief is expressed in his famous words: "God does not play dice." Although the quantum theory still stands despite the challenge the EPR experiment presents, the experiment (or various versions of it which have recently been actually performed) remains today as a reference point in the continuing controversy, physical and philosophical, over the interpretation of the quantum measurement problem.[11]

One version of the experiment involves observing two photons that are polarized. We have all heard of polarized light: the "crests and valleys" of the light wave can be thought of as oscillating in a plane aligned in a certain direction as in Figure 3a. Essentially polarized sunglasses are filters which preferentially pass the light whose waves oscillate in the same direction as the orientation of the filter.

In the experiment the two photons are polarized in the same plane (whatever the direction of the plane may be) and are emitted in opposite directions as depicted in Figure 3b. Suppose that two polarization filters, A and B, are placed at opposite positions, each 100 miles away from the emission point. Detectors are placed behind each filter to register the photons that pass through the filters. These filters, as with the sunglasses, will preferentially pass the light that is polarized along the direction of their orientation. Let both filters be oriented, say, in the vertical direction. Since the joint polarization of the two photons (remember their polarizations were assumed to be the same) can be in any direction, there is only a certain probability, according to the quantum theory, that, say, filter A will pass its photon. The greatest probability is when the photon's polarization has the same direction as the filter's orientation. Suppose we experiment using filter A and it passes the photon, whose polarization is now measured to be vertical, because the filter is oriented vertically. It turns out that filter B, 200 miles away and also oriented vertically, will pass its photon too. Furthermore, if photon A did not pass its filter, then photon B would not either.

The puzzling question is: how does photon B "know" instantaneously that photon A (which could have by the probabilities involved either passed or not passed its filter) indeed passed its filter so that it too should pass its filter at B (again, recall that both photons have the same polarization direction)? So both photons either pass, or both do not, in strict correlation. It does not happen that one does and the other does not.

How does one explain such an infallible correlative behavior that seems to be maintained instantaneously over a stretch of 200 miles or

---

[11]Especially in recent years there have been a plethora of remarkably subtle and ingenious experiments that are probing various aspects of the EPR challenge as well as many other facets of the quantum measurement problem (see Kafatos 89, Anandan 90, and Greenberger 94).

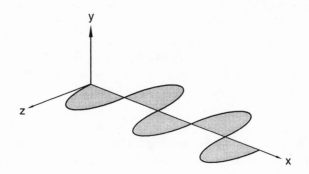

Fig. 3a–Simplified diagram of a light wave polarized
in the horizontal direction (z direction)

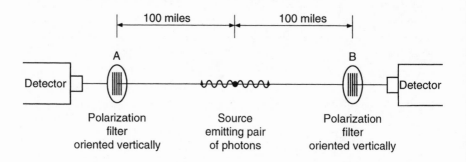

Fig. 3b–Diagram of an EPR experiment

any distance however large? A very significant contribution to understanding this problem was made by the now–famous Bell's inequality theorem published in 1964 (Bell 64). It is out of place here to render a detailed presentation of this theorem (see for example, Pagels 82, Herbert 85, Peat 90, Kafatos 89, or Anandan 90). A brief description of the salient features should suffice.

To begin with, the "common–sense" assumption that the two photons cannot communicate instantaneously is made. This is based in part on what we might expect in ordinary macroscopic experience. Then in essence the inequality states that the correlations one would expect to obtain between the photons counted at detector A and those counted at B when combined mathematically in a certain way, cannot exceed a certain numerical value. By correlation is meant the extent to which detection or non–detection of one photon will be correlated with detection or non–detection of the other, for various orientations of the polarizing filters. However, for appropriate settings of the filters quantum theory predicts that the numerical value in Bell's inequality is exceeded, there is more correlation than ordinary statistics predicts. And this quantum theory prediction has been experimentally confirmed[12] (Aspect et al. 82).

There seem to be two general approaches in attempting to explain this counterintuitive correlative behavior. The first is based on the assumption that underneath the "quantum veil" imposed by the uncertainty principle, particles are really behaving in a classical, non–quantal way which nature somehow does not allow us to see. Theories based on this concept are known as "hidden variable" theories (Bohm 80, Bohm et al. 87). The dynamical quantities, called variables, that we ordinarily work with in calculating the motion of a physical system are hidden. What has been shown using Bell's theorem in conjunction with the experimental results, is that for the strong correlations observed to occur in some of the hidden variable scenarios, there must be instantaneous (thus, superluminal, faster than light) communication between photons A and B as they reach their respective polarization filters.

Although some physicists are still working on hidden variable theories, most find them, and especially the idea of superluminal (faster than light) velocities, hard to swallow. So they accept the second

---

[12]It should be noted that a similar experiment could in principle be performed with any other simultaneously emitted, oppositely directed particles, e.g. electrons with a measurable correlated property, such as the polarization.

approach based on the quantum theory which, however defiant of common sense, gives the correct description. I have discussed the problem at length with many of my colleagues at Catholic University and elsewhere, including Joe Rosen, the son of Nathan Rosen of EPR, who visited us on sabbatical from the University of Tel Aviv. He and others feel, and I agree, that the quantum theory has been telling us all along about how the EPR experiment should be interpreted.

The atom or nucleus that emits the two oppositely directed photons is characterized by a wave function that contains all the information about the particle allowed by the quantum theory as constrained by the Heisenberg Uncertainty Principle. After emission of the photons the entire system, emitting particle and photons is still described by a total wave function. When this wave function is "collapsed" by an observation of the polarization of photon A, *the whole thing collapses*, and photon B, since it has the same polarization as A, has to do the same thing as A. That is, if A passes the polarization filter, B does also; if not, it does not.

Thus the whole wave function even though spread over 200 miles or more, behaves as an inseparable, coherent whole, and the "collapse" at the moment of the measurement is instantaneously active over the entire function. This behavior is generally termed by physicists as "non–local." Rosen feels that this phenomenon indicates that the quantum realm, the deeper realm hidden by the uncertainty principle is predominantly nontemporal and nonspatial. More precisely, as this deeper level is approached nontemporal and nonspatial characteristics become evident so that time and space as we know it begin to lose relevance. This in turn means that in this realm our usual concept of motion also loses validity (Rosen 91).

I believe that these ideas, as interesting as they are, will need considerable qualification and refining. In particular they need to be reconciled with what was said earlier about the dynamism of the vacuum. More about the nature of this unseen vacuum, this quantum underworld, will be treated in Part III.

In any event perhaps it is now evident how there is a nebulous border at the microscopic extreme of our cosmic cocoon, a cocoon that represents the world within which we feel we have cognitive access. Its gossamer–like border, whose measure is Planck's constant, is different from that of the other equally hazy extreme of the astronomically large, because the latter is expanding at such a tremendous speed. Yet my colleague, Joe Rosen, sees some connection between these two extremes in that the photon, an inhabitant of the quantum world moves at the speed of light, which so intrinsically characterizes our astronomical frontier. Whether at the microscopic or cosmologic level, the photon, the quantum of electromagnetic radiation, seems to play a large role in our understanding of time. So let us next turn to an examination of time in electromagnetism.

Summary

Probably the most apparent time–related feature of the quantum theory is to be found in the Heisenberg uncertainty relation involving time and energy. The two cannot be measured simultaneously with ultimate accuracy. This result comes into play in a variety of physical phenomena in the microscopic world, such as in calculating the average life–time of the radioactive decay of a nucleus. The time–mass version of the uncertainty principle finds use in the study of masses and lifetimes of short–lived subnuclear particles. It also places limits on the extent to which the Law of Conservation of Energy can be violated in terms of how massive and how long–lived virtual particles emerging from, and returning to, the vacuum can be.

Another very important time–related aspect of quantum theory is revealed in the measurement process that irrevocably converts or collapses a wave function, which gives a probability for every possible result of the measurement, to a specific one of those possible results. This is another example of an irreversible process that reveals time's irreversible character.

We saw how the Heisenberg Uncertainty Principle when applied to its extremes, either full knowledge of position or of momentum, yielded the dual modes of particle and wave addressed by Bohr's Complementarity Principle, as well as how the wave function could describe both possibilities. The wave function indeed has unusual properties since in principle it can stretch, however small its effect, to the far reaches of the universe. Also it is the uncanny coherence of the wave function that provides the most sensible explanation so far of the EPR experiment involving, for example, detection of the polarization of widely separated, oppositely directed photons. These phenomena among many others illustrate the various ways by which the Heisenberg Uncertainty Principle with its Planck's constant defines the microscopic limit of our cosmic cocoon.

5 TIMING AND SENSING
OUR COCOON THROUGH
ELECTROMAGNETISM

"The theory which I propose may therefore be called a theory of the
Electromagnetic Field, because it has to do with space in the
neighborhood of the electric and magnetic bodies."
—James Clerk Maxwell

There are four known forces in nature. The strongest of these is the
nuclear force, which, for example, keeps quarks together to form
protons and neutrons and also keeps protons and neutrons together in a
nucleus. Next in order of strength is the electromagnetic force which we
will see in this chapter is the fundamental mechanism that makes
possible the operation of us and most of the world to which we usually
relate. The third is known as the weak force, which comes into play in
the radioactive decay of a nucleus and many other elementary particle
phenomena. By far the weakest of the four is gravity. We can get an idea
of just how weak gravity is, say compared to electromagnetism, by a
simple experiment of using a small bar magnet to lift a nail from a
tabletop. The little magnet is able to do so against the gravitational
attraction imposed by the whole earth.

It has always been the mission of physicists to be able to describe
and predict the behavior of as large a range of physical phenomena as
possible with as little mathematics as possible. That is, they are always
striving for an "economy of equations." In particular there have been
continuing attempts to unify two, three, or all of the four forces into one
theory so that one set of equations describes all phenomena instead of a
set for each force (or interaction, a term most physicists use). Einstein
tried unsuccessfully to do this with electromagnetism and gravity for a
major part of his life. More successful has been the theory unifying the
electromagnetic and weak interactions, which received its first strong

support by experiments early in the last decade. This unification will be discussed further in Chapter 7.

THE GREAT THEORETICIANS OF ELECTROMAGNETISM

However, the first major unification of this kind was accomplished by James Clerk Maxwell in a paper entitled "A Dynamical Theory of the Electromagnetic Field," published in 1864. With a set of four equations of elegant simplicity and symmetry he was able to give a unified description of the electric and magnetic forces. Maxwell thus showed that electricity and magnetism were simply aspects of one force, electromagnetism.

Born in 1831 in Edinburgh, Maxwell as a boy possessed "agile strength of limb, imperturbable courage, and profound good nature" (Richtmeyer and Kennard 47, pgs. 46–8). He studied three years at the University of Edinburgh, but finished his schooling at Cambridge, from which he graduated with high honors. Early on he demonstrated outstanding ability in both theoretical and experimental physics, which he used in publishing some 100 papers on electromagnetism as well as molecular theory and color vision. His "Treatise on Electricity and Magnetism," published in 1873, ranks with Newton's "Principia" as one of the most important books in the history of science (Richtmeyer and Kennard 47, p. 49).

Maxwell's four equations describe the characteristics of stationary electric and magnetic fields as well as the intimate interaction between dynamic or changing electric and magnetic fields. A stationary electric charge can cause a static electric field. When the charge is moving at a constant velocity it additionally generates a static magnetic field. With one exception to be discussed in Chapter 8[1], this seems to be the only way a static magnetic field can arise, because, in contrast to electric charges, no magnetic charges have thus far been found to exist.

That is, all bar magnets and other magnetic materials possess their magnetism primarily by virtue of the electrons swirling about the nucleus in an atom, thus producing a small magnetic field, which, when aligned with its neighbors, sum to a stronger composite field. It is as if each atom were a tiny bar magnet with a north and south pole, each atomic magnet then aligning itself with the many other atoms in the

---

[1]In Chapter 8 we will discuss how at the most fundamental microscopic level many elementary particles such as electrons possess an intrinsic magnetism and behave like microscopic bar magnets.

James Clerk Maxwell
1831–1879

By permission of Niels Bohr Library, American Institute of Physics

material to yield the aggregate effect of the bar magnet stuck to your refrigerator.

Because they have north and south poles bar magnets, tiny or otherwise, are called magnetic dipoles in physics. Electric dipoles also exist, with a positive charge on one end and a negative charge on the other. But the fundamental difference between the magnetic and electric case is that in the latter the positive and negative poles can be separated as positive and negative electric charges. The magnetic poles cannot be separated this way, hence there are no magnetic charges. Thus it is the unit electric charge (positive on the proton and negative on the electron) that is the fundamental measure of most of the aggregate electromagnetic phenomena we experience at the macroscopic level.

The equations also describe how a changing electric field can generate a changing magnetic field, and vice versa. An oscillating electric charge or an oscillating magnet can generate an electromagnetic wave of combined electric and magnetic fields which are constantly linked and alternating as in Figure 4. But one of the most important results of the theory was that this electromagnetic field predicted by the theory turned out to propagate at a speed about equal to the speed of light as experimentally measured at that time. It was soon realized that the whole spectrum of radiations, radio waves, infrared, visible, ultraviolet, X–rays, and γ–rays, were all electromagnetic radiations moving at the speed of light.

However, the epitome in electromagnetic theory was reached soon after World War II when Richard Feynman, Julian Schwinger, and Shinichiro Tomonaga formulated quantum electrodynamics, often simply called Q. E. D. This theory reconciled Maxwell's theory for electromagnetic phenomena with the universally applicable basic theories of relativity and the quantum. In particular it was reconciled with quantum mechanics by describing the quantum behavior of light as photons. That is, the theory in effect extended Maxwell's theory, which described the electromagnetic field only in terms of waves, to include a quantum photon description. Q. E. D., although applicable only to electromagnetic phenomena, is by far the most accurate theory in all of physics, predicting numbers that agree with experiment to better than one part in a billion. In Feynman's words: "But so far, we have found nothing wrong with the theory of quantum electrodynamics. It is therefore, I would say, the jewel of physics—our proudest possession" (Feynman 85, p. 8).

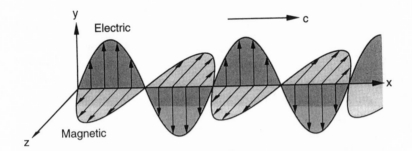

FIG. 4–Alternating electric and magnetic fields in an electromagnetic
wave moving at the speed of light, c. The polarization direction
is taken to be that of the electric wave.

THE PERVASIVENESS OF ELECTROMAGNETISM

In part because of the accuracy of Q. E. D. but also because of the wide technological application of electromagnetic theory, the electromagnetic force or interaction is known far better than the other three forces. Its effect and presence in all aspects of our life and relation to the world is ubiquitous. Electrons are constrained to orbit around the nucleus of an atom by the electromagnetic force. The interactive "glue" that keeps atoms together in a molecule is electromagnetic, so that all of chemistry and biology at root operate via this force. This means that we ourselves, and all our organs, are run by this mechanism, from the interactions of blood cells to the activity of neurons in the brain firing signals to each other across the synapses that separate them. Thus our most intimate interaction with matter is via the electromagnetic interaction. Indeed the dependence of the brain on electromagnetism for its operation has prompted some scholars to wonder if this very fact is not the reason why we know the electromagnetic interaction so accurately (Park 89).

Fire, gasoline consumption, and explosives (except for the nuclear bomb) all proceed via this interaction. It is the same force that governs the incessant interplay of the molecules in air and water that collectively unite their motion to give us sound and ocean surf. While it is gravity that keeps us, all earthly objects, and the atmosphere attached to the Earth, it is the electromagnetic force binding the atoms and molecules tightly together in solid objects that keeps the table lamp from falling through the table, and the table from falling through the floor. Although gravitational effects in terms of accelerations provide the cause, the disastrous effects of a car crash occur fundamentally from the power of the electromagnetic force.[2] It is this force that makes possible all modern communication: telephone, radio, TV, satellite, etc.

Whether we are examining the microscopic realm of elementary particles with particle accelerators and sensitive, sophisticated instruments or probing the heavens with giant telescopes, the knowledge we gain is mediated by the electromagnetic interaction. Virtually all experimental studies of the other three forces, whether in

---

[2]There is in addition a quantum effect that comes into play when atoms (or nuclei) are compressed tightly enough together. It is described by what is known as the Pauli Exclusion Principle, named after its discoverer, Wolfgang Pauli. In effect it says that, depending on the characteristics of an energy state of the atom (or nucleus), only a certain maximum number of electrons (or protons and neutrons) can occupy that state, others are excluded. That is, no more can be "pressed" into the state, unless a black hole is involved; then "all bets are off."

the microscopic or the cosmologic realm, are conducted through an electromagnetic "filter." This, of course, includes the operation of all the computers and complex electronic instruments that store and analyze the data, and that make calculations based on the data.

ELECTROMAGNETIC TIME

The time relevance of the electromagnetic interaction comes in many guises. It is this interaction that vitalizes the timing mechanism in the suprachiasmatic nuclei (SCN) in the hypothalamus that entrains our approximate living cycle. It likewise operates the timing device in an arctic gull's brain that makes it possible for it to navigate a round trip migration of 14,000 miles. Electromagnetic pulses with the fixed speed of light in vacuum and their somewhat lower, but well–known, speeds in other media such as copper wire and optical fiber make possible all of the complex timing mechanisms used in computer controlled experiments in the physical and life sciences.

Among the most significant time–related feature of the electromagnetic interaction is that it has provided us with the most accurate clock in use thus far. The now–famous cesium atomic clock is based on the fact that the cesium atom in one of its transitions between energy states emits radiation which oscillates at precisely 9,192,631,770 cycles per second. This has now become the time standard accepted universally throughout the world. In the United States the primary standard cesium clock is located at the National Institute of Standards and Technology (NIST) in Boulder, Colorado. Each time the cesium atoms accumulate the 9,192,631,770 oscillations, a beep is generated for the precision timing of the nation (Fraser 87, p. 72).

Recent cryogenic experiments involve techniques which can cool (and thus slow down) individual atoms to extremely low temperatures. Under these conditions it is claimed that the atoms can emit resonant signals 50 times more accurate than any other atomic clock (Kleppner 91). Also the use of lasers in a process known as optical pumping may yield a more precise clock (Itano and Ramsey 93). However, it may be some time before the technology utilizing these phenomena can be perfected.   Another interesting competitor of the cesium clock is a pulsar in outer space. These are stars consisting of extremely compressed neutrons which form a dense superconducting medium. By virtue of the superconducting currents a dipole magnetic field surrounds the star. Since the star's rotation axis and the axis of the magnetic field are generally not aligned, the precessing field generates a periodic electromagnetic pulse of remarkable regularity. Some of the fastest rotating pulsars produce pulses with periods as short as a few milliseconds with an incredible regularity that approaches that of the radiation from a cesium atom (Manchester 92). In any case, whether our clocks are atomic, astronomic, or conventional, all of our timers of any precision are ultimately electromagnetic, and the most accurate in use thus far is the cesium clock.

The accuracy of such a clock, atomic or astronomic, depends on its degree of isolation. The less subject it is to external perturbations, electromagnetic or gravitational, the more accurate it will be. Under appropriate conditions two similar clocks experiencing the same perturbations can jointly yield more accurate time when the ratio of their frequencies (instead of either individual frequency) is used as a standard. That is, if the disturbance affects both clocks in essentially the same way, then although the frequency of each clock individually may be rendered less accurate, the ratio of the two frequencies can be quite precise (Coe 69). In effect the disturbance is being "subtracted out." It is an extension of this basic technique that is now being put into practice using a global network of cesium clocks. Currently the timing data from some 200 cesium clocks around the world are correlated via a computer algorithm devised at NIST in Boulder.

Time–relevance is also apparent in the emission of electromagnetic radiation, which can be considered as one of the physical phenomena that serves as a gauge or indicator of the irreversible advance of time. Light from a candle in the dining room is emitted in all directions, and, except for chance reflections, the vast majority of it never returns to the source.

However, from the viewpoint of physical theory this irreversibility is considerably more subtle than might at first appear. Maxwell's equations as well as the Q. E. D. equations that can describe the behavior of the light are symmetric in time. That is, they work equally well whether the electromagnetic radiation proceeds in one direction with time progressing, or the opposite direction with time regressing. So that the equations are capable of describing the reverse of the above case: when light is emitted from the dining room walls and focused on the wick of the candle, even though we have never seen that happen. Although such an occurrence is extremely unlikely it is still in principle possible, and the theoretical equations can include that possibility (Morris 85, p. 142).

In 1945 John Wheeler and Richard Feynman showed how the time-symmetric equations might be reconciled with the time-asymmetric emission of light from a source (Wheeler and Feynman 1945), but their theory has not been experimentally confirmed and the quantum version of it has never been formulated. In reality, however, time asymmetry characterizes the multitude of electrodynamic processes which underlie and activate all of earthly nature. Atoms and molecules are continually absorbing and emitting mostly low energy photons. Such low energy photons are also emitted whenever these particles collide. All of this radiation from emissions and collisions is ultmately degraded in energy and lost in the complexity of the medium. Even though in principle, according to the theoretical equations, an isolated event is time-symmetric, where in nature on this earth is there such an isolated event? Although in Chapter 3 we saw that relativity tells us times are different for frames of reference in motion relative to each other, here I am not thinking cosmically, but locally, i.e., the reference frame of the earth, or any other planet where electromagnetism dominates its nature. So that for such cases electromagnetic phenomena underlie and drive the time asymmetry of what I call the thermodynamic gauge of time discussed in Chapter 9.

OUR "MYOPIC" ELECTROMAGNETIC LOOKING GLASS AND THE FINE STRUCTURE CONSTANT

It should now be apparent how pervasive the electromagnetic interaction and its temporal aspects are in our daily experience of ourselves and the world. It not only colors how we see ourselves and our earthly environment, but also qualifies how we see beyond to the microscopic and cosmologic realms. It is as if the only "glasses" available to us are electromagnetic and we are thus encumbered with a certain "myopia." It is myopia in the sense that the electromagnetic interaction is almost the sole mediator between us in the macroscopic world, the "middle–world," and our knowledge of the worlds of the very small and the very large.

In some strange way that has haunted my thoughts for many years, the mediative quality of electromagnetism and the median position of our macroscopic world between the other two I believe is embodied and crystallized in still another constant of nature known as the fine structure constant. The reason for this is that the fine structure constant, which physicists denote by α, is a combination of all three of the crucial constants we have been discussing in this Part of the book: h (Planck's constant), c (the velocity of light), and e (the unit electric charge).

Specifically α is the square of the unit electric charge divided by the product of Planck's constant times the velocity of light.[3] Its value turns out to be very close to 1/137, not a number with much simplicity or symmetry.

Nevertheless h, c, and e, which are the fundamental measures of each of the three worlds we have been discussing, come together in this fine structure constant. It is like a crystal or diamond, centered in the macroscopic world in which we live, but giving the view allowed us to the microscopic and cosmological worlds. So that, with the aid of the fine structure constant our view of these other worlds is mediated by the electromagnetic interaction with the unit electric charge as its basic measure. It is via these "myopic electromagnetic glasses" that information about our cosmic cocoon filters through to us. It is a cocoon described with *space*, vitalized by *time*, and infinitely provident in potential *knowledge*, the three elements which, at the beginning of this Part, Raimundo Panikkar described as fundamentally limiting to us humans.

SUMMARY

Of the four forces of nature, the most familiar and best understood is the electromagnetic, whose fundamental measure is the unit electric charge. This force is ubiquitous in all aspects of our lives in the macroscopic world. Chemistry, biology, the operation of all living things, including humans and their brains, surf and sound, all modern communication, scientific measurements, and computers, rely on the electromagnetic interaction. It has provided us with our most accurate timing device, the cesium clock. With its irretrievable emission from a source such as a candle it provides us with another example of a phenomenon by which time has been gauged.

For me it seems that the three worlds, microscopic, macroscopic, and cosmic with their respective gauges, Planck's constant (h), the electric charge (e), and the velocity of light (c), all come together in what

---

[3]Mathematically this is expressed as

$$\alpha = \frac{e^2}{hc}$$

In mathematical calculations in Q. E. D. α gives the relative strength of the electromagnetic interaction. Again, I find it challenging to the imagination that, α giving the strength of the electromagnetic interaction which dominates our "middle world," also contains the factors h and c characterizing the microscopic and cosmologic worlds.

is known as the fine structure constant (α), which somehow serves as an "eyepiece" to view all three worlds of our cocoon.

6 Probing Beyond: Spiritual Perceptions of Our Cocoon's Temporality

"But it is reasonable to enquire whether, in the mystical illusions of man, there is not a reflection of an underlying reality."
"Heaven is nowhere in space, but it is in time."
—Sir Arthur Eddington

Again recall at the beginning of this Part of the book (Part II) it was noted that *time, space,* and *knowledge* are the three fundamental limitations encumbering us according to Raimundo Panikkar. For example, on the human level we have only one lifetime, the space on Earth seems to get smaller and smaller, and we rarely seem to have enough knowledge to make a fully comfortable decision. On a more cosmic level the sun will only shine for another six billion years or so, the limited velocity of our spacecraft confines us to a small region of our galaxy, and with the universe so vast and diverse we will undoubtedly never know all there is to know.

As we have seen, so far as the physical world is concerned, we can find some understanding of the time, space, and knowledge limitations in terms of the relativity, quantum, and electromagnetic theories as discussed in the last three chapters. However, Panikkar also said that attendant with the above limitations there was the "almost irresistible desire to peer over at the 'other shore.'" This "other shore," this "beyond," represents the apprehension of an underlying, ineffable reality, which some may associate with an attribute of a transcendent Entity or God.

The "Map" and the "Terrain"

What can we say about this underlying reality? It is a reality the physical aspects of which are only approximated by such mathematical descriptions as the theory of relativity, etc. Any thoughtful physicist will readily admit that, however reliable and encompassing these theoretical constructs are, from a more sweeping long range viewpoint, they are only temporary. They will probably be either fine–tuned or subsumed by a more encompassing theory, which in turn will probably be subsumed. We seem to continue in the unshakeable, abiding belief that some kind of ultimate reality does exist, a reality the knowledge of which we are approaching ever more closely, but never quite reaching.

Thus our physical theories are but "maps" of our cosmic cocoon, and although they are continually being made more accurate, they are not the "terrain" itself.[1] They constitute our best effort thus far at understanding the order of the physical world, the cocoon around us, and as such serve as mediators between us and the "terrain," the underlying reality.

In my opinion nowhere is the idea of the mediating "map" and the "terrain" more masterfully and comprehensively described than in Edward Harrison's "Masks of the Universe." Harrison shows how during every major period in mankind's history a believable universe or world view was developed, which was rationally understandable and emotionally, as well as spiritually, acceptable. The earliest universes were ones of animism endowing the surrounding world of rivers, trees, and animals with spirits. As history unfolded, mankind's idea of a credible universe changed. Each universe, however awe–inspiring in its day, was superseded by a grander scheme: e.g. there was the "geometric universe" of the Greeks, the "medieval universe" of Christianity and Islam, the "mechanistic universe" of the Enlightenment, etc. (Harrison 85). But all of these universes, including the one we tentatively accept today, are only model universes (with lower case u). They are not the real Universe (with capital U). Mankind's universes are masks of the Universe which Harrison suggests may be identified with God (Harrison 85).

Regardless of whether we call this underlying reality, the "terrain," the Universe, or God, perhaps we may learn a little more about it by using knowledge gained through intuition and spirituality to complement our scientific view. Furthermore is it not possible that such intuitive and spiritual insight could occasionally furnish us with at least

---

[1]Perhaps one exception to this statement might be quantum electrodynamics (Q. E. D.) which uniquely demonstrates that we can understand at least some part of nature with incredible accuracy. However, some aspects of Q. E. D. and why it works so well are still not fully understood today so that it continues to be subject to signficant study.

a dimly perceived hint of scientific things to come, or occasionally, even what course to follow scientifically. Perhaps we should go back and extract from the treasure of these more spiritually oriented universes or cosmologies those components, which will help form along with science a more complete picture of our cocoon and its temporal aspects.

Since we ourselves are part of the universe and its constituents (atoms and molecules) are constantly in vibrant motion in our bodies, we cannot fully know the Universe. We cannot extract ourselves from it and get a transcendent view. This being the case, perhaps we should exploit this fact, the fact that we are truly part of nature imbedded in its cosmic temporal flow like a school of small fish moving with the surge of the sea. As a living part of this universe that has evolved consciousness, maybe we can somehow use the spirituality with which we and our forbears were endowed in an approach to reality unmediated by mathematial theories, to help see the way to a more holistic "map."

Accordingly, let us look at how some religious traditions see the "terrain," especially its time–related aspects. Perhaps this is best done by examining the cosmologies characterizing these traditions. Most religions have their own cosmology, their own view of the universe. Although the cosmologies often may incorporate some rather specific physical features, their purpose is primarily theological; they provide a world view, a setting, for the abiding spiritual guidance and sustenance needed by worshippers in dealing with themselves, others, and nature. However, generally at its core the theological motive undergirding the cosmology is to provide a "path" to salvation. The cosmology of the natural world is endowed with a soteriological (salvational) meaning by using it as a metaphor in describing this path. In a word, religious cosmology and salvation generally go hand in hand.

The achievement of salvation, the end of the "path," is usually associated with gaining unity with an ultimate Reality or God, and is often described with rich and inspiring imagery. This "end–time" theology, or eschatology, is the completing feature of a cosmology that is pervaded with temporal implications. Indeed temporal insights, implicit and explicit, generally characterize a cosmology throughout, whether it is everlastingly cyclical or unrepeatable with one beginning and ending. In what follows let us see what cosmologies from a few religious traditions say about the "terrain" of our cocoon, and in turn what that may tell us about time.

PRIMITIVE CYCLICAL RITUALS

Undoubtedly primitive man and woman must have experienced a profound awe for the manifold variety and fecundity of the natural world that enfolded them. They somehow made their peace with the power, beauty, and terror of nature, and in so doing closely identified themselves with its cycles: the sun's daily passage, the moon's periodicity, and the changing seasons.

However, they also had to face a more personally terrifying natural phenomenon, that of their own ultimate death. It was thus quite understandable that they looked to nature with its yearly rebirth for a consolation, a security against the terror of death and time. Since nature is reborn with periodic frequency, perhaps they too could experience this rebirth by identifying themselves with it. Thus in their most religious moments it is reasonable that they might have developed a cyclical view of time. On the other hand in their daily pursuits they were able to observe progressive (non–cyclical) changes as they constructed a domicile, watched the continual growth of a tree through the seasons, or noted the aging of their parents. With some awareness of such sequential change they must have had at least some sense of the advancing, unrepeatable character of time in their day–to–day living.

This contrast between these two time views (cyclical and sequential) of archaic peoples is evident in the work of Mircea Eliade (Eliade 71). Basing his conclusions on common features found in many (but not all) primitive religions throughout the world, he sees an interesting pattern of cyclical religious behavior among these traditions wherein there is a regularly recurring need to return to some mythical beginning.

Eliade associates what he terms "sacred" time with such cyclically governed religious times and "profane" time with ordinary daily temporal existence. In these periodic religious celebrations the experience of rebirth for these archaic peoples was extremely profound. It was usually based on a ritualistic yearly repetition of some mythical creation act, often involving some hero–god who brought about creation and order by fighting and overcoming the forces of darkness, evil, and chaos (Eliade 71, p. 17ff; p. 57ff).

The power of the ritual lay in the visceral belief of the participants that they were in reality reliving the creation act. A coincidence of the mythical event with the present moment was realized, so that profane time, regarded as essentially unreal, was erased. The result was a total sense of renewal because the accumulation of all sins, miseries, and tragedies of the past year was also erased. Thus in effect time itself was regenerated. In this way these early peoples dealt with what Eliade called the "terror of history" (Eliade 71, p. 141ff).

The practice of reproducing such an act of a mythical archetype had not only a temporal aspect but also a spatial aspect. The cyclically repeated rituals were always performed at the same hallowed spot. Regardless of what marked this location, be it a monolith, icon, or altar, the place was looked upon as the Center, the cosmic Center where the mythical creation act occurred (Eliade 71, p. 12).

Such was the way that many archaic cultures saw time and the underlying reality or "terrain;" it was their spiritual view of the cocoon. With this heritage in mind let us briefly examine the time–related aspects of some present–day religious cosmologies East and West.

SELECTED EXAMPLES OF EASTERN TEMPORAL WISDOM

Hinduism. The oldest of today's major religions is Hinduism. With some notable exceptions it can be regarded as a "mother of Eastern religions," because its complex and variegated development has not only insured its durability but also made it a spawning ground for other religions. For example, in the 6th century B.C. it survived the severe schisms of Buddhism and Jainism. Buddhism itself fragmented into many sects and spread to Sri Lanka, Southeast Asia, Indonesia, Nepal, Tibet, and in a considerably modified form to China, Japan, and Korea. Ultimately it left India almost entirely. Thus Indian religious thought, enormously diversified, has had, in one form or another, an extensive influence throughout most of Asia.

Although Hinduism (often called Brahmanism) remained in India, it nevertheless underwent prodigious diversification in its growth. This is due in part to its age, in part to its not being based upon the teachings of one person with a centralized clergy, and in part to the prolific intellect, intuition, and imagination of its many leaders. Indeed it is a religion of such unparalleled richness and heterogeneity that some of the beliefs and philosophies actually contradict one another.

The growth and the attendant vast spectrum of thought can be traced from the earliest group of scriptures (known as the Sruti), which among others includes the Vedas and Upanishads, to the later group (known as the Smriti) including among others the Sutras and Puranas (Nikhilananda 63, p. 22). The Epics, also a member of this latter group, contain the Mahabharata of which the Bhagavad Gita is a part. The Mahabharata, with 100,000 verses, is probably the longest epic poem in history.

The diversity of the religion is apparent in the Sutras, which contain the religious philosophy of the six major schools of Hindu or Brahmanical thought. In terms of basic philosophic premises the six schools can be reduced to three groups. The first, including the Vedanta and Purva–Mimamsa schools, is monistic, holding that there is only one fundamental reality. The Sankhya and Yoga schools are dualistic in this respect, while the Nyaya and Vaisesika see a universe based on plural realities.

Despite this abundant variety of religious philosophic positions, all six schools adhere to some common time–related views. This is because the problem of time has been a central concern in the historical development of these positions. So that in the rich tapestry of Brahmanism time is interwoven with such basic concepts as being and becoming, change and causality, and creation and annihilation (Balslev 83, p. 15). Thus the concept of repeated creation and dissolution of the universe is accepted by all schools, except the Purva–Mimamsa. Also all traditions, drawing on the Upanishads, maintain that being cannot arise from nothing; being is uncaused, indestructible, beginningless and endless (Balslev 83, p. 20ff):

> Of the non–existent there is no coming to be:
> of the existent there is no ceasing to be.
>
> —Bhagavad Gita 2:16

Notwithstanding these common beliefs, there is much more that distinguishes the schools. For example, in the Nyaya–Vaisesika pluralistic system time along with space are but two of nine equally fundamental realities (Reyna 71, p. 202). As one of the transcendent realities, time is conceived as static; it does not flow as described by Newton. As such it cannot be directly perceived, only inferred from motion and change. Nevertheless, time is regarded as a necessary condition for change and movement. In other words changes are *in* time; time itself cannot change (Balslev 83, p. 29ff).

For the dualistic Sankhya–Yoga schools there are two irreducible realities: Purusa (consciousness) and Prakriti (the underlying ground or principle which makes possible all movement and becoming). In these traditions time is considered absolutely inseparable from change and motion, which are essential characteristics of Prakriti.

However, of all the schools it is essentially the monistic philosophy of the Vedanta school with its offshoots, embodying the views of such great leaders as Shankara, Ramanuja, and Madhva, that now dominates the mainstream of Hindu thought. And it is Shankara's

Advaita Vedanta that most eloquently and beautifully expresses the monism, or non–dualism (Nikhilananda 63, p. 21), that courses through the center of this mainstream and represents "the culmination of the Brahmanical tradition" (Balslev 83, p. 57).

The Advaita Vedanta tells us that the ultimate deity, from which all other deities derive their power, is Brahman. Brahman is the only Absolute Reality: beginningless, endless, changeless, ineffable, and beyond good and evil, time, space, the universe, and causation. In particular since only the timeless Brahman is real, time itself has no absolute reality. The ultimate individual Self, also beyond the ensnaring concerns of this world, is Atman, the indestructible spirit of Brahman in man and woman.

Time, space, and the universe are seen as but transient manifestations which arise from, and return to, Brahman repetitively.[2] The vast scale of this periodic creation and destruction of the universe is described in the Puranas. The smallest period of this cosmic process is the yuga, of which there are four of progressively shorter duration, but which total 4,320,000 years, a mahayuga. This in turn is but an increment in a succession of periods of larger and larger scale, the largest of which is the "100 year" life of Brahma,[3] 311,040 billion years (Hopkins 71, p. 101). Hinduism is the only major religion that envisions specific time durations of such colossal scope.

It is important at this juncture to examine the intimate relationship between this cyclical cosmology and salvation. Given the age–old belief in reincarnation and karma,[4] the endless periodicity of creations and annihilations seems to be presented deliberately as a metaphor for the painful monotony of continuous deaths and rebirths through which one must suffer if what is known as *moksha* is not achieved. With moksha one is released from the ensnarements of the natural world, from the bonds of karma and the interminable chain of rebirths, worldly lives, and deaths known as Samsara. The release from Samsara is to a

---

[2]Brahman is the cause of the manifested universe, but not in a temporal sense, i.e., antecedence in time, otherwise some fallacious temporality could be attributed to Brahman.

[3]Brahma, the creator, is one of the trinity of gods, along with Vishnu, the preserver, and Shiva, the destroyer, which are manifestations of the supreme god, Brahman.

[4]Karma, sometimes called the law of cause and effect, essentially expresses the belief that one's fortune in this life is affected by one's actions in a past life, and one's future life will be affected by one's present action.

transcendent state of consciousness wherein one is totally identified with Atman, the spirit of Brahman.

The awesome periodicity of the Brahmanical cosmology is often cited by Western writers as the basis for a general claim that a strictly cyclical view of time characterizes this tradition. As will be discussed further in Chapter 9, this claim has only very limited validity. Firstly, the yugas are not equal in duration, and even if they were, it is the karmic growth and progression of the soul through this periodicity that is the essential salvational feature. Secondly, as we have seen there is a voluminous scriptural literature in the tradition that meticulously expounds on an incredibly broad spectrum of time concepts, most of which are not cyclical (Balslev 90).

Buddhism, Nirvana, and the Moment. Nevertheless, the concept of rhythmic repetition, but in altered form, also found its way into the cosmologies of most Buddhist sects (Eliade 71, p. 115). Again the cosmologies provide a milieu for the path to salvation. In this case it means transcending the samsaric cycle of births, deaths, and all attendant suffering, and achieving nirvana.

According to Edward Conze: "Nirvana is the raison d'etre of Buddhism, and its ultimate justification" (Conze 67, p. 71). Human words are considered inadequate to describe the Absolute Truth or Ultimate Reality which is nirvana. Although meditation and following the Buddha's doctrine, called the Eight–fold Path, (symbolized in Figure 5), have generally been found helpful, there are no set prescriptions for its attainment. All desire must be abandoned, including the desire for nirvana itself, or even the desire for death. But with nirvana time is transcended.

Particularly with respect to reaching nirvana, there are some general differences between the two main branches of Buddhism: the Hinayana, holding to the earliest orthodoxy, and the Mahayana, which arose roughly 700 years after the Buddha's ministry. In the more conservative Hinayana, dominated by the priesthood, usually only a priest could reach nirvana. The Mahayana tended to be more democratic; the path to nirvana was open to all, and the salvation of one's neighbor and universal enlightenment were stressed.

These differences are reflected generally in their cosmologies. Some Mahayana sects visualize endless worlds throughout space inhabited by

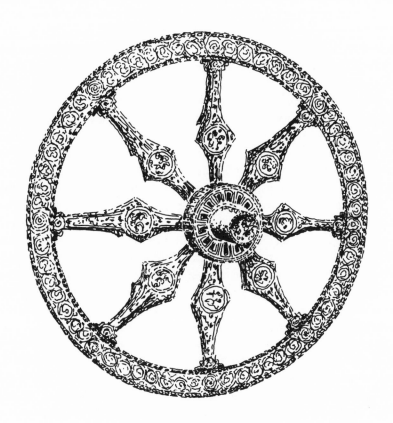

FIG. 5–Symbol of the Eightfold Path.

Buddhas. This accommodates the belief that nirvana or Buddhahood is available to all. Therefore their cosmologies tend to place an emphasis on space. In contrast, in the Hinayana some sects hold to the belief that there was a succession of some seven Buddhas, the seventh being the historical Buddha. Thus their cosmologies tend to be dominated by time.

It is in the concept of time that most all of Buddhism[5] differs fundamentally from Brahmanism. The depth of this difference can be seen when it is realized that it goes hand in hand with another profound difference, concerning the concept of self. For the Buddhist, flux and change characterize the world, so that only the "moment" is real, the "point–instant" in space and time. This view is intimately consistent with the belief in "no–self," because, if only the moment is real, then there is no abiding self that persists from moment to moment. There is no real essence by means of which man and woman can be distinguished from anything else in this world of flux. This belief in no–self, or anatman, is in direct opposition to the Brahmanical doctrine of a constant abiding self, ultimately represented by Atman.

Hence for the Buddhist duration and continuity are only conceptual constructions, and change is not just modification but substitution of one entity by another. The annihilation of the entity of the previous moment is total and spontaneous, so that being is absolutely instantaneous (Balslev 83, p. 80). Thus the reality of change and the present moment is essential, but only fully understood in the reality of nirvana.

The Tao te Ching. The importance of the spontaneous and the moment finds some approximate congeniality with the Taoist philosophy of China, but in a somewhat more softened, diffuse, and humanly subjective sense. That is, the Tao te Ching, reputedly written by Lao Tzu, tells us to do nothing that is not spontaneous and genuine. We should release our free–flowing native instincts in serene, but uncompromising naturalness and enlightened passivity. This is expressed in Lao Tzu's doctrine of *wu wei* (not doing), which is applied to everything from personal relations to politics and war.

One useful way of applying wu wei is to perceive that every action provokes a reaction, more often an undesired one. It is better to do nothing about evil and let it run its self–defeating course. For every time an attempt is made to correct evil, the evil only becomes reinforced by

---

[5]It must be remembered that there are a large number of Buddhist sects, each of which has a somewhat different concept of time. Here for the purposes of this book we are attempting to describe concepts thought to be generally characteristic of Buddhism.

the importance that has been accorded it. In the words of the *Tao te Ching*: "The more laws you make the more thieves there will be" (Welch 57, p. 20). Thus the best thing to do is to return good for evil, or as Lao Tzu puts it, "requite hatred with virtue (te)" (Welch 57, p. 21). This sounds quite similar to the teachings of Jesus[6], but Taoists see this behavior as practical and the best way to get people to do what you want, not as a holy duty. Thus inaction succeeds by *being* rather than doing, by attitude rather than act (Welch 57, p. 21). Indeed the best symbol for Tao is water:

> That which is best is similar to water; Water profits ten thousand things and does not oppose them. It is always at rest in humble places that people dislike. Thus it is close to Tao. [Tao te Ching, Chap. 8] (Chung–yuan 75, p. 27).

Thus the Tao is the mysterious quiet that pervades all nature. This is reflected in the Taoist cosmology, which reveals two aspects of Tao. There is an *apparent* aspect manifested by the order of the universe and an *absolute* aspect which is the Essence from which the order arises. This Essence or Absolute Tao is often referred to as the Nameless or Non–Being. This is nonbeing in the sense that it cannot be classed with anything we know as being; it is rather "no–thing":

> The Tao that can be Tao'd is not the Absolute Tao. The name that can be named is not the absolute name (Welsh 57, p. 55).

The world and all its creatures emerge from and return to the Absolute Tao, which is ineffable and timeless. There are no time scales, as in the Hindu and Buddhist cosmologies, only a gentle unspecified rhythm. An aura of quiet natural beauty, living serenity, and immanent mystery therefore pervades the cosmos of the Tao. Salvation involves a gracious, relinquishing of all that is not natural and instinctive, a healing return to the Absolute Tao (Girardot 90).

In our survey of the foregoing religions three general features may be apparent: 1) a cyclical or rhythmic cosmology of some kind, 2) the salvational goal of transcending this rhythmicity and identifying with a timeless reality, and 3) varying concepts of temporality in lived life. Thus, while there is indeed a considerable cyclical aspect to Eastern concepts of time, it is erroneous to assume that it constitutes the whole temporal picture. Other properties of time play an equally important role. Among these properties is the ongoing, irreversible quality of time,

---

[6]For some remarkable parallels between the New Testament Gospels and passages in the *Tao Te Ching* see Welch 57, pp. 5-6.

a feature which is the dominant temporal component that evolved in the Judeo–Christian–Islamic tradition.

JUDEO–CHRISTIAN–ISLAMIC EMERGENCE INTO UNREPEATABLE TIME

Earlier in this chapter we learned from the work of Mircea Eliade how archaic peoples dealt with the "terror of history" by totally immersing themselves in their yearly rituals of complete renewal. Eliade goes on to compare this primitive cyclical experience with that of the early Israelites, and suggests that the Israelites began to deal with this terror from a considerably different spiritual posture, namely that of *faith* (Eliade 71, p. 109). It was this faith that was the undercurrent nourishing the seeds for the gradual growth over many centuries of a sense of time as progressive and non–cyclical. I believe it is a profound insight that faith and subjectively experienced advancing time go hand–in–hand. If we think on it, to live and live fully in the relentless evolving of time, which is open ended and fraught with chance–taking and vulnerability, requires an enormous amount of faith, whether conscious or subconscious.

What role did faith play in developing the temporal concepts of the biblical era? The power of biblical faith was first exhibited by Abraham's willingness to sacrifice his only son, Isaac, if God, Yahweh, so commanded it. Abraham's interaction with Yahweh was the beginning of an almost 2000–year dialogue between the Israelites and God in which there was not just one divine event which was periodically celebrated, but a number of them. Undoubtedly the most significant episode in this dialogue was the Exodus from Egypt, led by Moses, empowered by faith. This saga found a spiritual fulfillment with the receipt of the Ten Commandments.

Later, after the Israelites led by Joshua invaded Canaan, they adapted the Canaanite festivals, which celebrated gods of fertility and nature in a yearly cyclical fashion reminiscent of the archaic cultures described by Eliade. These festivals were transformed by the Israelites to celebrations of some of the major past events in their interaction with Yahweh, e.g., the Passover celebrating the Exodus, the Feast of Tabernacles celebrating the covenant renewal at Shechem, etc. In effect they began worshipping a single God of evolving history instead of gods of cyclical nature (von Rad 65, p. 81). So that in about the 10th century B.C., looking back in the light of the Exodus, the first writers of the biblical scriptures realized that there were many holy occasions on which Yahweh intervened on behalf of the Israelites. The account of this succession of divine events of which none could be omitted developed into a sequential history (von Rad 65, p. 83). It spanned the entire period starting with Abraham and the succeeding patriarchs, through the period of the Judges, such as Deborah and Samuel, and into the period of the Kings.

Nevertheless it was many centuries before the record of these events was looked upon as a chronological history in the modern sense. One of the reasons for this was that the priests and religious leaders wanted the events to maintain their spiritual vitality and not to slip forgotten into the irretrievable past. Thus these holy occasions were originally regarded as separate, temporally disconnected "times" by the Israelites, who had no comprehension, as we do today, of a universal chronological time, proceeding independent of individual occurrences (von Rad 65, p. 78).

In fact the Hebrew language lacked a word for time in this sense, or for history. This biblical view of time, or "times," was later expressed primarily in terms of two Greek words,[7] "kairos" and "chronos," endowing time roughly with quality and extensiveness, respectively. Kairos had the general purport of "decisive moment," with powerful elements of fate and crisis. It was believed that Yahweh governed and dispensed these crucial moments, a prototype for which would be the "Time of Judgment" (Delling 65, p. 455). On the other hand chronos could mean time in general, duration, lifetime, or age.

The periods of time characterizing chronos lacked the precision of modern time increments. Since the Bible was written as narrated history of the spiritual interaction of men and women with God, time tended to be "measured" in humanly graspable intervals, such as a person's life time (Yeide 90). Thus, for example, we see the orgy of "begats" in the Gospel of Matthew (King James version): "Abraham begat Isaac; and Isaac begat Jacob; and Jacob begat..." (Matthew 1:1).[8]

The early Christians quite naturally continued the Israelite tradition of "event–oriented" time. With the Christians there were also many decisive sacred events, compressed, of course, into a much shorter

---

[7]The use of Greek is especially important because of the *Septuagint*, which was a Greek translation of the scriptures begun by Jewish scholars in Alexandria in the 3rd century B.C.

[8]However, here it must be emphasized that the primary purpose of this genealogy, as seen by most biblical scholars, was to establish the authenticity of Jesus' messiahship (e.g. Brown 77).

period of time. By far the most crucial of these was the crucifixion and resurrection of Jesus. In the light of this central divine episode the many inspired spiritual acts, especially in the ministries of Jesus and Paul, were each suffused with a profound holy import. Although it was not viewed so in biblical times, for Christians in later centuries and today Jesus stands forever at the center of history, B.C. and A.D. years being numbered from this time.

In any case in the Christian era also, the sense of sequential history and time inherited from the Israelites was maintained and propagated. According to the biblical scholar Gerhard von Rad, this development of serially progressing history which Israel bequeathed to the West was one of its greatest achievements (von Rad 65, p. 84).

If we look back at the sweep of biblical history, the reality of time seems to have been experienced and viewed on three different levels (Yeide 90). The first is that of human subjectivity, time as realized in the worldly and religious life of persons and communities. The second is the cosmic level based on the understanding of the order of the natural world, which exhibits a manifold diversity of temporal aspects. The third level is that realized by the divine encounter with God; it is God's eternal time:

> "...with the Lord one day is as a thousand years, and a thousand years as a day."
>
> Peter II 3:8

It is the interplay of these last two levels that provides the fabric of the Judeo–Christian, as well as the Islamic, cosmologies. They are "one–time" cosmologies characterized by one unrepeatable beginning and evolving redemptively to a specified end, involving an eschatology of final salvation and judgment. With rich imagery the eschatologies feature the coming of the Messiah as set forth in Daniel, the second coming of Christ as described in Revelation, and the Day of Judgment as depicted in the Koran (e.g., Suras 73, 75, 82, and 99). Therefore in addition to a sense of the sequential advance of time inherited from the dialogue of the early Israelites with God, these cosmologies clearly establish a sweeping spiritual view of time's progression.

The validity of this progression is reaffirmed by many Islamic thinkers. For example, the 17th century Islamic philosopher Mulla Sadra, building on the thoughts of Heraclitus concerning change (see Chapter 2), was the first philosopher in Islam to establish a philosophy of flux. He saw movement as the only reality in the world, and superimposed onto the concept of advancing time the belief in irreversible progress to ever greater excellence or perfection. For Mulla Sadra a movement backward, from the more perfect to the less perfect, is impossible (Hourani 75, p. 230). Thus Moslem sources contributed to the irrepressible belief in progress, which is still with us today.

However, in the world of Islam the irrevocable unfolding of time is no more conclusively expressed than by the great Persian poet and scholar of science, Omar Khayyam:

> The Moving Finger writes; and, having writ,
> Moves on: nor all your Piety nor Wit,
> Shall lure it back to cancel half a Line,
> Nor all your Tears wash out a Word of it.

> (Fitzgerald 42)

On the other hand the full scope of cosmic time and its relation to judgment of our acts in this world is beautifully captured by scholar L. E. Goodman: "Time in the Koran is the precarious moral span of history suspended between judgment and creation. Here we act and choose and are tested, with results that endure through eternity" (Goodman 93, p. 139).

In this overview of selected religious concepts of time we see that both the irretrievable advance of time and cyclical characteristics of time play a role, a role empowered and vivified by an unceasing spiritual quest. The quest is firmly based on the belief, for all religions discussed, in an ultimate Reality, a timeless Absolute; whether it is Brahman, the Reality of Nirvana, the Absolute Tao, Yahweh, God, or Allah. And as will be discussed in Chapter 12, all tell us in varying degrees that some quality of timelessness or eternality may characterize the underlying reality of our cosmic cocoon.[9]

Especially with this powerful suggestion of the reality of timelessness, I believe that we bring to the picture of our cosmic cocoon an enhanced sense of completeness and richness by supplementing our physical concepts of time with temporal views drawn from spiritual insight. The evolution of our cocoon has resulted not only in physical order, but also in consciousness. This being the case, the deepest

---

[9]As discussed earlier the Israelites and early Christians did not have a concept of time as we know it today; thus no idea of timelessness either. The notion of timelessness was introduced primarily by Augustine and succeeding theologians. Many theologions now maintain that this was a neo-platonic legacy, not part of biblical Christianity, and generally argue for an eternity seen as a "fullness" of time, arising from the Trinity (e.g. see Pannenberg 91; Torrance 69; Peters 93). Nevertheless, as discussed in Chapter 12, I hold that a Christian God that has an aspect of timelessness is meaningful.

intuitive, religious perceptions of that consciousness should be put to use in its description. The religions may not be able to provide us with many concrete details of the "terrain" of our cocoon, but I believe they do give testimony to its existence and its spiritual access.

SUMMARY

We complete this brief survey of our cocoon by examining it from the intuitive and spiritual perspectives afforded by some of the major world religions. This is primarily because of the realization that the mathematically based physical theories in the three previous chapters furnish only a "map" of the universe's "terrain." Although the map is continuously being made more accurate, it cannot fully describe the "terrain," the underlying reality, which the religions address intuitively and spiritually, thus serving to complement the scientific picture.

A number of the relevant time concepts characterizing a religion are found in its cosmology, which is a theological world view providing spiritual sustenance and hope by providing a milieu for the "path" to salvation, a salvation involving enlightenment or unity with an ultimate reality or god. Many primitive cultures realized a "yearly salvation," a total renewal, in celebrations of the creation act of a mythical hero god.

In dealing with the problem of salvation Hinduism experienced a growth over millennia from the earliest Vedic tradition to the Vedantic adherence to the timeless, attributeless Brahman, which is considered as representing the mainstream of the religion today. The salvation of moksha was achieved by transcending the ensnaring train of births and deaths, envisioned by their periodic cosmology, and identifying with Atman, the Self, the spirit of Brahman. A roughly similar transcendence of a repetitive, but essentially non–theistic, cosmology, by the attainment of nirvana is the goal of the devout Buddhist. The Tao tradition also provides a diffusely cyclical cosmology wherein the world and all its creatures emerge from and return to the timeless, ineffable Absolute Tao.

The Israelites altered the Canaanite festivals celebrating gods of cyclical nature to ones worshipping Yahweh, a single god of history. It was the Old Testament record of the many events of God's divine intervention that was the seed for the ultimate conception universally progressing time. Consistent with this concept, Judeo–Christian and Islamic cosmologies envision one irreproducible beginning ineluctably leading to an End, the Day of Judgment. However, in all of the religions discussed, East and West, there is the spiritual insight giving testimony in varying degrees to a timeless or eternal, indescrible Reality, or God, somehow characterizing the "terrain" of the cosmic cocoon.

Part III   THE NATURE OF TIME

"Whether dealing with the nature of nature or the nature of the self...,
the question of the nature of time is at the core of every question we
ask."

—Charles Sherover

There are many questions we can ask about the nature of time. Did it have some kind of beginning? How is time distinguished from motion? What is its relation to space? What role do cyclical and irreversible phenomena play in our gauging and understanding time? Is timelessness real? What is the peculiar character of "now," the present moment? Is time continuous or composed of elementary, irreducible increments, i.e., is it quantized? Here in Part III we will attempt to address these questions.

We will do this by keeping in mind the material presented in Part II, which was essentially a survey of some key temporal concepts characterizing our cosmic cocoon. With these concepts as a basis, we can now examine in somewhat more detail the above mentioned facets of time primarily from the joint viewpoints of modern physics and selected world religions. However, some relevant material will be drawn from other disciplines, such as philosophy, psychology, and biology.

7   Did Time Begin?

"You (God) made all time; you are before all time; and the 'time,' if
such we may call it, when there was no time was not time at all."
                                                              —St. Augustine

The question as to whether time began or whether it stretches
infinitely into the past has undoubtedly haunted the contemplation and
thought of scholars and mystics since the dawn of consciousness.
Although obviously the notion of a beginning[1] of time is intimately linked
to that of a beginning of the universe, one does not necessarily follow
from the other. That is, the problem of whether time began reduces to
the fundamental question: even if the world had a beginning, was time
created with the world, or was it preexistent so that the world was
created in time? In what follows let us try to extract from religious and
physical cosmologies what we can to bring to bear on this and related
questions.

THE CREATION INSIGHT

A crucial element in the cosmology of many religions and cultures
throughout the ages has been the instinctive conviction that the world
had a beginning; its existence did not extend forever into the boundless
past. The presence of what I will call a "creation insight" is clearly
manifested in the creation myths of many primitive, as well as modern,
religions throughout the world. These creation myths serve as a

---

[1] Indeed even the notion of a beginning of time is fraught with philosophical
problems. Since we are in time, part of the temporal process, how do we think of
a beginning when there is nothing antecedent providing the contrast necessary to
distinguish a beginning. With this thought in mind for lack of a better expression
I will nevertheless occasionally use "beginning of time."

spiritual fountainhead for the religion and as the opening act in a cosmology that characterizes the drama of salvation.

Throughout the world there is a rich variety of creation scenarios. There are what C. H. Long (Long 63) terms "emergence" myths, that is, birth from Mother Earth, to be found in the Navaho, Pueblo, and some South Pacific cultures. Closely related are the "world–parent" myths of Babylonia, Polynesia, Egypt, and the Zuni, wherein, for example, the Earth is mother and the heavens, father. Greek, Finnish, Upanishadic, and Tahitian traditions depict creation from chaos and from a "cosmic egg." There are also the engaging "earth–diver" myths describing a divine being (usually an animal) who dives into the water to bring up the first particles of earth, the germs from which the whole universe grows. Finally there are the "creation–from–nothing" (*ex–nihilo*) myths, found among others, in Australian, Mayan, Vedic, and Maori traditions (Long 63).

Clearly whatever the form it took, from this abundant testimony a case can be made for some universality of a "creation insight." I feel we do a disservice to the intuition and intellect of these early peoples by dismissing such myths simply as metaphors drawing on the dawn of the day, the emergence of spring, or childbirth for some kind of parochial ritualistic purpose. On the contrary it has been said that a myth expresses such a powerful instinctual insight that its meaning cannot be conveyed by direct words, but only by a story. And ritual is the reenactment of a myth (Campbell 88, p. 82).

Therefore I believe that creation myths may have been generally a means of expressing a primal spiritual apprehension of a cosmic creation. Anthropologists tell us that the human brain has not gained very much in size for the last 100,000 years. Thus primitive man and woman could easily have been equally as intelligent as we, and what they lacked in modern technological expertise they more than made up for in intuition and spiritual insight.

Probably the most familiar creation myth in the Western world is that which opens the Bible:

"In the beginning God created the heavens and the earth. And the earth was without form, and void; and darkness was upon the face of the deep. And the spirit of God moved upon the face of the waters. And God said, 'Let there be light,' and there was light."

—Genesis 1:1–3

This is followed by a description of the next six days of creation. The consensus among biblical scholars is that some of the themes in the

Genesis account were borrowed from earlier Mesopotamian and Canaanite creation myths, but appropriately altered to suit the theological needs of the Israelites, in particular by providing a starting point and setting for Israel's spiritual history.

There are three apparent features of the cosmology described in the above quotation and the ensuing verses. The first is the simple statement that there was indeed a beginning. Secondly, accompanying this beginning was light: the production of light occupied the first day of creation. The third is the fact that the creation was done in stages, that is in six days, the last of which saw the creation of man.[2] This creation scenario is also supported in Islam (e.g., Koran, Sura 7:54 and Sura 23:12–14).

However, the biblical cosmology is not the only one that describes a beginning attendant with light and/or creation in stages. Consider the Polynesian myth of creation by the god, Taaroa (Long 63, p. 172):

> He existed, Taaroa was his name. In the immensity. There was no earth, there was not sky, there was no sea, there was no man. Above Taaroa calls, he became the universe. Taaroa is the origin.... It is thus that he is named. Taaroa is the light....

Also in the world–parent myths of the Egyptians and Zuni, light and order shine forth when the parents are separated (chaos prevails while they are joined!). The Yoruba of Nigeria and Togo are the most numerous of the some 1,200 ethnic groups in Africa. For them it was the god Olodumare who created the world in four days, and rested on the fifth[3] (Salami and Friaca 92).

Accordingly, I believe that a case can be made not only for some universality of a creation insight, but also for it being attendant with light, and perhaps also with creation in stages. Concerning such stages, much has been made of the days of creation in Genesis by attempting to

---

[2]A well-known Christian interpretation of the Genesis account is that the days of creation were not intended to represent any temporal duration but were meant to convey metaphorically the absolute eternality of God as the non-temporal cause of creation. Other interpretations while holding to God's non-temporal causation, nevertheless invest temporal duration to the seven days. One way these views can be reconciled is by a Koranic interpretation of the six days wherein they indeed involve temporal extent because this is the way time-yoked mankind see God's creation. But for God, creation was totally non-temporal, consistent with God's eternity.

[3]In many cultures the week is not seven days.

correlate the time scale of a day, for example, to the stages of physical and/or biological evolution involving millions or billions of years.

For some that may be a comforting exercise of the imagination. However, I believe that the essential common feature to be drawn from creation accounts, whether religious or scientific in origin, or whether a stage lasts for a microsecond or a billion years, is that creation *did not happen all at once* (Fagg 85, p. 138). This realization is not as trivial as it at first may seem, and has in fact been of relevance in philosophic thought for centuries. Indeed there are manifold viewpoints concerning the duration of the initial creation process.[4]

In any case with respect to time itself the biblical account of creation received a brilliant and incisive interpretation at the hands of St. Augustine. As already noted in Chapter 2, Augustine clearly states that antecedent to creation there was no time. God preceded creation and time but not in any temporal sense. God created the world and time along with it (Augustine 61, p. 263).

Although today's physicists and cosmologists obviously are not usually prone to claim God as a cause for creation or time, we will see that many believe that time somehow began. Let us see how this may be so.

THE BIG BANG

Until early in this century it was believed by many that our galaxy, the Milky Way, essentially constituted the universe. However, it soon became apparent that nebulous objects originally thought to be stars were actually galaxies. This set the stage in the 1920's for the pivotal work of such astronomers as Vesto Slipher and Edwin Hubble which established that these galaxies are receding from us at great speeds and the further away a galaxy was the faster was its recession. In fact Hubble showed that there is a direct linear proportionality between a galaxy's distance and its recession velocity. Internally the galaxies themselves do not expand; they are being swept along by the expansion. Again, keeping in mind the two–dimensional analogy of the ink dots on the expanding balloon surface (See Chapter 3), our position in the universe is not sacrosanct. Wherever we are in this cosmic complex of galaxies, they are all receding from us and from each other in a roughly similar fashion.

---

[4]A wise elderly lady I know, Ida Levine, maintains that God must be a male, because if God were female, instead of seven days, she would have taken nine months and done the job right.

This behavior, having at least some of the characteristics of an explosion, undoubtedly prompted Georges Lemaitre, "father of the big bang theory," to propose that the universe resulted from the explosion of a "primeval atom" (Pagels 85, p. 150). The first modern mathematical expression of the big bang theory was developed in 1948 by George Gamow and his collaborators. He was among the first to write popular books about modern physics. His "Mr. Tompkins Explores the Atom" and "One, Two, Three... Infinity," among others, were a delight to lay readers and physicists alike. The theory of Gamow and his colleagues not only described the universe's expansion but also predicted that it consists of about 75% hydrogen, 24% helium, and 1% the rest of the elements. Experimental evidence so far confirms this.

However, the most dramatic experimental support came in 1965 with the discovery by Arno Penzias and Robert Wilson of very low–energy, long wavelength electromagnetic radiation coming uniformly from all directions, which was also predicted by the theory. This pervasive remnant radiation is the afterglow of the final stage of the primordial explosion to be described shortly. It is called the cosmic microwave background (CMB) and is among the oldest directly observable features of the universe. So that with the CMB we are truly looking back in time at one of the earliest epochs of creation. At the time of its emission it was roughly 1,000 times more energetic than now but with the universe's expansion it has, and will continue to, cool to lower and lower energy, and longer and longer wavelengths.

How did the CMB come to be? To understand this we must look at some of the more recent theoretical and experimental work in cosmology. Especially in the last fifteen years physicists in two subfields of physics previously thought quite disparate, cosmology and elementary particles, have been jointly focusing on understanding events in the early universe. Why is it that cosmologists, studying physics "in the large," and elementary particle physicists, studying physics "in the small," would unite in such an enterprise? We can start to answer this question by observing that, since the universe is now expanding with time, we can logically infer that if we look back in time, it would be contracting. Like taking a moving picture of an explosion and reversing the film, the galaxies would progressively join each other, and ultimately end in a roiling inferno of extremely high temperature and incredible mass and energy density.

Indeed the compression was so intense that all matter existed only in its most elementary components, and at some time in the various stages of the process every form of elementary particle came into existence. So it is in this early regime that cosmology merges with elementary particle physics. This in turn means that in order to describe the process, the quantum theory (of the microscopic world) and the general relativity theory or gravitation theory (of the cosmologic world) must both be used and thus somehow be reconciled. Despite prodigious efforts by theoreticians this reconciliation in the form of a theory of quantum gravity has not so far been achieved. The fact that quantum theory has been successfully applied to the other three forces of nature is a powerful motivation for finding such a theory. Many have been proposed. For example, quantum gravity is contained in various of the proposed "Theories of Everything," e. g. string theories wherein the ultimate elements are tiny strings instead of point–like matter (Barrow 91, p. 77).

Nonetheless, drawing on the accumulated knowledge gained from high energy particle accelerators, astronomical observations, and "state–of–the–art" theoretical study, physicists have attempted to extrapolate back in time to about 10^{-43} seconds (based on our present-day time scale) after the initiation of the big bang.[5] Doing this they have come up with what is considered, as of this writing, a "most likely" scenario for the beginning epoch of the universe. Accordingly, keeping in mind that the very earliest stages of this picture may never be experimentally substantiated, let us take a very brief, hypothetical journey through the earliest stages of the universe's evolution.

Earlier than about 10^{-43} seconds, an "epoch" known as the Planck regime, the universe is so compressed that quantum effects dominate, and time and space as we ordinarily know them no longer have any clearcut meaning. It is in this "era" that all four forces, gravity, weak, electromagnetic, and nuclear are thought to be unified, in principle describable by a single set of equations (which have yet to be found). At around 10^{-43} seconds (see Figure 6) gravity separates from the other three which remain unified and are in principle delineated by one of several candidate theories known as Grand Unified Theories, or GUTs. This name seems inappropriate since the theories cover only three forces, not all four. In any case one of these theories or variation thereof is waiting for confirmation which may be a long time in coming.

---

[5] 10^{-43} is a very small fraction: one divided by a number which is one with 43 zeros behind it.

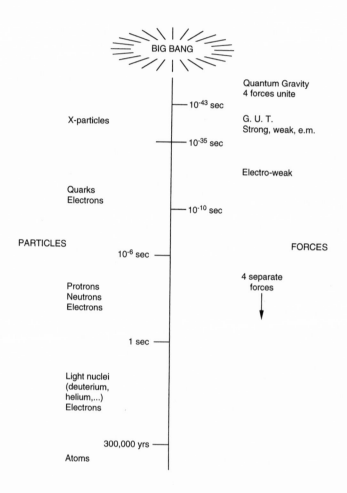

The GUT unification is supposed to have lasted until roughly 10^{-35} seconds, at which time the nuclear force broke away from the remaining two, the electromagnetic and weak. This pair in turn continued together until about 10^{-10} seconds, after which they separated, thus leaving the total of four distinct forces as they exist today.

In contrast to the as yet unsuccessful unifications of all four forces or the GUTs, a thus far successful unification of the electromagnetic and weak forces, called the electroweak theory, was formulated by Steven Weinberg and Abdus Salam over twenty years ago. Support for their theory, the first major unification since Maxwell unified electricity and magnetism, came in 1983 from experiments using the European high energy particle accelerator at CERN. This huge facility circles four miles underneath the countryside, straddling the French–Swiss border near Geneva. The particle energies it produced were such that energy densities high enough to give evidence of electroweak unification were achieved. However, to test the GUT theories Stephen Hawking estimates that it would take an accelerator with dimensions comparable to those of the solar system or more. It is "unlikely" that Congress will appropriate funds for such a facility.

In contrast to the forces being united at the earliest stages of the creation event, particles of matter existed in their most elemental, irreducible form. So that in the "era" previous to about 10^{-35} seconds two of the most elementary particles we know today, quarks and electrons, were considered to be indistinguishable. After 10^{-35} seconds these two particles assume form and become prime ingredients of a universe that can be described as an extremely high temperature "soup" (roughly 10^{13} degrees Kelvin[6]). Then similar to steam condensing to water, or water freezing to ice, at about 10^{-6} seconds the quarks began to join in groups of threes to form protons and neutrons and "freeze" down to a lower temperature soup of these two triune particles along with the electrons as salient components. The next "freezing" to a still lower temperature soup occurred at roughly one second when the protons and neutrons began to combine to form light nuclei such as deuterium (heavy hydrogen) and helium (Weinberg 77, p. 100ff).

A final "freezing" took place at around 300,000 years, when the expansion allowed the temperature to cool and the attendant chaotic motion to quiet enough for the positively charged nuclei to hold on to the

---

[6]The Kelvin temperature scale is based on absolute zero, not on the freezing point of water.

negatively charged electrons to form atoms. Since the electric charges in the atoms were thus balanced, this final soup consisted of electrically neutral particles. From the viewpoint of modern physics, this final stage represents the completion of the birth of the physical universe, the universe that evolved to what we see today. The electrical neutrality of the universe finally made it possible for light, photons, to radiate freely without being trapped in continual interaction in the ionized media of electrically charged particles characteristic of the higher temperature soups. It is the remnant of this light, further cooled and degraded in energy, that is the cosmic microwave background (CMB) which permeates the observable universe today.

In our preoccupation with the behavior of forces and particles we have bypassed two vital features of the early evolutionary process that now need to be examined. The *first* is a feature common to all of the GUT theories. Previous to the conception of the GUTs virtually all physical theories formulated equations that were symmetric in time, being capable of describing processes advancing with time as well as their reverse, whether such reverse processes ever actually happened or not. However, according to the GUT theories there is a time asymmetry wherein some percentage of the processes do not possess this advance–reverse time symmetry, but only advance. With this time asymmetry the theory also includes another asymmetry, the small dominance of the amount of what is known as baryonic matter over baryonic antimatter. Baryonic matter is matter made up of various combinations of quarks, such as protons and neutrons.

A similar asymmetry was first shown to exist experimentally by J. W. Cronin and Val Fitch in their study of the decay of the short–lived, neutral K–meson[7]. In one mode of the decay of this particle, they found that the decay, which amounted to a break–up into smaller particles, was not exactly balanced by the decay into their antiparticles. Balance was missed by about two parts in one thousand. It can be shown that according to presently accepted theory this indirectly implies a complementary time asymmetry of the same small magnitude.

It is the time and baryonic matter–antimatter asymmetries that may have played a key role in the evolution of the early universe. According to the GUT theories there was a small preponderance of this matter over antimatter by about one part in 10^{10}. Although proportionately very

---

[7]The neutral K-meson is one of many kinds of particles called mesons, some neutral, some charged, which are heavier than electrons, but have a different composition of quarks than such particles as protons and neutrons.

small, it was nevertheless large enough to yield the universe we know today. Without it we would not be here. This is because, if the amounts of matter and antimatter were exactly equal they would have annihilated each other, ultimately leaving mostly energy in the form of radiation. Indeed Stephen Hawking points out that the fact that we are here can be regarded as giving some qualitative (not quantitatively accurate) support for the GUT theories (Hawking 88, p. 78).

Some physicists disagree with me, but I cannot help speculating that this time asymmetric description of processes in the early universe may possibly be extremely important. I believe it may be describing phenomena which played some role in the establishment of the irreversible characteristic of time for the universe at the most fundamental level, a level which may underlie all of the other irreversible phenomena by which we commonly gauge time. Indeed we will later discuss how quantum cosmologists, by applying quantum theory to the whole universe, are attempting to link the advance of time indicated by thermodynamic processes with the expansion of the universe (Zeh 89; Halliwell 91; Hawking *et al.* 93).

The *second* very important point that we need to examine has to do with the fact that while the basic features of the big bang theory are still considered valid, there are several observed properties of the universe that it cannot predict. Most of these problems can now be dealt with by a significant refinement to the theory known as the inflationary universe theory, the initial elements of which were first proposed by Alan Guth in 1981. Several improvements on Guth's theory have been developed in the last decade (Linde 87). Among the most recent are the so–called chaotic inflation theories which do not require a high temperature, at least for the very initial instants of the universe's beginning (Linde *et al.* 94).[8]

However, most versions of the inflation concept indicate that approximately between 10^{-35} and 10^{-30} seconds the universe completed an extremely rapid expansion, due to an inversion phase which made gravity repulsive instead of attractive. This inflationary expansion was far greater than that which the universe experienced before or after that time period (Guth and Steinhardt 84). Then after about 10^{-30} seconds the inflationary scenario merges with that of the standard big bang theory.

What are some of the features of the universe encompassed by inflation theory and not by the big bang? One important feature is the

---

[8]For an historical survey of the inflation theories see Linde *et al* 94.

existence of galaxies and clusters of galaxies; the big bang theory cannot predict their formation. How the galaxies evolved is a central issue in cosmology and astronomy today. Inflation's answer to this problem is that the galaxies and clusters of galaxies were germinated from quantum fluctuations during the inflation process. These quantum fluctuations are similar to the spontaneous appearance of particles from the vacuum discussed in Chapter 4. The important difference is that during the inflationary stage space–time may have been so curved that the Heisenberg Uncertainty Principle, valid in ordinary flat Euclidean space, could have been altered (Pagels 85, p. 340). So that particles which spontaneously materialized did not vanish as ordinarily is the case, but remained to gravitationally attract others. The galaxies are thought to have grown by gravitational accretion of neighboring matter building from these nascent quantum fluctuations.

This hypothesis for galaxy and cluster formation is but one among several others. There are a number of such hypotheses because the birth of the galaxies is generally thought to have taken place roughly between 300,000 and one or two billion years after the bang, a period about which little seems to be known. In fact it is believed that less is known about this period than the earlier period between 0.01 second and 300,000 years (Turner 91).

Another important property of the universe specifically predicted by inflation and not encompassed by the standard big bang theory is its average homogeneity. Even though the universe exists in clumps, i.e. galaxies and clusters of galaxies, on very large scales the average number of these bodies is expected to be the same everywhere. Until recently it seemed as if there might be a problem of reconciling the joint existence of homogeneity and the "lumpiness" embodied by the very large galactic clusters observed in the last decade or so. The galaxies seem to cluster in a roughly soap–bubble–like configuration, being distributed around the surface of the "bubble," so that there appear to be large voids with essentially no galaxies in the interior. Nevertheless homogeneity on very large scales is still thought to exist. One reason for this is that as astronomers look out to distances comparable to, and exceeding, the dimensions of the clusters, the universe appears to become progressively more homogeneous (Peebles 92). However, homogeneity also got powerful support from the observation of the cosmic microwave background (CMB) which has been measured by the COBE satellite to be uniform to better than one part in 10^5. In fact the CMB was observed to be so uniform that this result began to seriously challenge the idea of galactic evolution arising from early quantum fluctuations. How could galaxies have evolved from what appeared to be such a smooth universe?

A major step toward reconciling the large scale galactic structure with the smoothness of the CMB was taken in April 1992, when George Smoot of the University of California at Berkeley made the dramatic announcement that further COBE observations at the accuracy level of six parts in 10^6 had revealed small temperature variations in the CMB (Smoot *et al.* 92). These variations are considered to be reflections of inhomogeneities in the matter density of the universe at times as early as 10^{-35} seconds after the bang (Physics Today 92) involving a thus far undetermined form of matter. The small density concentrations in this matter would then be the seed attractors for the more familiar and detectable ordinary matter, which ultimately formed the galaxies and clusters we see today. Observations taken from very high altitude balloons corroborate the COBE data. Although the early balloon and COBE data only detect matter variations on very large scales, seven times larger than the largest galactic clusters, recent balloon experiments revealing much more detail give clues about the future course and ultimate fate of the universe. Let us now turn to this question.

A *third* characteristic of the universe that is treated by inflation and not the big bang (without invoking special initial conditions) centers on the burning question of whether the universe is open, closed, or precisely in between. If it is open, then the expansion velocity is so great that it overcomes the mutual gravitational attraction of the galaxies and clusters of galaxies, and the expansion continues forever. If it is closed, then there is enough mass in the universe for the mutual attraction to ultimately halt the expansion and reverse it, the resultant contraction finally leading to what John Wheeler has called the "Big Crunch."[9] However, the universe could also be delicately balanced exactly in between being open or closed so that the expansion will continue to gradually slow down to ever slower speeds, but never quite come to rest.

For the last scenario to occur the universe would have to be at precisely the right mass density, called the critical density, above which the universe closes, below which it is open. Astronomic observations

---

[9]If this is the case, a few cosmologists (Dicus *et al* 83) have taken seriously the possibility that the universe would then "bounce" back with another big bang, and in fact continue this cyclical behavior indefinitely. However, such an eventuality is not presently considered likely by most cosmologists.

thus far indicate that the luminous matter in the universe, i.e. light–producing galaxies, accounts for roughly one percent of the matter required for the critical density. However there is evidence for a considerable amount of non–luminous matter, i.e. ordinary non–visible matter such as dead stars and black holes, which is indirectly detectable by its gravitational effects on luminous matter. It is presently estimated that the sum of both luminous and non–luminous matter brings the mass density to some 5 percent of the critical value.

This means, of course, that experimental evidence thus far tells us the universe is open. However, while 5 percent may seem rather far away from the critical value, from the viewpoint of cosmologic calculations it is not. The universe is actually extremely close to being exactly balanced, because these calculations show that at one second into its evolution the universe had to be balanced to one part in 10^{15} for it to be the way it is today (Guth 86). If it departed even a little from this precision, the universe would either have contracted by now or have expanded and cooled well beyond its present state. In either case we would not be here. The fine tuning that yields a universe precisely balanced at the critical density is an integral part of inflationary theories. Previously, this tuning had to be injected ad hoc as a starting condition for the big bang theory.

Detailed analysis of the results of ongoing balloon flights measuring the CMB continue to yield evidence that the universe may indeed be at the critical density. But cosmologists estimate that only 35% of this density is due to matter; and most of it is not ordinary matter (protons, neutrons, etc.), but an unknown form called dark matter. However, the density gap may not be filled by matter alone. Studies are being made of supernova explosions, which occur when a star exhausts its nuclear fuel, implodes due to gravity, and ends as a star made only of very tightly packed neutrons. Analysis of light from a type of supernova called SN1a indicate they are receding from us at an accelerating rate, considerably greater than that expected for a universe at the critical density with a slowing expansion rate. The latter rate, however, is determined assuming that it is gravitationally interacting mass that governs and slows expansion. Many cosmologists now believe that some 65% of the density gap is not filled by mass but by energy (recall $E=mc^2$). It is an inherent energy characterizing space. It has a repulsive effect causing accelerated expansion. So maybe we have 5% ordinary matter, 30% unknown (dark) matter, and 65% energy of space, called dark energy; stay tuned.

In any case the search for such dark matter is very intense, and experimental results are expected in the 1990's which may shed some light on the question of its existence and characteristics as well as further test the inflationary big bang hypothesis and its prediction of a universe poised between being open and closed.

THE ANTHROPIC PRINCIPLE

A delicately balanced universe near or at the critical mass density is not the only kind of balance that has made it possible for us to be here. If the nuclear force were 1% weaker, hydrogen would be the only element, the sun could not burn as it does, and we would not be here. If it were 1% stronger, too much helium would exist in the universe, and we would not be here either. If the expansion rate of the universe had been smaller by one part in 10^{17}, the universe would have collapsed before now (Hawking 88, p. 121). The universe had just the right size and balance between mass and expansion velocity along with just the right physical constants to make possible the some 14 billion year "cooking" time of the soup of nuclei and electrons in the correct proportions to make stars, planets and humans (Wheeler 76).

It has been thoughts such as these that in part have given rise to what is known as the Anthropic Principle (see Barrow and Tipler 86). As the name may suggest, the principle has to do with the relationship between humans and the universe and has been considered useful by some cosmologists. In essence the principle makes use of the simple fact that we humans have evolved. That is, the fact of our evolution is employed to place restrictions on the range of possible models of the universe and its beginnings that can be considered. So that, a valid model must be consistent with our presence here. Thus our very existence may give cosmologists some guidelines as to what the behavior of the early universe must have been.

There are much stronger versions of the Anthropic Principle which reverse the logic somewhat by saying in effect that our evolution is a necessary condition for the universe's coming into being in the first place, instead of simply saying that theories of its coming into being have to take into account our existence. In fact John Wheeler goes so far as to suggest: "The universe could not have come into being unless it were guaranteed in advance to be able to give rise to life at some point in its history–to–be." To quote Wheeler: "… Why then is the universe as big as it is? Because we are here" (Wheeler 76).

I can comfortably accept the weak version of the principle because it seems logical that a viable model of the universe must be consistent with our presence. However, I among many other physicists hesitate to endorse Wheeler's strong version. Nevertheless, I firmly believe that it is very important that he expressed it, because for me the idea is one that will probably stimulate my imagination and challenge my thought for the rest of my life.

Indeed the problem of what our place is in the universe and how we might figure in its future will probably be with us all as long as our species exists. The wonder of the evolution of consciousness will provide an abiding motivation in the search for answers. As Edward Harrison puts it: "We are a part or an aspect of the Universe experiencing and thinking about itself" (Harrison 85, p. 1). Perhaps it may reinforce our sense of intimate immanence in the universe to realize that although there are roughly 10^{11} stars in a galaxy and some 10^{11} galaxies in the observable universe, there are also approximately 10^{11} neurons in the human brain.

One must be careful about drawing too profound a conclusion from a comparison of these numbers, but I suggest that it may indicate some potential for the human brain to encompass the concepts of the universe that it needs to know. We are a part of the universe and, along with any possible extraterrestrial intelligent beings, participate in its consciousness.

When we look out at the stars and galaxies scattered throughout the vast heavens, we and our consciousness may seem incredibly insignificant. But this is because we are only thinking in spatial terms. We may not be significant in space, but it is quite possible we are specially significant in time.

Did Time Begin?

Our inescapably intimate involvement with time is cause enough to contemplate the question: "Did time begin?" Maybe we will never really know, but there are physical phenomena available to us which allow us to infer that it might have had some sort of a beginning. We have already seen how astronomers can probe back into the universe and see quasars and proto galaxies believed to be representatives of the earlier stages of galactic evolution. The CMB which everywhere surrounds us is among the oldest remnants of the big bang. Furthermore, the theories of elementary particle physics, such as the electroweak unification theory, contribute along with astronomic evidence to an increasingly consistent scenario of an evolution in phases from an early state of unimaginable heat and energy density.

All of this seems to indicate that the universe in its relentless expansion is behaving as a gigantic cosmic clock ticking off the eons of evolution, a clock that was somehow wound up and started with the primordial fireball. But again, was there a specific instant when all of this got started? Certainly not in terms of thinking of instants as the temporal counterpart of geometric or spatial points. Recall that back at the very earliest theoretical epoch, the Planck regime in the time frame of 10^{-43} seconds, general relativity (gravity) meets the quantum theory, and time and space as we know it become diffuse and impossible to define. This must at least mean that perhaps the best surmise is that time somehow "emerged" from this primal state, with no clear cut initial instant.

This view of some form of emergence from an ill–defined, fuzzy source of intense energy is essentially the scenario portrayed in some of the theories of the early universe put forward by quantum cosmologists. Without directly coming to grips with the problem of quantizing gravity, these theories are based on the somewhat controversial assumption of applying quantum mechanics to the entire universe. They set up a wave function (see Chapter 4) for the whole universe and attempt to determine the initial conditions from which the inflationary phase of expansion began.

Two such efforts, which have drawn attention in the last decade, are called the "no boundary" and the "tunneling" theories (Halliwell 91, 92). In the "no boundary" theory, proposed by James Hartle and Stephen Hawking, the universe in its earliest stage when subject to quantum effects is seen as having no specific spatio–temporal initial state or "beginning boundary" (Hartle and Hawking 83). For this to be true, according to the theory, time must become "imaginary." This is not imaginary in the conventional sense; it is a mathematical term (any number multiplied by the square root of minus one, $\sqrt{-1}$, is imaginary), which in this case endows time with another kind of dimensionality. Thus as represented in Figure 7 there is no clear cut point at which time began. Time has no real meaning in this beginning era just as north has no meaning at the north pole (Halliwell 91).

In the "tunneling" proposal, the universe "tunnels" from nothing to the inflationary condition (Vilenkin 84; Linde 84). It is out of place here

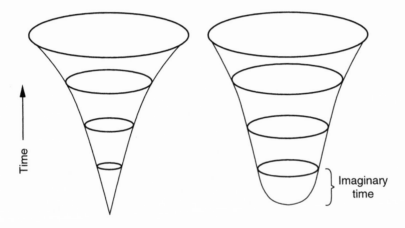

FIG. 7–Representation of an expanding universe with a definite beginning (left), and with imaginary time (right)

to describe the mathematics that justifies this, but the tunneling process is roughly analogous to that which occurs in the radioactive emission of an α–particle. This particle is a helium nucleus (two protons and two neutrons) and is emitted by heavy nuclei such as uranium. The α is trapped in such a nucleus and ordinarily can only get out if it receives enough energy to overcome the average nuclear attractive force imposed by all of the other protons and neutrons in the uranium nucleus. However, by the quantum theory it is possible under certain conditions for the α–particle to "tunnel" through this nuclear force barrier to freedom. This process then bears some rough similarity to the tunneling of the universe from nothing.

While these two scenarios have some degree of plausibility and certainly engage our thought and imagination, the idea of working with a wave function for the whole universe is subject to some question. This is in part because: since we are part of the universe, there is no observer exterior to the universe to make a measurement on it and "collapse" its wave function (see Chapter 4).

Nevertheless, such imaginative and ingenious theories are very important. They constitute a valuable way of framing questions about a universe, of which there is only one, and aspects of which may never be fully available for experimental study. Again, one of the most significant of these aspects hinges on the question of whether time had some form of a beginning. From the physical point of view a case can be made for some kind of a beginning for time by considering all of the self–consistent evidence supporting the big bang picture in the light of what we know about how spacetime and matter behave.

Furthermore, I feel it would be somewhat self–limiting and myopic not to consider religious viewpoints concerning this question. We have already noted the impressive array of creation scenarios embodied in myths from a spectrum of cultures worldwide. St. Augustine, in developing the myth narrated in Genesis, eloquently maintains that time did begin with God's creative action. The Genesis account as well as myths from other religious traditions maintain that there was indeed a beginning, attendant with light and/or evolution in stages. While still other myths do not specifically cite a beginning of time, it is often implied.

These features—the creation of time and the universe, the emergence of light, and evolution in stages—seem to roughly correlate with the current generally accepted physical picture. However, in the light of the salvational motivation of these religious cosmologies, we obviously must be careful about making too trivial or superficial a comparison with physical cosmology. It is not a matter of religion being right about cosmology all along, or of science proving the validity of a religious claim. It is a matter of according some credibility to the profound spiritual insight that vitalizes these religious traditions. It is a matter of sensing that when the scientific and religious descriptions of something have such general similarity, a special immanence of meaning, a special inner resonance is accorded that description that it otherwise would not have (Burwasser 88). It is a matter of realizing that a world view that is solely scientific is incomplete and unsatisfying.

Furthermore a salvational motif should not necessarily be relegated solely to religious cosmologies. Can we not be probing the universe scientifically with some partially unconscious, inarticulable motivation involving at least our, and/or our progeny's, physical salvation? Already Congress is considering the appropriation of funds to track potentially threatening asteroids, ones whose impact with the Earth could extinguish us. This was the probable fate of the dinosaurs 65 million years ago. We may now have the technology to nudge at least some of these objects off of their deadly course. So I cannot help but feel that the exponential growth in science and technology may have the underlying, as yet unexpressed, purpose of the physical salvation of the human species, not to mention its spiritual salvation. I believe as time goes on that the two may become more closely linked.

I also feel it is possible that some of this yearning for salvation may stem in part from a primal apprehension that the enveloping time of the universe and our own brief lifetime are awesome and precious gifts. This somehow lends a subtle sense of immediacy to our search. In any event, though we may never really know whether time began in some way, there is support from two disparate sources, religious and physical cosmologies, that this may be the case.

SUMMARY

In many religious cosmologies and belief systems of diverse cultures throughout the world there is a central feature, which can be termed a creation insight. Most of these traditions have in common the conviction that there was a beginning, and with many, creation was accompanied with the emission of light and/or occurred in stages, not all at once. Though some traditions do not explicitly hold that time began with creation, St. Augustine, in his penetrating interpretation of the Genesis account, lucidly states that in creating the world God created time along with it.

The observation of the universe's expansion, the ratio of hydrogen to helium abundance, and the cosmic microwave background (CMB) provided convincing support for the basic features of the big bang theory. Additional evidence, especially the recent discovery of low–level inhomogeneities in the CMB, provides growing support for the inflationary refinement of the big bang. Further support may come from the intense search for more bizarre forms of dark matter, other than electrons, protons, etc. In any case the emission of light and evolution in stages were among the characteristics of the big bang process that are shared by many religious cosmologies.

Where humans fit into a coherent picture of the universe brings the Anthropic Principle into consideration, which at the very least maintains that any theory of the universe's creation must account for our existence. Although it is not considered useful to compare the big bang scenario with that generically extracted from many world religions in terms of mutual evidential support, such comparison may provide a texture of meaning to the events of the universe's evolution. Though time cannot be said to have commenced at a specific instant, there seems to be support from both physical and religious cosmologies that it somehow emerged with the rest of the universe in the process of its coming to be.

8 TIME AND MOTION

"Time is the number of motion..."

—Aristotle

CHANGE AND PERMANENCE

Whether or not we know how long time has existed, it seems to be with us now. How do we sense this? Essentially by interpreting motion and change. Sitting on a park bench we see leaves rustling in the breeze and pigeons waddling about, heads bobbing, in their endless search for food. We observe a rich diversity of motions.

But how are we aware of motion or change? How else but by comparison with something that is not changing or moving (at least at the same velocity). Thus, in the park we observe motion by distinguishing it from our stationary surroundings, the park bench, the sidewalk, etc., which are fixed references. These are things that we consider as "permanent." Of course from a more cosmic point of view there is probably little in our natural world that is really permanent.

However, if we can accept the idea of permanence as we experience it in the macroscopic world of our daily lives, then the awareness of change comes to us fundamentally through its contrast with permanence (Benjamin 81, p. 7). Heraclitus, who held that only change was ultimately real, and Parmenides, who espoused the reality of permanence, should have gotten together and agreed that, at least in a sense, they were both right. Perceptions of change and permanence go hand in hand and are mutually necessary in understanding ourselves and our world. If everything were permanent, we would not know it, because there would be no changes around to provide contrast and let us know that we were fixed. If everything were change, we might not fully realize it, for there would be nothing abiding and constant providing a reference to inform us that we were being swept along in the flow of change. Thus the perceptions of change and permanence work in conjunction and underlie our awareness of motion and its twin sister, time.

However, from the spiritual viewpoint of most religions change and permanence are but aspects of an all encompassing God. This God, whether Yahweh, Allah, or Brahman, represents the only true and ultimate permanence. The apparent "permanences" as viewed by men and women on this earth all have finite temporality. For the religions both these "permanences" and the changes experienced by all living creatures arise from an everlasting and timeless God. So that while time and motion in particular may characterize mankind's view of the cosmos, it is God's eternity that consummates the cosmic picture.

CYCLICAL AND IRREVERSIBLY EVOLVING PHENOMENA

A contrast and attendant comparison somewhat analogous to that for change and permanence come into play when we consider cyclical and irreversibly evolving phenomena. Both of these processes are needed for us to establish our sense of time (Schlegel 68, p. 14). From the daily course of the sun to the radiation from a cesium atom, cycles have been invaluable to humankind for the measurement of time. It is by comparison with such phenomena that we sense the irreversible advancing nature of time. Indeed it is only by being imbedded in the on–going, unrepeatable passage of events that we can fully appraise the usefulness of cyclical phenomena as measures of time.

That is, if all phenomena were cyclical we would be enveloped in an ever–reproducible state of quasi–permanence. But we would never know it because there would be nothing undergoing unrepeatable change to exhibit contrast to the cyclical process. On the other hand if everything were involved in a flux of unrepeatable change we might have difficulty sensing it for there would be no cycles by which to pace or measure the change. So that cyclical and unrepeatable processes go hand in hand and are mutually indispensable in developing our realization of time. Examples of these two kinds of processes are all about us. Let us take a brief survey to see just how universal they are.

CYCLES

Whether it is orbital, rotary, or oscillatory motion, cyclical behavior is ubiquitous throughout the physical universe at every level of observation, cosmologic, macroscopic, and microscopic. In the cosmos each cluster of galaxies moves about its common center, and even clusters in a supercluster can move in a roughly similar fashion. The stars in a galaxy course at hundreds of kilometers per second about the galactic center. Following the rotation of the Milky Way, our sun completes a circuit every 250 million years. The Earth and its sister planets pursue their unique elliptical orbits about the sun, as do moons about the planets.

In the macroscopic world of everyday living, pendulums monotonously pace our time with their measured "to and fro." The lapping waves on a breezy lake caress the shore with remarkable regularity. The soaring strains of the Brahms violin concerto consist of sonic vibrations modulated with exquisite delicacy.

At the microscopic level the atoms in a molecule rotate and vibrate about the molecular center. Electrons busily orbit about the atomic nucleus in a flurry of quantum "fuzz." Protons and neutrons similarly describe diffuse envelopes of orbits about the nuclear center. Furthermore, in undergoing a transition from a higher energy to a lower energy state, molecules, atoms, and nuclei can emit electromagnetic radiation detectable in the form of oscillatory waves. It is such an emission that is the basis for the highly accurate cesium atomic clock.

For me a most fascinating suggestion of cyclical motion in the microscopic world is one which cannot be directly observed as a motion at all, namely the intrinsic or internal spin of elementary particles. Such particles as electrons, quarks, photons, and neutrinos (electrically neutral particles of extremely small mass) for example, have a fixed, discrete value of intrinsic spin which is either an integer or a half–integer multiple of h, Planck's constant. Neutrinos, quarks, and electrons have spin $1/2$ h and are called fermions (named after the great physicist, Enrico Fermi), while photons and some other elementary particles have spins that are integer multiples of h, and are called bosons (named after the Indian physicist Bose).

The existence of such intrinsic spin is an ultimate example of the extreme application of the Heisenberg Uncertainty Principle. That is, we are allowed absolutely precise knowledge of the internal angular momentum (spin) of the particle, but know absolutely nothing of its angular position in any rotation about the spin axis. Angular momentum (or spin) and angle (or angular position) are conjugate quantities, just as are momentum and position or time and energy as discussed in Chapter 4, and thus are subject to the Uncertainty Principle. In a word, with spin we are dealing with quanta of motion, cyclical motion, at the most fundamental level. In the case of the electron, by virtue of this undetectable spin motion and the electron's charge, it behaves like a tiny bar magnet, even tinier than the atomic magnets discussed in Chapter 5, which possess their magnetism by virtue of the orbital motion of electrons in atoms.

Whether or not intrinsic spin is involved, the ceaseless cyclical activity at the microscopic level also provides the grounding for the vital universality of cyclical mechanisms in all of biology. All organisms more complex than bacteria have internal clocks. These clocks help maintain the organism by coupling it to the cycles of the environment (Menaker 89). That is, the creature's internal chronometer is approximately synchronized by the earth's cycles, but not precisely driven by them. For example, a house sparrow's perch–hopping activity follows a 25 hour cycle. By implanting the pineal gland of one sparrow into a second, the latter is then found to follow exactly the same periodicity as had the donor, all of this independent of the earth's motion. The clocks of mice can be interrupted and reset; those of hamsters can be progressively entrained to periods anywhere between 20 and 24 hours (Menaker 89).

Most birds and bees navigate directly or indirectly through the joint use of their clocks and the sun. There is evidence that some birds orient themselves using the stars or the earth's magnetic field in conjunction with the partially polarized light from the sky (Browne 93). The correlation of the bird's internal clock with such natural phenomena and the length of the day can be remarkably accurate. The greater yellowleg makes the 16,000 mile roundtrip to Patagonia in the autumn and back to Canada in the spring, where it invariably lays eggs between May 26 and 29 each year (Whitrow 1980, p. 137).

Although humans seem to be considerably less coupled to the earth's cycle, internal chronometry nevertheless plays a vital role. This is most evident in the diurnal sleep cycle, and the menstrual cycle of women. It is well–known that women living in dormitories or convents gradually synchronize to the same menstrual periodicity. At a somewhat more precise level, an EEG with a sensor placed at the back of the head can detect some four rhythms emitted by the brain, the strongest, known as the α–rhythm, is about 8 to 12 cycles per second in normal humans. Much more precise, and indicating how fundamental our linkage to the earth may have been, the excretion of potassium from the human kidney occurs regularly every 24 hours, independent, for example, of whether or not one lives 22 or 26 hour days in a cave (Lobban 60; Whitrow 80, p. 160). This along with the other human rhythms is clear evidence of our entrainment with the sun; and the periodicity of menstruation is undoubtedly a legacy of entrainment with the moon.

The pervasive presence of this rhythmic activity, being attuned to the cosmos, probably provided a natural background and intuitive basis for cyclical religious cosmologies throughout the world. As we have already seen, this included the power of repetition in the yearly rituals of re–creation in many primitive societies as well as cyclical characteristics found in the Hindu, Tao, and most Buddhist cosmologies.

Persistent remnants of cyclical observance still overlay the time–directed progressive societies of the West. For example, there is a noticeable sense of renewal that occurs every four or eight years with the election of a new American president. The yearly celebration of Christmas, Rosh Hashanah, and Ramadan remain as fixed components of Western culture.

IRREVERSIBLE, PROGRESSIVE EVENTS

Just as with cyclical phenomena, irreversibly progressive phenomena are apparent at every level of the physical universe, cosmologic, macroscopic, and microscopic. Stars in the heavens are continually being born by progressive accretion of dust and gas. Compressed by gravity, they heat to searing temperatures, burn their nuclear fuel, and die. Galaxies, carried by the universe's expansion, recede from us never to return.

At the macroscopic level of our worldly life, we see trees grow from seedlings to majestic heights and rivers slowly shape and erode their banks on their relentless way to the sea. We are born, age, and die, irrevocably weaving our short thread into the time–bound tapestry of humankind. In the microscopic world molecules in a gas pursue their random course never to return to exactly the same place at exactly the same velocity (see Chapter 9). Electrons and alpha particles emitted by a radioactive nucleus will never return to exactly the same state again.

The consistent temporal behavior of a number of phenomena like those described above allow us to sense time's ongoingness. For example, many modern thinkers maintain that we gauge the passage of time in everyday life through the awareness of a few physical and psycho–biological phenomena, whose chronological implications have undergone extensive scientific study. These irreversible phenomena are often sorted into some five categories, which I believe can be reduced to an essential three.

The first of these is based on the general tendency of physical systems ultimately to pass to greater and greater states of disorder and is the essential characteristic of the first temporal gauge, which I will call the *thermodynamic* gauge. The physical quantity that is a measure of this disorder is entropy; the greater the disorder, the higher the entropy. Some aspects of the thermodynamic gauge are exceedingly diverse and complicated, and as discussed in the next chapter, can, in some circumstances, actually lead to prolonged states of order or organization. This is because the Second Law of Thermodynamics, which tells us how entropy behaves, is so all embracing. So much so that it can include the possibility of far–from–equilibrium processes resulting in the evolution of self–organization or regulated chaos (Coveney and Highfield 91, p. 183ff; Prigogine 80, p. 103ff).

Some processes involve so much self–organization, such as plant and animal species, especially the human species, that their evolution and continuance are generally considered the basis for the second gauge, which I label the *psychobiologic* gauge. Because these are examples of high development of order or organization they have often been termed anti–entropic.

The third process by which the irreversible character of time finds a measure, as we have seen, is the expansion of the universe, which I term the *cosmologic* gauge. Significant underlying aspects of these gauges, especially the second, will be treated in some detail in the next chapter.

Such gauges and the phenomena on which they are based, as well as a host of related phenomena, provide the physical background for the goal–directed, spiritually progressive temporality to be found in a number of religious traditions, East and West. This is in contrast to the cyclicity noted in the previous section. These progressive characteristics are inexorably bound up with the notion of a spiritual path to salvation. We saw in Chapter 6 how the inescapable dictum of karma regulates the spiritual progress of the Hindu and Buddhist devotees through the prolonged series of burdensome reincarnations in their striving for moksha or nirvana. Also in that chapter it was described how the dramatic sequence of divine interventions in Israel's spiritual history vivified a cosmology which irrevocably progressed from an unrepeatable beginning to an end involving judgment and salvation. The consecration of time whose goal is salvation also characterizes the unrepeatable Christian and Islamic cosmologies as well.

However, whether we consider the evolving drama of sacred time or the physical and psycho–biological processes of gauged time, common to all of these temporalities is the underlying reality of motion. Without motion there would be no time. Let us examine this seemingly obvious, but actually quite complex, basic fact a little more closely.

TIME AND MOTION

Aristotle was among the first in recorded Western history to seriously analyze the relationship between time and motion. He reasoned that, while there is not time apart from change and motion, time is nevertheless not identical to motion. Therefore time must be some aspect of change and motion (Aristotle 83, p. 43). That is, time cannot be specifically identified with motion in general, for motions can have various speeds which are judged and measured by time (Whitrow 80, p. 25). Yet time cannot be defined without the use of motion.

Aristotle observed that time exists not only as a measure of motion but also of rest, for time passes when a body is at rest. A similar argument was taken up eight centuries later by St. Augustine in his probing investigation of time:

> It is clear, then, that the movement of a body is not the same as the means by which we measure the duration of its movement....The same body may move at different speeds, and sometimes it is at rest, and we measure not only its motion but also its rest by means of time (Augustine 61, p. 273).

Although he disagreed with Aristotle concerning other aspects of time, this observation, that motion in general could include the state of rest, was the final argument in his agreement with Aristotle that time and motion were not identical. If this is the case, then what is the relationship between time and motion. For Aristotle it was the awareness of "before" and "after" that makes possible time's measure of motion:

> But time, too, we become acquainted with when we mark off changes, marking it off by before and after, and we say that time has passed when we get a perception of the before and after in change (Aristotle 83, p. 44).

Developing this line of thought, Aristotle finally associates number with time in its measure of a motion's progress through before and after: "For that is what time is; a number of change in respect of the before and after" (Aristotle 83, p. 44). Thus time is dependent upon motion, or an aspect of motion, in a way that somehow makes possible the numbering of the successive states, from before to after, reached by motion (Whitrow 80, p. 26). Temporal order seems to have something in common with real numbers which it does not have with a dimension in space (Denbigh 81, p. 23).

How is this numbering accomplished? In the earlier parts of his discourse he maintains that it is by sensing the "now," which divides the before (past) and after (future). The now is not a fixed instant, but a continuously changing event serving as the end of before and the beginning of after:

> For it is by the moving thing that we become acquainted with the before and after in change, and the before and after, considered as countable, is the now...and the now is, as the moving thing is, like a number (Aristotle 83, p. 45).

It may be apparent that we are not left with much of a clear cut prescription of how to count the nows, whether they are considered as instants or not. In the end he finally seeks recourse, as we do today, to cyclical motion as a measure, something we can count: "then uniform circular motion is most of all a measure, because the number of turns is most easily known" (Aristotle 83, p. 53). Indeed Aristotle carries the circular concept much further in holding that time was essentially the cyclic motion of the celestial sphere, i.e. the apparent movement of the heavens around us. It was this circular motion that he thought was the most fundamental reference for time measurement. But it was this very concept, incidentally, with which St. Augustine emphatically took issue (Augustine 61, p. 272).

Another criticism that might be leveled against Aristotle is that he only briefly discusses the central question of whether or not the relationship of time and motion is dependent only on the presence of the soul, as he puts it, i.e. on human awareness. He poses the basic question pondered on by philosophers through the centuries to this day: is there time, if there is no one to observe or measure it? Although Aristotle seems to answer no, in a rather unclear statement he also seems to allow for the possibility of some form of time via change, independent of human presence. Certainly a principal reason for his generally negative position is that without the human mind there would be no abstract numbers with which to count time (Aristotle 83, p. 52).

Clearly what is intended here is the *ability* of the human mind to count time (e.g. as done by St. Augustine, see Chapter 2), because there is still a non–quantitative human awareness of time in its relation to motion without measuring it and giving it number. Modern thought, perhaps drawing on philosophy as far back as Immanual Kant, seems to center around the opinion that time is a human abstraction from motion, change, and process. Postponing until later the whole question of a definition, or component definitions, of time, the haunting question persists: does some form of time exist in the presence of motion independent of human awareness?

On many occasions I have tried unsuccessfully to address this question. However, it has occurred to me that one way to sense the profundity of the problem is through a very elementary, but rather unorthodox thought experiment. Let us imagine that the universe consists of just two essentially point–like particles, that is, with no internal parts or mechanisms. Let us further suppose that the particles are very unusual and, hopefully without stretching your imagination beyond the breaking point, that somehow both particles nevertheless are endowed with the capacity to sense some external properties, such as distance and motion.

Finally, suppose these two "sentient" particles are moving at some small velocity with respect to each other (so that for all practical purposes we can ignore the theory of relativity). Question: will they be able to determine how far apart they are? In a discussion with Joe Rosen, he convinced me that the answer is no, because, despite their inherent ability to observe distance, there would be nothing else in the universe by which distance could be gauged. Nothing would be around to help them determine what is near or far. If they could not determine distance, they also would not be able to sense their relative velocity. As they recede from each other or approach each other, they would only sense each other's presence, nothing else. It would be a very dull one–dimensional universe, because, as we learned in geometry, two points determine a line.

Let us now try to improve this boring situation by adding a third such particle moving at its own velocity relative to the other two. Under these conditions each particle now has some kind of reference for distance. Each can observe the separation between the other two particles and then use that as a comparison to obtain some gauge of its own distance from the two. Furthermore, it can observe the relative velocity of the two, and also have some gauge of its velocity relative to them. But this more sophisticated universe is nevertheless only two dimensional, since we also learned in geometry that three points determine a plane.

If we finally add a fourth particle, we arrive at a three dimensional universe (ignoring the special case of the fourth particle being in the plane of the other three). Does this mean that the interrelationships of distance and velocity have now made evident some primitive notion of time? In addressing this question we can also ponder on what happens when all four particles reverse their velocities. Is time reversed or not, or, again, is there any time at all? Perhaps not, but I feel these questions may possibly be moot and require further examination. Accordingly, they also will be considered further in the next chapter. In any case, despite the fact that this little thought experiment cannot earn the stamp of scientific or philosophic rigor, it does serve at an elementary level to stimulate thought about the relationship of time and motion, and about whether it is only a matter of human awareness.

It also raises the question: at what level of complexity can a concept of time make any sense? Does the complexity have to be such that only a large, statistically meaningful assemblage of particles passing to or from higher or lower states of disorder (entropy) can have time as a characteristic? Could time be a thermodynamic quantity along with temperature and entropy?

Undoubtedly this general and preliminary discussion of time and motion will not settle the question raised in Chapter 2 as to which of the two constitutes the higher order of reality. But it may evoke some tentative speculations about their relationship. For me time seems to link a complex of motions in a common, intrinsic, undefined even pace, a pace that has no specific measure as we know it, e.g. seconds or minutes, until we impose one on it. Time is like an holistic, unseen network bringing organization and synchronism to the motions of a system, regardless of the relative velocities of the particles therein. It somehow is the underlying dynamic grounding of an assembly of motions. It is the conductor of a symphony of motions. Let us see how these rather broad and qualitative speculations fare under the more detailed scrutiny of the irreversible gauges of time in the next chapter, and what this scrutiny may reveal about whether there is time independent of human observation and conceptualization.

Summary

Change and permanence go hand in hand as equal orders of reality to be considered in developing a concept of time. However, religions tell us that only God or Reality is truly permanent. The changes represented by time and motion as well as the apparent permanences in the world that humans experience are but limited manifestations of an eternal Reality or God. Cyclical and irreversible, progressive phenomena are apparent in essentially all domains of the natural world as well as in the realm of animals and humans. Through comparison they provide indicators and gauges of time and its relentless advance. In particular cyclical motion appears at every level in the physical world: microscopic, macroscopic, and astronomic; irreversible processes do also and in addition furnish us with three common gauges of time: thermodynamic, psycho–biologic, and cosmologic.

The fundamental nature of the intimate relation and inseparability of time and motion was extensively explored by Aristotle who in essence concluded that time is an enumeration of change in the context of before and after. The questions on which Aristotle pondered are still with us today, especially the one he posed but did not really answer: "Is there time if no one is there to observe it?"

In addressing this question, one possible approach that has occurred to me is to consider the dynamic relationship between a small group of "sentient" point–like particles. This thought experiment is suggested as one way of speculating at what level of complexity might a primitive concept of time be valid. Many of the issues introduced and surveyed in this chapter will be considered in more detail in the next chapter.

9 IRREVERSIBLE GAUGES OF TIME

Threefold the stride of Time, from first to last:
Loitering slow, the Future creepeth—
Arrow–swift, the Present sweepeth—
And motionless forever stands the Past.
                    —Johann Christoph Friedrich von Schiller

One never says: "It's getting early"
                              —Mary Skipp

In 1927 the British philosopher J. M. E. McTaggart of Cambridge University published a two volume work: "The Nature of Existence." In this study he pondered extensively on the nature of time, particularly its fundamental transience and irreversibility (Whitrow 80, p. 345ff). In doing so he formulated the problem in terms of two fundamental modes of ordering temporal events, which he labeled the A and B series (McTaggart 27, vol. 2, p. 9ff).

With the A series temporal sequence is established through awareness of past, present, and future. The B series is time–ordered seem to be little to distinguish the two modes, they each generally find use in quite different contexts. Some philosophers may disapprove, but I see the A series in a more dynamic, humanly subjective context because it is characterized by the continuously changing present, providing a constantly progressing division between past and future. On the other hand the B series is most applicable in a more objective, essentially static context, because past applicable in a more objective, essentially static context, because past events can be ordered with respect to before and after by the memory (or some recording device), and future events so ordered by knowledgeable anticipation.

Thus, for me, the A series generally characterizes the temporal experience sensed by human consciousness; the B series usually comes into play in objective observations, such as recording history or making theoretical predictions in the physical sciences. These two temporal modes have been used to a considerable extent as references for an incredible amount of philosophical discussion ever since McTaggart set them down. I have been to conferences on time where prolonged and laborious philosophical discourses, some of consummate rigor, others of bewildering convolution, have grappled with which series truly represents temporal reality.

In any case the two series highlight the contrast between the subjective and objective views of time cited at the beginning of this book, and serve as a helpful starting point for our treatment of the three main gauges of time cited in Chapter 8. Recall that these were: 1) the cosmologic gauge, 2) the thermodynamic gauge, and 3) the psychobiologic gauge. As we will see, there may be some bases for linking the three. Let us first turn to the cosmologic gauge.

The Cosmologic Gauge

Perhaps the simplest, most fundamental, and universal physical phenomenon by which we can observe the passage of time is the expansion of the universe. This is essentially the basis for the cosmologic gauge. Although this could change, from what is known as of this writing from astronomic observations, the universe appears to be open because not enough mass has been found with any certainty to support the claim that the critical density defined in Chapter 7 has been reached or exceeded. In this case the universe will expand, and our cosmic clock will tick, forever. However, as discussed in Chapter 7, many theoretical cosmologists maintain that the universe is exactly in between being open and closed, and that the missing mass, which provides the necessary gravitational attraction to slow the expansion by just the required amount, will some day be found. Here also the universe will expand forever, but at a continually decreasing rate, never quite stopping.

If more than the critical amount of mass is present in the universe, then it is closed. The expansion will ultimately cease, reverse, and irreversible contraction will occur. Many writers, including reputable scientists, such as Stephen Hawking, have speculated that under these conditions "time would reverse." I do not believe this would be the case. Several who initially maintained that this might be so have since recanted, including Hawking (Hawking 88, p. 150).

Indeed it is difficult to understand, even in a contracting universe, what it means for time to be reversed. Presumably it means that the succession of all temporal events is reversed. But if this were the case, we would supposedly be caught up in these ongoing events and not know we were "in reverse." These events could be rather weird. Imagine unreading a book. As you read the book backwards from end to beginning, your memory would continually erase the information it had. A bouncing tennis ball would increase its height with each bounce, instead of decreasing it.

However, another phenomenon which I believe may be fundamental to the cosmologic gauge of time is a phenomenon similar to the time asymmetry found in the decay of the neutral K–meson,[1] discussed in Chapter 7. It may be recalled that the decay into one set of product particles exceeded that into the set of their antiparticles by about two parts in a thousand. I feel that a process similar to this may be an essential feature of the cosmologic gauge and may be in part responsible for its existence. This is because, as cited in Chapter 7, the GUT theories applicable in the early universe predict not only such time asymmetry but also the concomitant incremental predominance of matter over antimatter. Without this predominance the matter would have annihilated with the equal amount of antimatter and we would not be here. So that again, as Hawking has said, "our very existence could be regarded as a confirmation of grand unified theories" (Hawking 88, p. 78).

In fact I feel it can even be suggested that this phenomenon may have been what started the cosmologic gauge. There are those who disagree with me, but others (Penrose 89, p. 345) believe that time asymmetry may be a feature of any successful theory of quantum gravity (Coveney and Highfield 90, p. 288).

THE THERMODYNAMIC GAUGE

Despite the fundamental, universal grounding for evolving time provided by the cosmologic gauge, currently it is the thermodynamic gauge that seems to attract the most interest as an indicator of progressive time. This is undoubtedly because it is the thermodynamic gauge that underlies our usual experience of the world around us. We simply take for granted in our day–to–day living that events transpire with irreversible progress and never reverse. Spilt milk does not leap up from the floor and collect back in the bottle. A skier does not reverse

---

[1]Some authors (e.g. Morris 85) judge the neutral K-meson time asymmetry to represent a separate gauge of time. Due to its essential similarity with that predicted by the GUT theories, I do not ascribe it a separate status.

direction and slide back up the mountain.[2] Given such facts of daily experience in our macroscopic world, it may seem at least a waste of time if not ridiculous to give serious thought to the idea of reversible motion in time. Indeed this would be true were it not for the fact that in the quantum description of the microscopic world, and in many classical physics descriptions of macroscopic phenomena, the concept of reversibility turns out to be an extremely useful and meaningful concept. **Reversible Motion.** Some sense as to the validity of such a concept may be gained by considering a collision of two balls on a pool table shown schematically in Figure 8. A collision with the arrows reversed is described equally well by the physical laws (and corresponding equations) governing the collision process. That is, as far as the laws are concerned, they embrace both the case shown in Figure 8 and the case where the arrows are reversed with no preference for either.

Perhaps the most convincing way to grasp the notion of reversibility in the above example would be to take a motion picture of the collision between the balls. Suppose the film were taken off the spool and thrown on the floor in a tangled mess. How, in principle, would one know which way to wind the film on the spool again. Either way a perfectly valid example of the physical laws involved would be shown by the projector, one collision being the reverse of the other (Park 80, p. 50).

Although there are some small frictional heat losses of the energy of the balls to the felt on the pool table, the example at least approximates an ideal frictionless collision. Even more ideally reversible collisions are experienced, for example, by a pair of molecules in a gas. Here the motions involved in individual molecular collisions can also be described in a way that is completely symmetric in time.

This time symmetry of the physical laws is reflected in the mathematical equations the physicist utilizes to represent the motion. That is, regardless of whether the physicist uses +t (denoting advancing time) or -t (denoting its reverse) in the equations, the form of the equations does not change. An equally valid physical solution is obtainable either way. Indeed, excluding the decay of the neutral K-meson mentioned earlier (and possibly another known as the neutral B-

---

[2]Because of the essential irreversibility involved in the emission of electromagnetic radiation discussed in Chapter 5, e.g. the emission of light from a candle, I have included in the Thermodynamic Gauge what some authors have called the Electromagnetic Gauge.

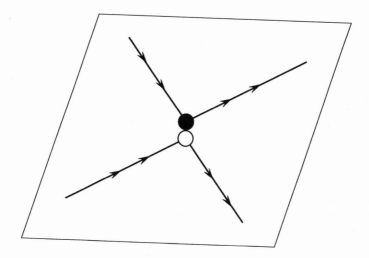

FIG. 8–Billiard balls in collision

meson), this is true of all interactions, between all particles in the microscopic world. This is an extremely powerful statement.

It may now be understandable why so much thought has been given to the irreversible nature of time in our everyday macroscopic world. For the profound question immediately arises: How is it that the phenomena in the macroscopic everyday world are characterized by irreversibility, while almost all of the individual microscopic events comprising this macroscopic world are amenable to a reversible motion, or time–symmetric, description? A little thought should indicate that this is far from a trivial problem. The answer is not at all obvious even after rigorous scientific analyses, and many aspects of it are still subject to intensive study as well as controversy today.

From Microscopic Reversibility to Macroscopic Irreversibility. In order to take some preliminary steps toward understanding the transition from microscopic reversibility to macroscopic irreversibility, it may be of use to return to the example of our "sentient" particles discussed in the last chapter. If we start with our universe of one particle and then add another, we will find that already in principle we are running into complexity at a primitive level. It can be argued on quite general logical grounds that while a single entity (particle or whatever) is indeed a simple system, adding another complicates things noticeably. The two now constitute in general a new and different system, a new whole. This system often has new and different properties and is not just simply two separate particles. Why? Because we must now consider not only: 1) each particle singly, but 2) the relation of the particles to each other, as well as 3) the relation of each to the whole (Puddefoot 92).

An example might be the very short–lived positronium atom, consisting of an electron and a positron (positively charged electron). This system only exists for a time that averages to about 10^{-8} seconds before the two particles annihilate each other, giving up their mass energy with the emission of gamma ray photons. However, during that brief duration it has been shown experimentally that the system manifests many similarities to an ordinary hydrogen atom (one proton and one electron), which can exhibit quite a complex behavior.

Admittedly, this example may not be totally fair in representing the foregoing simple general arguments, because the particles are microscopic and electrically charged, thus bringing in all of the complications of the quantum theory and the electromagnetic interaction. But perhaps it has been helpful in illustrating the generalization. If we now add a third particle, one can guess that the complications multiply. There is not only the three separate singles and their relation to each other and the whole, but also the relation of each particle to combinations of the other two (Puddefoot 92).

Although, again, almost all simple microscopic systems of two or very few particles can generally be treated in a time–symmetric fashion, we perhaps can begin to see the complications ahead when a system of even a few particles is considered. Indeed the dynamics of a system of three interacting particles is not exactly solvable by analytic mathematics (Coveney and Highfield 90, p. 267), and generally has to be determined by successive approximations using computers. These complications at such an early stage of complexity may show that the cumulation of reversible events at the microscopic level summing to irreversible temporal behavior in the macroscopic world is not a simple hypothesis to prove.

It was the statistical theory of thermodynamics,[3] developed in the last century primarily by Ludwig Boltzmann, which constituted the first step toward showing that this hypothesis might be valid. From the statistical analysis of the motion of molecules in gas it was possible to derive mathematical expressions for such thermodynamic quantities as temperature, something which is commonly measured for all kinds of macroscopic objects from humans to electric power transformers. The temperature of such an object was directly related to a statistical averaging of the microscopic velocities of the molecules of the object.

Boltzmann derived the statistical counterpart for another thermodynamic quantity relevant to the "reversibility–irreversibility" question, entropy, cited in the last chapter. In essence he related the entropy of a given isolated system to the degree of molecular disorder in the system. As the disorder or loss of organization of a confined system increases, so does its entropy, the measure of its disorder. The essential basis for this is that disordered states are more plentiful and thus have a higher probability of being realized than more ordered states. It is this progressive entropy increase that many thinkers associate with the irreversible nature of time.

With some exceptions which will be treated later, a vast body of physical processes in the universe exhibit a steady advance toward disorder or entropy increase. Heat flows from a hot body to a cold one, never to be recovered unless by some kind of machine (e.g., a heat pump)

---

[3]Thermodynamics is the study of the transfer of energy, especially heat, within or between systems. Its most sophisticated expression is in terms of statistical analyses of the motions of the particles of the system under study.

that will have to expend energy in the effort to recover the energy lost to the cold body. A drop of ink placed in a glass of water will soon uniformly color the whole glass and is not expected to organize back into a drop again. The probability is extremely slight that a pack of cards originally ordered numerically and according to suits, once shuffled, will return to the initial order in any tolerable length of time. The refined and ordered configuration of gasoline molecules is disintegrated in the burning of the fuel in the engine cylinders of a car. The energy produced is not all transmitted to the order implicit in giving the car motion and direction. Much is irrevocably lost in the exhaust and heat radiated from the engine block.

It is obvious that there are endless examples of processes with a net gain in disorder or entropy and concurrent loss of order and organization. However, the most important characteristic of such entropy increase is its irreversibility, which brings us back to Boltzmann. Despite the time–reversible nature of individual microscopic interactions, he was able to make the first steps toward showing that the cumulative statistical randomness of these individual events add up to irreversible behavior of the gas at the macroscopic level. When it is realized that in a liter of air that we breathe there are of the order of 10^{23} molecules (1 with 23 zeros behind it), perhaps such a result may seem reasonable.

Much of what has been said here is summarized in, and can be inferred from, what is known as the Second Law of Thermodynamics. In essence this law states that any changes that occur in an isolated system are such that its entropy *never decreases*. The system can stay in the same state or change, but if it does change it is always to a greater state of disorder.

However, to some readers there still may remain the haunting speculation that, at least in principle, if there were a computer large enough and if we knew the initial positions and velocities of all of the trillions and trillions of gas molecules, we could keep track of their future motion and thus achieve a very precise prediction of the action of the collective assembly in the container, certainly more precise than the statistical averaging techniques mentioned.

Such a predictive power, even in principle, suggests the possibility of determinism, the belief that everything is wholly determined by a succession of causes, which held sway until the end of the 19th century. Thus, according to this principle, the behavior of a gas is determined, since the cause of the present and future motion of every molecule can be traced back through all of the collisions with its neighbors to the given initial state. In essence it was the belief in this ability to keep track of things at the microscopic level that led to one of the arguments forwarded against Boltzmann's statistical formulation. For, in addition to this belief making possible the idea of classical determinism, it also permits the possible, though highly improbable, return of a system to its original state.

For example, even if we grant that it is extremely unlikely that the playing cards when reshuffled will return to their original order, or the drop of ink to its original concentrated volume separated from the water, or the molecules of a gas to their original configuration of positions and velocities, there is nevertheless in principle a calculable probability, however extremely small, that such repetitions will occur. The length of time it would take for such a recurrence to transpire, of course, depends on the complexity of the system under consideration, but it has been estimated that for isolated systems of macroscopic size, the time involved would be incredibly long, trillions and trillions of years (see Denbigh 81, p. 101ff).

The reason for bringing up the matter of what has been termed "recurrence of physical states" (Whitrow 80, p. 331; Zermelo 1896) is that if such is the case, then how can the Second Law of Thermodynamics be valid? If a physical system can return to its original state, then its entropy (disorder) has not increased continually, but has had to decrease to accomplish such a return.

So how does such an association of advancing time with entropy increase have any validity if a system can ultimately return to its original state? The answer is that in reality it cannot return to that state. First, even if it could, the time it would take for such return is so incredibly long that for all practical purposes it is never. Second, the Heisenberg Uncertainty Principle tells us that both the position and momentum (or velocity) of a microscopic particle cannot be simultaneously measured with arbitrary accuracy. Thus we could never know whether all or any of the particles returned to exactly the same state. Third, even without the Uncertainty Principle it is easy to show that the slightest perturbation in the initial state of the system can lead to drastically different final results. This also happens to be an essential feature of chaos theory which, among other processes, we discuss next. These processes show that thermodynamics embraces broader possibilities for gauging time than envisioned by simple increase in disorder or entropy.

Modern Thermodynamics and Far–from–Equilibrium Processes.
While it seems predictable that essentially all systems characterized by
some form of order will ultimately evolve to greater disorder in the
long, long run, there are vast numbers of systems describable by
thermodynamics which progress to greater order or organization with
time as long as suitable conditions prevail. These are generally known
as far–from–equilibrium systems, which can evolve to remarkable
states of organization. A key characteristic of such processes is the vital
necessity to be able to exchange matter and energy with the
environment. The system must draw on the "food" furnished by its
environment in the form of the needed energy and appropriate chemical
compounds to build and preserve its organization, as well as discard the
molecular components it no longer needs (Coveney and Highfield 90,
p. 168; Prigogine 80, p. 103ff; Prigogine and Stengers 84, p. 177ff). Thus
the system gains its organization at the expense of its environment.
Nevertheless the Second Law of Thermodynamics still holds, for if we
consider the total of the system plus its environment, the entropy for the
whole never decreases.

This awesome ability of the molecules of such a system to
collectively communicate and organize is generally driven by feedback
processes which, with the aid of the appropriate environment, allow the
system's continued growth or maintenance with time. Such feedback
mechanisms are an example of why far–from–equilibrium processes are
described by laws of non–linear dynamics. What do I mean by non–
linear, say, as opposed to linear? In general a linear dependence on
something also involves a simple, direct proportionality. For example,
with constant velocity there is a linear relation between distance and
time. If you were to plot distance vertically and time horizontally on a
graph, a constant velocity would be represented by a straight line with a
given slope as in Figure 9a. A faster velocity would have a steeper slope.
An example of non–linearity would be the gravitational acceleration of
a walnut falling from a high tree. The distance covered after two
seconds is four times that covered in the first second, so that the plot of
distance versus time is a rising curve as shown in Figure 9b.

Non–linearity is an essential feature of the cooperative action of
the molecules in the temporal development of a far–from–equilibrium
system exhibiting self–organization. There are many examples of
chemical reactions which display beautifully ordered spatial patterns, as
well as others which reveal a clock–like periodicity with time
(Prigogine 80, p. 112; Coveney and Highfield 90, e.g. p. 220–1, 294–5).

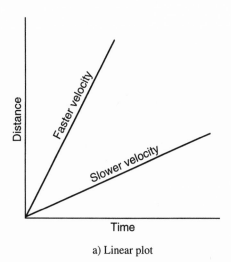

a) Linear plot

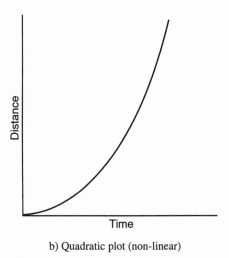

b) Quadratic plot (non-linear)

FIG. 9

Like soldiers in a brigade without a general, the molecules via subtle mutual electromagnetic communication assemble themselves in marching battalions revealing such patterns and/or periodicity.

In some of these chemical processes the system proceeds to a critical point where it bifurcates, or follows one of two branches in its continued temporal evolution. Each branch has an equal likelihood of being followed, and which is actually followed generally depends on the slightest undetectable perturbation of the system (Arecchi 92; Coveney and Highfield 90, p. 165ff; Prigogine 80, p. 105; Prigogine and Stengers 84, p. 160ff). A very simple example of a "one–time" bifurcation would be a magnetic material such as iron at a relatively high temperature exposed to a small magnetic field. At the elevated temperature the iron atoms, each of which behaves like a tiny bar magnet, will be randomly oriented. However, if the iron is cooled, a critical temperature will be reached when the slightest perturbation will cause all of the atoms to collectively align along the magnetic field in one direction or, almost as likely, all line up in the opposite direction, but not both.

However, there are systems which can undergo a multiple succession of bifurcations. Indeed one of the most well–known mechanisms leading to what is popularly called chaos is via an indefinitely increasing number of bifurcations (Gleick 87, p. 72ff; Arecchi 92). But it should be kept in mind that these bifurcations generally proceed by a well–defined law, or in many cases a relatively simple mathematical equation (Kadanoff 83). Thus instead of the implied randomness of the word "chaos," many such systems could better be described as ones of ordered or controlled progressive complexity. Indeed chaos has been described as "nothing but a delinquent form of self–organization" (Coveney and Highfield 90, p. 294). Nevertheless, the singular characteristic of a chaotic system is that the slightest change in its initial state generally leads to dramatically different resultant states.

Undoubtedly the most well–known figure in the modern study of far–from–equilibrium processes is Ilya Prigogine. Born in Moscow, his family moved to Brussels when he was ten years old. He expressed an early interest in thermodynamics and chemistry, and now divides his time directing experimenters and theoreticians at the Free University of Brussels and at the University of Texas. In 1977 he was awarded the Nobel Prize in chemistry for his seminal work in non–equilibrium thermodynamics.

Prigogine has devoted a major part of his life to developing a theory which somehow includes both reversibility and irreversibility in a way that not only bridges the microscopic and macroscopic worlds but unifies them. As already mentioned, a clear–cut construction of such a bridge from reversibility to irreversibility is not a trivial matter. Indeed according to Prigogine, "it is perhaps one of the hottest problems of our time, one in which science and philosophy merge" (Prigogine 80, p. 49).

Prigogine thus champions irreversible thermodynamic processes as playing an equally fundamental role with reversible processes in the physical world. He maintains that time–symmetry gives the later processes a static quality because how time progresses makes no difference. He feels that these essentially static descriptions afforded by classical and quantum dynamics represent a world of "being," while irreversible thermodynamics, because of its inherent, continual progression, reveals a world of "becoming." His principal mission has been to show that both reversible and irreversible phenomena are embraced in a much larger mathematical formalism, which is a generalization of the traditional "static" formalism (Prigogine 80, p. xiii; Prigogine and Stengers 84, p. xi).

So the equations in his theory contain both reversible and irreversible components. Moreover, he claims that time is irreversible at the microscopic level, a position I support, but for different reasons. As discussed in Chapter 5, it is the host of subtle quantum electrodynamic radiations resulting from atomic and molecular excitations, emissions, and collisions that underlie and drive the thermodynamic gauge of time. (See also Fadner 92; Verstraeten 91.)

In any case we witness the wondrous ability of some systems to evolve to remarkable levels of organization and to persist indefinitely as long as exchange with the environs is available. Such processes in their own way define their own "mini–gauge" of time, and on a local scale apparently defy the broad general tendency of nature to progress to greater states of disorder and increased entropy. Again, the Second Law of Thermodynamics is not violated, because taking both the system *and its environment* into account, order is still irrecoverably lost. Thus entropy is ever waiting in the background with its myriad of ways for the system and its environment to ultimately degenerate to irreversible disorder. Nevertheless the existence of such far–from–equilibrium processes sets the stage for our examination of irreversible temporality in very far–from–equilibrium systems, such life–forms as plants, animals, and humans. It is humans that represent the farthest–from–

equilibrium system of all and serve as the ultimate example of the next gauge, the psychobiologic.

THE PSYCHOBIOLOGIC GAUGE

We humans are continually dependent on exchange with our environment. We breathe and exhale, eat food and excrete waste. In the words of Henri Bergson: "Life ascends the slope that matter descends." This living process in its most fundamental aspects is similar to any other far–from–equilibrium process. So how can we humans lay claim to being the farthest–from–equilibrium system of all, the one with the subtlest and most exquisitely complex reproductive process of all? It is because we have evolved to the ability to be conscious of, among many other things, how far from equilibrium we really are. Not only that, but we are conscious of our consciousness of that fact. It is this consciousness of being conscious that especially distinguishes us from the other forms of life around us, miraculous though they are. Every living thing is a marvel of organization of vast numbers of mutually communicating molecules constituting organs and parts making up a concordant whole that is greater than the sum of its parts. But each human person is a symphony of cosmic proportions, a symphony of information–bearing neurons, coursing blood corpuscles, incessantly coordinating and vitalizing finely tuned organs, all synchronized to provide the material home for a transcending consciousness, and an even more transcendent consciousness of being conscious.

It is this faculty that makes us aware of the changing present, the marvelous realization of being in the present and becoming in the ever so subtlely succeeding next present with the change it brings. It is this awareness that brings together the two basic modes by which we personally sense the irreversible passage of time: 1) succession of events, 2) the interval between events or duration (Piaget 81, p. 208; Whitrow 80, p. 41). The succession of events is sensed by our experience or observation of each in the present, then with our immediate memory chronologically ordering these events. The events are given wholeness and completeness by duration. In any case this serial chronology remains as such in our memory. So that when we remember an important episode in our past, our rerunning of its events is generally in this same chronological order, not the reverse (Whitrow 80, p. 81). This is in part because the biological clocks ticking unnoticed in the subterrains of our physiology give durational measure to our memory's cumulative record of progressing time.

More generally, the irreversible nature of time that is associated with the psychobiologic gauge is revealed in humans by their growth and maturing, at least on the scale of their life–times. This growth and maturing can perhaps be somehow approximately quantified by the growth of information according to David Layzer (Layzer 75). The human being, representing the most anti–entropic of systems, is characterized by an irreversible accumulation of information. Information can be equated to order, the opposite of entropy, the measure of disorder.

However, the question immediately arises: what about an individual's aging and death, their ultimate disintegration, and merging into the thermodynamics of their environment? Indeed this occurs on a given human's life–time scale. But the psychobiologic gauge, in particular considered with respect to humans, can only achieve its full significance in terms of the historical growth of the species as a whole, the constructive nature of what is passed on from generation to generation. Certainly a measure for this growth is the accumulation of information in human history, which in the last 300 years has been awesome. In fact Layzer terms this gauge of time the "historical" gauge (Layzer 75).

Information is the food for consciousness, the growth of the two is mutual and concurrent. Consciousness in some collective form now envelopes the earth. Through its insatiable thirst for information it is in a significant sense spreading with probing fingers to the far reaches of the solar system, the galaxy, the observable universe. If we take the sanguine outlook that this growth will continue indefinitely, then the irreversible spread of consciousness in some form, or its effects, is an ultimate expression of the psychobiologic gauge of time.

Is There a Unity of the Three Gauges?

The relation of the three gauges and the question of their possible interdependence is the subject of considerable study currently. Many scholars maintain that the cosmologic gauge is the most fundamental, the "Master" gauge of time. We have already noted that Penrose believes that the cosmologic evolution of time will be an inherent feature of any viable theory of quantum gravity. Certainly on logical grounds a case can be made for its primacy, since without it the other two might not exist, particularly the psychobiologic.

However, it is possible to argue that the thermodynamic gauge is concomitant, or closely attendant, with the cosmologic. After all, thermodynamics played a central role in the earliest stages of the universe's evolution. H. Dieter Zeh in a detailed mathematical exposition attempts to show how the cosmologic and thermodynamic gauges are linked through characteristics of the wave function of the universe (Zeh 89) (for the concept of such a wave function see Chapter 7). The linkage of the two gauges is also supported by recent work of Hawking and his colleagues using the "no–boundary" approach to the big bang, which was also discussed in Chapter 7 (Hawking et al. 93).

Another basis for the unification of the two gauges might be seen in the claim of some scholars that the universe in its ultimate stages of expansion will finally reach full thermodynamic equilibrium when there will no longer be any exchange of heat, and entropy will have increased to its absolute maximum. Some have called this the "heat death" of the universe. Strictly from the point of view of the observable matter particles in the universe, this may be true. However, Heinz Pagels[4] has pointed out that by far the dominant portion of the universe's entropy resides with photons, particles of light, as well as neutrinos, particles of zero, or near zero, mass, which are very difficult to detect (Pagels 85, p. 236–7). These particles were already thermally equilibrated at early stages the of cosmic expansion. So as far as most of the entropy in the universe is concerned the "heat death" occurred eons ago.

There is also a linkage between the thermodynamic and psychobiologic gauges in that the latter could hardly exist without the former. Without the tendency in nature for systems to decay to greater states of disorder, greater entropy, the nutritive ingredients for progressively ordered processes such as trees, animals, and humans would not be available. Thus the two gauges may well continue their course indefinitely in a reciprocal or complementary relationship. In fact I wonder whether we, being made of matter, are not finally articulating the irreversible nature of time that inarticulable matter has been silently expressing all along. Indeed might there not be a primitive "now" immanent in nature, but inexpressible by humans? For me such conjectures might be worth considering in the heated controversy over which of McTaggart's series, A or B, has ascendance.

---

[4]Heinz Pagels was an excellent physicist and writer of books on physics understandable to the lay reader. In the last pages of his book "The Cosmic Code" he describes a dream predicting his death in a mountain climbing accident, which actually occurred a few years later.

For now, I see the three gauges as having successively evolved, first the cosmologic, then the thermodynamic, and finally the psychobiologic. But they are nevertheless concurrent, coexistent, and intricately interdependent, and each has the dual properties of irreversible succession and duration. However, for a different perspective as to their nature and reality we turn to a consideration of the spiritual aspects of evolving time as found in some of the world's religions.

SALVATION AND TIME

In Chapter 6 we cited how, in the biblical era, time seems to have been experienced and perceived on three levels: 1) that of everyday worldly and religious life, 2) that grounded on an understanding of the natural world and the cosmos, and 3) God's eternity. Clearly in very broad qualitative terms the first two levels cover roughly the same temporal spectrum as the three gauges we have been examining. But here we will look at the relationship of the third level, divine eternity, to salvation and time.

In a given religion its spiritually impregnated view of time is generally associated with the ideal of an irreversible path to salvation, the setting and background for which is represented by the religion's cosmology. The cosmology is a metaphor in terms of the phenomena of the natural world for the "spiritual geography" the adherent must pass through to reach the goal of salvation and be reconciled with God's eternity. Transient time, the time of one's days, stretches out from the eternal Essence like a light beam guiding the follower to the Source.

In one form or another an indispensable fuel for pursuing the salvational course is faith. As mentioned earlier, even in everyday living it takes faith to allow oneself to be swept along by relentless time and to muster openness to what the future might bring. It even takes faith, resting in the reality of one moment, to believe that the next moment will come, that God will provide it.

Recall in Chapter 6 how Mircea Eliade saw faith as providing the spiritual thrust for the Israelites to break out of the cyclical pattern of primitive worship of natural divinities. As we have seen, this was the beginning of a series of events of divine intervention which would not have been possible without faith. The scriptual writers by setting down the events produced a history which, according to many scholars, provided the first seeds of our modern sense of progressive time. For perhaps the first time a god of history was worshipped instead of a god of cyclical nature.

In addition to this detailed chronology the bible presents the sweeping cosmology discussed earlier, with one unrepeatable beginning proceeding ineluctably through salvational history to an End, the coming of the Messiah. This End is Christ's second coming for the Christians, and the coming of Judgment Day for the Moslems.[5]

In more recent times Teilhard de Chardin has developed an imaginative integration of the Christian biblical cosmology with the physical cosmology as it was understood before his death in 1955, several years after Gamow's Big Bang Theory was published. He saw the universe as evolving to progressive stages of ever greater complexity along what he has termed a "favored axis." As shown in Figure 10, this growth proceeds from inanimate matter, to animate matter or life, then to "Reflection," or humans and consciousness, next the society of humankind, followed possibly by a Christian society, finally reaching the Omega point, the goal of salvation, which may be associated with Christ's second coming (Teilhard de Chardin 68, p. 210ff). The irreversible evolving nature of time is clearly implicit in such a spiritual model of the cosmos.

But the Western religious traditions are not alone in providing a representation of a spiritually endowed progressive aspect of time. As we have briefly noted in Chapter 6, contrary to common thinking strong progressive, non–cyclical components are apparent in some of the major Eastern traditions (Balslev 90). Specifically Hinduism and Buddhism are often prematurely passed off as presenting purely cyclical cosmologies. Again, while it is true that the larger cycles in the Hindu cosmology exhibit a repeatable cyclicity, this is not true of the smallest period, the yuga. The four yugas comprising a mahayuga, are each of progressively shorter duration, possessing quite different dharmic, theological content. That is, they are not exactly repeatable by any means.

Much more important as an indication of progression is the realization that the entire cyclical cosmology is a theological metaphor for the repeated, painful reincarnations a soul must struggle through, unless by faithful karmic striving one is able to extract oneself from this process and achieve moksha, thus identifying oneself with the eternal, ineffable Brahman. The salvational course through this cyclical milieu can be considered just as valid a representation of a spiritually evolving

---

[5]For some Moslems, particularly the Shiites, the End occurs with the coming of the Mahdi, the Expected One. Through history there have been several false pretenders for this role.

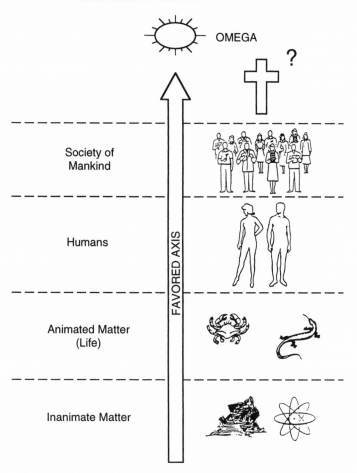

OMEGA

Society of
Mankind

Humans

FAVORED AXIS

Animated Matter
(Life)

Inanimate Matter

TEILHARD DE CHARDIN

FIG. 10

irreversible aspect of time as that characterized in Western cosmologies. A similar case can be made for many Mahayana Buddhist cosmologies which are also cyclical. But here again the cosmologies are representations of the progressive karmic struggle through many reincarnations that one must endure before hopefully reaching the eternal salvation of nirvana.

Another aspect of temporal irreversibility is revealed in considering the uniqueness of, and reverence for, the moment. Although this is the principal subject of Chapter 11, it is important to emphasize here that it is the incomparable singularity of each moment, each now, that directly implies the irreversible nature of time. For, if each moment is truly unique, then it cannot be repeated and thus helps define the irreversible character of time.

Both in the East and the West exemplary expressions of this uniqueness, and its implications for temporal irreversibility, are not hard to find. The full vividity of the living present is powerfully and poetically expressed by Martin Buber, who with exquisite but cogent strokes paints the delicate texture of a given now, which can never be repeated in the same way again (e.g. see Buber 58). In Whitehead's religiously impregnated metaphysics, as discussed in Chapter 2, a given "actual occasion" is an unique event and can never be exactly reproduced, hence the irreversible nature of time (Whitehead 19, p. 63). Furthermore as we have seen, Buddhist tradition confers an ultimate reality to the moment, each now being a new creation, irreplaceable and unrepeatable. These examples will be more fully treated in Chapter 11, but are relevant here by showing that a reverence for the moment, East or West, brings a consummate unique fullness to it, which cannot again be realized in the same way. This therefore implies the irreversible character of time and invests it with a spiritual essence.

So we see that world wide, there are rich examples of salvational cosmologies and the moments that comprise them, which consecrate time with a spiritual content of hope, faith, and redemption. It is a value–endowed, faith–pervaded, and goal–directed time that lends a quality of meaning to the three gauges discussed above, a meaning they otherwise would not have, a meaning that is the most inspiring and challenging that the spiritual revelation of God's eternality can provide. God does not reverse events, time proceeds relentlessly. Both in the East and the West this fact could be interpreted as suggesting that theologically the path to salvation and judgment is presented also as irreversible in order to encourage the irreversible commitment of the worshipper to a life justifying salvation.

In any case both religious and physical sources give testimony to the relentless, irreversible, and evolving nature of time. But in addition the religions spiritually enrich this time with a value–endowed, goal–directed quality.

SUMMARY

The irreversible passage of time can be sensed in two fundamental modes, the subjective mode of human experience and the objective mode of rational recording and prediction. These modes roughly correlate with those more specifically defined by McTaggart as the A series (past, present, future), and the B series (before, after).

Although several gauges of time have been proposed, I believe that they can be distilled to a fundamental three. The first is the cosmologic gauge based on the expansion of the universe. Next is the thermodynamic gauge which reflects the ultimate tendency of all nature to pass to greater states of disorder, or increased entropy. However, this gauge is fraught with complexity, because many far–from–equilibrium systems can develop to remarkable states of organization provided they can exchange matter and energy with their environment. Nevertheless, considering the system plus its environment, the entropy of the total will never decrease, and the Second Law of Thermodynamics is ultimately obeyed.

The third, the psychobiologic gauge, is based on the growth of very far–from–equilibrium systems such as plants, animals, and especially human beings. Though humans can be considered as extreme examples of such a system, their most distinguishing feature is consciousness, as well as consciousness of consciousness. But the ultimate expression of this gauge is the growth of information acquired by the species as a whole through ongoing generations.

From the viewpoint of the major world religions time's advance is associated with the sacred goal–directed course toward salvation, as well as the sacred unrepeatable moments that make up this course. Thus both physical and religious sources attest to the unrelenting becoming of time, but it is a time impregnated with spiritual value and purpose by the religions.

10 Time, Space, and the Dynamic World: The Spatialization and Liberation of Time

"Nobody has ever noticed a place except at a time, and a time except at a place"

—Hermann Minkowski

"Where flies the arrow that cannot point,
Whence time and motion find their joint?"

—L. W. F.

Experiencing Time and Space

Very often in one context or another we mention time and space together with an implied understanding that they are closely related parts of some ill–defined whole. There is an unexpressed assumption that some degree of mutual interrelation characterizes the two. That this might be the case should not be surprising considering what is now known about the sense of time and space in modern psychology or what can be learned from the wisdom of spiritual leaders of the past. Indeed nowhere does the relation of time and space appear more intermeshing than when it is experienced psychologically, or intuited spiritually.

Time and Space in Psychology. For example, interdependence of time and space is quite apparent in a number of revealing tests in experimental psychology performed with a human subject. In one test the subject is asked to close her eyes and bare one of her forearms. The experimenter then makes three light pin pricks along the forearm. The first and second are closer together in distance than the second and third. However, if there is a greater time duration between the first and second pricks than between the second and third, the subject will erroneously conclude that the distance between the first and second is greater than between the second and third (Helson and King 31; Whitrow 80, p. 71).

In another example the subject is presented with successive flashes of light from three sources spaced again so that the first and second are closer together in distance than the second and third. She is then given control of the timing of the second, or middle, flash, and asked to time it so that it comes exactly half way in time between the first and third flash. She will tend not to allow equal time intervals between the flashes, but to give a longer time interval between the first and second flashes, which are closer together spatially (Cohen *et al.* 55; Whitrow 80, p. 71).

Among other things these tests suggest that different sense organs possess different capacities to gauge time and space. Consider two apples falling from a tree at different speeds, but striking the ground simultaneously. If you hear their impact you can tell that indeed they landed at the same time. However, if their impact is out of earshot, your visual comparison of their motion will lead you to claim that the faster apple arrived first. Thus under these circumstances the ear seems to be our best sensor of time (Whitrow 80, p. 73).

In any event, it is the brain which sorts and interprets the data from all of the sensory organs. Via an intricate system of interactions the brain presents the mind with a total picture, an integrated evaluation. While the brain exists in three dimensional space as well as in time, the mind results from an exquisitely complex interaction of various parts of the brain and is not localized in any one of them. Thus, although the mind has an encompassing cognizance of space, the mind is more deeply aware of time (Whitrow 80, p. 113; Denbigh 81, p. 153). All of this tells us that at the psychological level time and space are interwoven in an extremely complex way.

Spiritual Conceptions of Spatio–Temporality. The degree of this complexity may be apparent in the profound apprehension of the breadth of space, the depth of time, and their harmonious unification that has been accessed by mystics through spiritual contemplation. This holistic sense of the intimate interdependence of time and space is evident in many descriptions of the states of consciousness reached in Hindu and Buddhist meditation. Such a perception of temporal and spatial interrelatedness is expressed very powerfully by D. T. Suzuki, well–known scholar of Eastern religions, in his discussion of the meditative state achieved in the practices of the Avatamsaka school of the Mahayana. A condition is reached wherein there is no longer consciousness of any distinction between mind and body or subject and object. In this situation:

> ...every object...is related to every other object and penetrated by it not only spatially but temporally. For this reason, every minute we live contains eternity....It is the same with the idea of space. The point I occupy is the center of the universe, and it is mine and with me that it subsists. As a fact of pure experience, however, there is no space without time, no time without space; they are also interpenetrating (Suzuki 38, p. xxvii).

This sweeping sense of the integration of time and space is also expressed by the great Tibetan Buddhist mystic Lama Govinda in his discussion of the experience of space in his meditative practice:

> And if we speak of the space–experience in meditation, we are dealing with an entirely different dimension....In this space–experience the temporal sequence is converted into a simultaneous co–existence, the side–by–side existence of things into a state of mutual interpenetration, and this again does not remain static but becomes a living continuum in which time and space are integrated (Govinda 69, p. 116ff).[1]

Thus as a profound awareness of space is experienced in meditation, one arrives at an encompassing state of total presence where the full extensiveness of time and space can be viewed, and they become one dynamic, interrelated whole.

This realization of the enveloping interdependence of time and space is in some fundamental respects congenial with some Western religious philosophies dealing with the subject. Again recalling the penetrating thought of Whitehead to be discussed further in Chapter 11, he saw the universe as evolving via a complex of "actual occasions," each influenced but not determined by God. These events were regarded as quanta of experience defining some finite duration and spatial extent. For Whitehead there was no time without space and no space without time; they become commingled in the concrescence of an actual occasion (Whitehead 20, p. 142).

In his two volume work *Space, Time, and Deity* the incisive philosophic and religious thinker Samuel Alexander represented a closely related perception of time and space. But in contrast to Whitehead, he thought in terms of points and instants and saw the world as a complex of point–instants, which he labeled "pure events" (Alexander 20, p. 48). He argued that time as such could not exist

---

[1]Portions of the foregoing two quotations are also discussed in Capra 77.

without space and vice versa and went so far as to insist that "space is in its very nature temporal and time spatial" (Alexander 20, p. 44). The intimate relation of time and space was imaginatively described using the human body as a metaphor: time is the mind of space and space the body of time (Benjamin 81, p. 28).

Actually a spiritual integration of time and space has probably been a central feature in the worship of men and women ever since they developed a thoughtful reaction to the world around them. In Chapter 6 it was described how archaic cultures celebrated a mythical creation event at the same time each year and at the same holy place. Space and time were fused in the divine events of Israelite biblical history. So today worshippers around the world bring time and space into a sacred synthesis by celebrating holy events yearly at the same church, synagogue, mosque, temple, or hallowed ground. Thus the spiritual coalescence of time and space to capture the holiness of a sacred event is a primal need set deep in the hearts of men and women everywhere.

The Interpenetration of Matter. Another aspect of the interdependence of time and space is revealed in considering the concept of interpenetration. This concept was specifically mentioned in the two above quotations concerning the Buddhist space–time experience. These Buddhist schools extend the concept to include the interpenetration of matter, wherein all things are seen as mutually pervading and interactive. For example, the message of the *Avatamsaka sutra* as expressed by Buddhist scholar Charles N. E. Eliot tells us:

> In the heaven of Indra there is said to be a network of pearls so arranged that if you look at one you see all others reflected in it. In the same way each object in the world is not merely itself but involves every other object and in fact is everything else (Eliot 35, p. 109).

A similar perception is implied in the words of D. T. Suzuki:

> When the one is set against all the others, the one is seen as pervading them all and at the same time embracing them all in itself (Suzuki 68, p. 52).

These two quotations[2] clearly transmit the universal sense of interpenetration that characterizes the views of some of the Mahayana mystics.

Such perceptions of the interpenetration of matter bring us back to the physical world in that they suggest a provocative analogy with the idea of overlapping wave functions in quantum mechanics discussed in

---

[2]These quotations are also discussed in Capra 77.

Chapter 4. Remember it was learned there that all matter, in particular all microscopic matter such as electrons, protons, atoms, and molecules, could be characterized by a probability function or pattern. The probability is greatest that the particle is at the center of the pattern where the curve is maximum. Each side of the pattern trails off to very low probabilities. Nevertheless, the probability that the particle might be located at those extremes, though very slight, is nevertheless not zero, even out to the far reaches of the universe. It is in this probabilistic sense, and only in this sense, all particles of matter are interpenetrating.

However, since we as observers are also made of matter, the related problem of observer theory also is affected by our concept of interpenetration. That is, where do the limits of the observer's domain end and those of the object observed begin? This suggests the haunting and imaginative question: how do thought, insight, and emotion operating in the human brain affect the atoms and molecules therein, which in turn through interpenetration relate to all matter in the external world (Toben and Wolf 83, p. 36, 37)?[3]

But what might the notion of matter interpenetration in the physical world have to do with linking time and space? For one linkage that suggests itself we must turn back to general relativity theory discussed in Chapter 3. Recall that in the proximity of a large mass time slows and space curves. Indeed in dealing with some aspects of general relativity certain large concentrations of matter are often considered as an extreme convolution in the curvature of space–time. Although these remarks are primarily valid for large masses of matter, they nevertheless seem to suggest some kind of fundamental linkage of time and space via matter. In fact, as suggested in Chapter 3, one wonders whether, instead of speaking about "space–time," we should not be speaking of "space–time–matter" (or considering $E = mc^2$, "space–time–energy").

Of course, such a term may not come into use until general relativity, with its ability to slow time and curve space, is reconciled with quantum theory by a successful theory of quantum gravity and applied to the microscopic particle that our universe presumably was at its beginning. More will be said about this and the concentration and quantization of time and space in the next chapter. For now, having turned to thinking about spatio–temporality in the dynamic physical

---

[3] Another conceivable mechanism by which the brain could affect the external world would be subtle electromagnetic waves generated by the brain.

world, let us continue by examining some ideas about how velocity relates time and space.

TIME, SPACE, AND VELOCITY

Have you ever watched a baseball fly through the air, I mean really watched it closely? As you carefully watched its movement you may have soon become cognizant of the intimate relationship of time and space when you pondered the mystery its motion. Looking at the baseball's movement, it traverses a certain space in a certain time. Is the elemental basis of its motion a sequence of instantaneous states analogous to the successive frames on the film of a motion picture camera? As discussed earlier, Aristotle devoted extensive study to the analysis of motion, especially in the seventh book of his Physics. His meticulous study in this particular treatise was based on assuming the reality of points and instants in space and time. Zeno before him reasoned from a similar point–instant basis in formulating his famous paradoxes, one of which was cited in Chapter 2, and all of which are still discussed to this day.

As we have seen, the power of Zeno's paradox of the arrow is that it highlights the problem of assuming points and instants. For again, if the tip of the arrow that is in motion coincides with a given point in space at a given instant, how can one distinguish that situation from the case when the tip occupied that position all the time? Perhaps the difficulty with the point–instant assumption can be sensed since it renders it hard to conceive how motion proceeds. How does something get unstuck from one point and proceed to the next?

However, the mathematical analysis of the role of time and space in motion received its most successful treatment with the invention of calculus independently by Newton and Leibniz. With calculus the idea of velocity being determined by the ratio of a certain distance traversed to a corresponding time duration was given a rigorous mathematical definition. How this is done can perhaps be understood if we imagine a process by which the value of the velocity is determined by taking the ratio of a very small increment of distance to the correspondingly small increment of duration. By allowing these increments to progressively become infinitesimal in a consistent way, the value of the velocity is obtained. This is a rough qualitative description of the analytical basis for differential calculus in general, where differential ratios representing all kinds of quantities, not just velocity, can be obtained.

In any case it appears that velocity can only be rigorously defined using the concept of such infinitesimals of time and space. Thus velocity, when considered in and of itself, brings time and space together at a very elemental level. Let us pursue other ways in which velocity brings time and space into interdependence by looking again at some effects described by relativity theory.

Time and Space in Relativity

In Chapter 3 we discussed in general terms how relativity required an interflexibility of the time and space scales involved when comparing measurements made by two observers moving at some high velocity relative to each other. Recall that each observer saw the other's clock to be slower and ruler to be shorter the greater their relative velocity. Remember also it was noted that the development of relativity theory and such attendant effects were primarially the result of an analysis of the temporal and spatial relationship of events. It is events that constitute an elementary link between time and space. Let us examine in somewhat more detail the nature of the interdependence of time and space in the observation of an event.

Imagine that Lucy, the astronaut, is moving at a very high, but constant, velocity with respect to Willie in his laboratory on the ground, and they are both observing the same event, say a burning meteorite falling to the earth. Suppose that Lucy, out of curiosity, decides that, instead of her own time and space scales, she would like to use Willie's time and space scales, as she sees them from her spaceship, to make measurements on the event. That is, she is going to take the time given by Willie's clock, slower than her own, and the distance measured by Willie's ruler, which is shorter than hers for her measurements of the meteorite's motion.

In order to know exactly how much Willie's time and space scales differ from hers she must use equations which mathematically relate her scales to his. These are known as transformation equations which transform the spacetime scales of one observer to those of another moving at some relative velocity with respect to the first. They were originally devised by H. A. Lorentz, and later Einstein incorporated them in his relativity theory.

In using these equations Lucy immediately sees when calculating Willie's time scale that it is not only related to her own time scale but is also affected by her distance scale. Furthermore Willie's distance scale will not only be related to her distance scale but also be affected by her time scale. Moreover if Willie similarly wanted to relate his scales to Lucy's, he would find the same effects. Of course, it should be remembered that this is a hypothetical example, and that these effects would only become easily noticeable at relative speeds much higher than those of present spaceships.

However, the example illustrates how intimately interdependent time and space are in our relativistic world. This relationship can perhaps be made clearer by further noting that Lucy will discover that the contraction of Willie's ruler and the slowing of his clock will be by just such an amount that the total change of all four dimensions, three space and one time, will be zero. Willie would see the same effect on examining Lucy's measuring system. It is only by the time and space scales reciprocally trading off in this way that Lucy and Willie could measure the velocity of light to be the same regardless of what their relative velocity is.

WHAT ARROW OF TIME?

It was the necessity to bring time and space together in this integrated, interdependent way that principally generated the notion of four–dimensional space–time. Time could apparently be made like another spatial dimension essentially by multiplying it by the velocity of light. If you are driving to New York at 50 miles an hour with 2 hours to go, you spatialize this time by multiplying the two numbers together and seeing you have 100 miles to go. In any case primarily because of relativity theory the concept of four–dimensional spacetime has gained universal acceptance, and has in a sense developed an independent reality of its own.

Although, it is readily acknowledged by any physicist that, despite relativistic time and space interdependence, time is nevertheless an essentially different and separate quantity from space, the mathematical treatment of time as a space–like quantity has had its effect. Indeed in my opinion the popularization of the concept of four–dimensional space–time has done more to propagate the notion of time spatialization than any other influence.

Of course, if we think about it, it is almost impossible to express time, or to measure it, without using a spatial description or mediary. We look at the position of the sun or the minute hand on a clock. We plot time versus space on a piece of graph paper. All of these are spatial representations of time. In the words of Henri Bergson: "When we evoke time, it is space that answers the call."

In fact just about everywhere we turn, we see evidence of temporal spatialization. Numerous quite credible books have been written and many articulate, scholarly lectures delivered, all using words such as "the arrow of time," "the direction of time," "the linearity of time." *Tell me! Where does the arrow point? In what direction is it flying? Along what spatial line is time proceeding?*[4]

Of course, an answer to these questions is that: "well, these are simply convenient metaphors used to express the advance of time." This is true, but I cannot help feeling that their universal and constant use tends to rigidify our perception of time and to rob it of its unique and dynamic nature.

Can we not at least try to do something about this? In fact I myself have made an attempt. You may or may not have noticed it, but, despite the ubiquitous general usage of such metaphors, until now *I have not once mentioned such words as "arrow," "direction," or "linear" in reference to time in this book.* I have done this with the deliberate intention of demonstrating that it may be possible to express concepts of time in non–spatial terms. This despite the fact that I may have sacrificed some clarity by depriving myself of the use of such metaphors and also have resorted to words that may not be entirely devoid of spatial overtones. Nevertheless this has constituted one small effort among many much more reputed in the last century or so to express the special character of time. These efforts arise from the instinctive sense that nature is telling us that a realistic view of the world is much better described, not by the spatialization of time, but by the dynamitization of space (Capek 81, p. 473).

THE LIBERATION OF TIME

Among the better known efforts to allow time its uniqueness, there have been several valiant attempts to develop a mathematical theory that provides a measure for time, but in non–spatial terms. These are attempts to rigorously describe in some form of mathematics the essential progress of time as an ordinal succession of instants or moments of some kind. The essential nature of the problem was cogently expressed by Jean Piaget who maintains that we: "have geometry derived from an abstraction of space, but no chronometry derived from an abstraction of time" (Piaget 81, p. 203).

---

[4]For those who imaginatively wish to integrate cyclical and advancing time by invoking the spiral as a metaphor, I ask: "Where is the spiral spiralling?"

One impressive effort to devise such a chronometry was made by Sir William Rowan Hamilton over one hundred and fifty years ago. He was a brilliant scholar who at age 13 had mastered 13 languages, and who at age 22 was appointed to a professorship at the University of Dublin. In 1837 he published a 130 page paper a large section of which was entitled: "Preliminary and Elementary Essay on Algebra as the Science of Pure Time" (Hamilton 1837). His efforts were later shown to be unsuccessful, but his work ultimately lead to his invention of a novel, but now well-known, form of mathematics involving what he termed as "quaternions."

Nevertheless to this day such efforts are continuing. Probably among the most notable and persistent has been the work of David Finklestein, now at the Georgia Institute of Technology. I can recall attending a lecture of his some twenty-six years ago in which he presented his ideas for an algebra that avoided the use of points and instants, an algebra which accorded elements of spacetime some spatio-temporal extensiveness (recall that this is consistent with Whitehead's spacetime philosophy). In fact he entitled his lecture "Pointless Physics"! Finklestein has continued his efforts to find a more viable representation of time as well as space with an imaginative use of sophisticated mathematics (Finklestein 89; Finklestein and Hallidy 91).

All such theoretical efforts have been attempts to capture self-consistently and coherently both the essential ordinality or sequence of some kind of temporal increments (instants, moments) and the progressive duration underlying their becoming. Although they are thus far unsuccessful, they are attempts that reveal the depth and complexity of the problem and show us the challenge we have to meet. If we are to liberate and despatialize time, we must somehow describe it in, and on, its own terms, and we must find what those terms are. Among other things we need to realize that time truly is different from space in a very fundamental way. With space we can move up or down, forward or backward, right or left, i.e., either way in all three dimensions. But with time we proceed only from past to future (Rosen 93).

Thus time needs to be free to recapture its holistic vitality. It needs to again take its place beside space as an equal partner. It needs to be rationally and sensibly understood as a unified becoming, which is generally comprised of a synchronous assembly of becomings, and which can be measured by another regularly paced becoming.

An essential element in this understanding, attempted in this chapter, is an elucidation of time's role as an equal partner with space in their interrelation. The intimate nature of this interrelation is revealed from physical, religious, psychological, and philosophical viewpoints. However, a still fuller understanding of the symbiosis of time and space is afforded by an examination of the concept of the moment. Whether seen as a spiritual integration of time and space in a holy event or as a temporal quantum in the natural world, the moment plays a vital role in a more coherent description of time. It is the subject of the next chapter.

SUMMARY

Whether in ordinary daily living or in deep contemplation, we humans experience time and space as intimately interrelated. Examples of this can be found in a number of tests on human subjects by experimental psychologists. On a more spiritual level a conception of intermixing and integration of time and space characterizes certain Buddhist meditative practices. This temporal and spatial intermixing is a central feature in the religiously oriented metaphysics of such philosophers as Alfred North Whitehead and Samuel Alexander. The spiritual fusion of time and space has characterized the yearly celebration of holy events since archaic times.

The concept of interpenetration when extended to matter also reveals itself in Buddhist meditation and finds a provocative analogy with the idea of overlapping wave patterns in quantum mechanics. From general relativity we know that matter can influence time and space and in doing so may serve as some kind of intermediary linking the two.

A much more obvious linkage is afforded by consideration of velocity, the careful analysis of which reveals the inextricable relation between time and space. Velocity reveals another way in which time and space are interdependent by the interflexibility of the time and space scales of two observers moving at high speed relative to one another. Relativity brought about the general use of the concept of four dimensional spacetime which was one of the principal causes of the now universal tendency to spatialize time through the use of a number of spatial metaphors. This tends to rob time of its unique and dynamic character. Attempts to quantify this character by means of some mathematics delineating the sequential and durational nature of time have thus far proven unsuccessful, but will undoubtedly continue. In any event it is apparent that religious, psychological, and physical sources in each case give abundant testimony to the intimate relation of time and space.

11 THE MOMENT: INCREMENT OF TIME AND SPACE

"Moments, moments, moments, notes in the symphony of time."
—L. W. F.

"The sacred moment, the limpid eye of eternity."
—L. W. F.

THE SACRED MOMENT

In those rare and precious moments when we wholly open ourselves to our vibrant surroundings, time and space take on a different appearance and seem to reveal a deep essence of integration. The living "now" assumes a pervasive immanence; we are in tune with the Eternal Now. Our surroundings, our space, become the universe in the sense that we are totally at peace with our place in it and feel a full relation to it, all of it. In effect, we are a microcosm of the universe; all space and time are distilled into the "here" and "now" (Fagg 85, p. 157).

Let us examine some of the ways a reverence for the moment is expressed from a few selected sources.

Martin Buber. It is Martin Buber who for me expresses most powerfully the unparalled access to the vivid fullness of the "here" and "now." No other 20th century religious scholar captures such a harmoniously blended integration of the reverence and the vibrancy of the moment as does Buber. No one so cogently articulates how the moment challenges us to expose ourselves to its depth with total, vulnerable openness. For Buber: "One does not withhold oneself from the moment to buy a richer one later on."

Martin Buber
1878–1965

In his studies as a young man Buber proved to be an impressive interdisciplinarian. He did not believe in extensively restricted specialization, feeling that there was always some significant relationship between things and ideas to which men and women devote their attention and study. It was his conviction that a broad approach led to an inner sense of unity and self–integration. Generally disdaining the practices of classification, systematization, and rigorous philosophical or rational thought, he might best be termed a phenomenologist or existentialist. However, in keeping with his cultural holism he did not wish to be labeled. Although many have called him a theologian, philosopher, or educator, all with very good reason, he personally felt his interdisciplinary efforts could best be described as "philosophical anthropology."

Buber's fascination with the Eastern religions, Hinduism, Buddhism, and Taoism, undoubtedly helped contribute to the exquisite, incisive, and poetic perception that brings such vitality and presence to his religious writings. These included a broad spectrum of works on Judaism, Zionism, and biblical interpretation. However, perhaps the most important source for his thought arose from his life–long efforts to interpret 18th century Hasidism in Eastern Europe (Buber 60). For Buber, Hasidism is the greatest phenomenon in history of the human spirit, being a society that lived so completely by faith. He has been criticized for not giving more studious attention to the orthodox Judaic aspects of Hasidism, but his profound sense for Hasidic spirituality constitutes an invaluable contribution to modern religious thought.

For the Hasidim, according to Buber, holiness and spirituality entered all aspects of life. Life must not be compartmentalized into the holy and profane; it must be lived in the "here and now" in the spirit of faith which sanctifies each act with full presence and attention. It is the essential challenge of taking a chance on one's true feelings and stepping totally, without reservation, into the living present that Buber addresses in his extensive and well–known writings on interhuman relation, the most famous of which is *I and Thou* (Buber 58).

In his works he sets down the essential elements necessary for genuine dialogue, I–Thou dialogue. There must be sufficient "distance" for the persons so engaged for them to have "space" to freely express their individuality and personality (Buber 57). From this mutual posture each of the two parties turns to the other in complete openness and readiness for spontaneous and unanticipated dialogue. Such a dialogue is a unique happening in that moment and will never happen in the same way again. All concerns about making an impression, looking good, or image building have evaporated; the two in dialogue are sharing themselves in the unplanned grace of the living present. In Buber's words: "The Thou meets me through grace—it is not found by seeking....The primary word 'I–Thou' can be spoken only with the whole being....All real living is meeting" (Buber 58, p. 11).

The Thou, the other, need not necessarily be another person; it could be a dog, a tree, a work or art, or God. But in addressing the Thou with one's whole being one becomes I: "I become through my relation to the Thou; as I become I, I (can) say Thou" (Buber 58, p. 11). That is, in a dialogue the more totally I present myself, the better able am I to utter "Thou" with full grace and commitment.

Buber distinguishes two fundamental forms of relation, the "I–Thou" and the "I–It." In contrast to the "subject–subject" relation of I–Thou, the I–It is a subject–object relation. Here the subject tends to use, impress, inspect, or manipulate the other as if it were not a subject but an object. Buber further helps distinguish I–Thou and I–It in terms of the present and past: "The 'I' of the primary word I–It...has no present, only the past" (Buber 58, p. 12). In contrast I–Thou exists totally in the present: "True beings are lived in the present, the life of objects is in the past" (Buber 58, p. 13).

However, it should not be assumed from the foregoing that the I–It relation is necessarily evil. All people indulge in it in their conversations to a greater or lesser extent most of their lives. Because of its complete spontaneity, most people can number on the fingers of one hand the times they have truly experienced an I–Thou dialogue, for it is something that happens, and cannot be made to happen. Buber clearly states that I–It is necessary in life, but he warns: "In all seriousness of truth, hear this: without 'It' man cannot live. But he who lives with 'It' alone is not a man" (Buber 58, p. 34).

Many religions have celebrated each year a special sacred moment, a divine moment. As we have seen a number of primitive cultures celebrated the moment of creation by a mythical hero or god. Christians celebrate Easter; Jews, Yom Kippur; Moslems, Ramadan; etc. The spiritual power of these moments can be experienced as divine by devout followers of a given faith. But from Buber's words we may infer that individually the potential for not just one, but a life of sacred moments is in principle always available to us, if we can muster the courage to fully open ourselves to the here and now.

The Moment of Buddhism.[1] Whether the concern is with an individual involved in the here and now or with nature generally, from the viewpoint of religious philosophy the ultimate significance of each moment is nowhere more unequivocally emphasized than in the Buddhist tradition. If succinct generalizations can be made of Buddhist thought, one of them is that the reality of the moment is at the core of its metaphysics. That is, even in rigorous philosophic terms the instant (moment) has fundamental ontological reality (Balslev 83, pgs. 80, 85).

Each successive moment is a creation, entirely new, never seen in exactly the same way before. Since each moment is different, then change, absolute and unqualified, is necessarily an equally essential concept in the Buddhist ontological view. In the words of Anindita Balslev: "...the Buddhist understanding of change is thorough and total, there is no room for any notion of unchanging substance, no category of reality such as beginningless and endless" (Balslev 83, p. 121). So that change is not just modification, but replacement of one entity by another, completely and spontaneously. In a word, "The moment is change manifested" (Kawamura 92). Any ideas of continuity and duration are merely conceptual abstractions (Balslev 83, p. 84).

The central importance of change and the concomitant instant inescapably imply that being is instantaneous, so that time and being merge in the ever changing moment:

> Time as instant, being as instantaneous, are the inevitable concepts, when the problem of change is understood in the Buddhist manner. Even more, the instant and the instantaneous are conceived as coalesced, as fused with one another, giving rise to the Buddhist model of the point–instant (Balslev 83, p. 121).

Accordingly, in direct contrast to the Vedantic Hindu position discussed in Chapter 6, that the unchanging is real, the Buddhists hold that change is real, nothing is exempt from change. In fact their position on this doctrine is so fundamental that the world is seen not as matter undergoing change, but as change bringing about matter (Kawamura 92). It is in this context then that being is perforce instantaneous and time is seen as consisting of irreproducible instants or moments, only transcended by nirvana.

---

[1] As noted in Chapter 6, there is an extensive spectrum of religious metaphysical positions among the many sects of Buddhism. In particular, this holds true for concepts of time. Accordingly, while it is always dangerous to generalize, again for the purposes of this text I have tried to present what I consider a mean or balanced view of Buddhist temporal thought.

It is very important to realize the powerful implication that follows from these concepts. Since being is instantaneous and each succeeding instant is a new and different reality, there can be no such thing as a continuous or abiding self. Life is a chain of conscious moments, each expressing its unique reality.

Thus any notion of self is an intellectual abstraction, because there is no substantive continuity to realistically distinguish a self.[2] In any case the fundamental Buddhist concepts of instantaneity or momentariness and of no-self are mutually consistent and comprise an indispensable duality. The concept of no-self (or anatman) thus reveals another aspect of the polar disagreement with the Hindu position, which holds to an abiding reality of the self (Atman). Nevertheless, however distasteful the idea of no-self might be to the Western psyche, perhaps Buddhism's insistence on the reality of the ever-changing moment could still serve as an inspiration to open to the fullness of the here and now.

The I Ching. When Buddhism was imported from India via Tibet to China, the concept of anatman (no-self) ran counter to the sense of self characteristic of the Taoist and Confucian traditions. Not only was the idea of rebirth new to China, but also such notions as cosmology, worlds, and kalpas (cosmic periods in Buddhist cosmologies) conflicted with the deep-seated Chinese belief in China as the world center. Although the Chinese translated most of the Buddhist scriptures into their own language, there were many changes, adaptations, distortions, interpolations, and embellishments in translation. Nevertheless Buddhism gradually developed into a strong religious and cultural force in China and took its place beside Confucianism and Taoism.

In the Confucian system the Chinese monarch was a son of heaven, providing the human link between earth and heaven. This was the zenith of a social and political hierarchy characterized by propriety in all human relationships and deference for superiors and ancestors. This attitude was particularly apparent in the profound respect given Confucian literature, especially as embodied in the five great Classics (Wu Ching). For the Chinese these works were endowed with an authority possessed by no other books and offered precedents par excellence for all aspects of living.

---

[2]However, contrary to the mainstream of Buddhist thought, a Hinayana sect, the Pudgalavadins, believed in the existence of some form of self or soul, called the "Pudgala," representing a kind of integrating essence, but not a self in the Western sense.

The most well-known of the Classics is the *I Ching*, the *Classic of Changes*, which describes a cosmological structure that encompasses both humans and nature in a single system (Legge 63). It can be regarded as a manual for interpreting moments, events, and inner states of mind. A unique feature of the *I Ching* is its system of sixty–four hexagrams, which if properly understood supposedly reveal profound and subtle meanings applicable to daily life.

The hexagrams (an example is shown in Figure 11a) are comprised of all combinations of eight trigrams each of which in turn consist of a column of three full or broken lines such as shown in Figure 11b.[3]

The whole concept is intended to represent the Chinese cosmic view of the interactive harmony of the yin–yang principle (symbolized as in Figure 11c). The yang (full line) is male, active, and identified with heaven; yin (broken line) is female, receptive, and identified with earth. The yin and yang principles, inherited from the earliest stages of Chinese culture, enjoy universal application and are regarded as explaining all being and all change by their ceaseless interplay.

A multitude of arrangements of the symbols are possible, so that in general between the extremes of yin (earth) and yang (heaven) all intermediate realities and situations can be portrayed using appropriately varying proportions of yin and yang. In particular the quality of a given moment can be succinctly expressed. This means any moment of any situation with all of its diversity and subtle nuances can be captured using the appropriate hexagrams of the I Ching, from fateful moments of decision to meditative moments of peaceful awareness.

The reciprocal harmony of yin–yang in the I Ching found an especially congenial synthesis with the Tao concept of return to the primal grace of the living moment immanent in all of nature. The hexagrams when used with care, thoughtfulness, and sensitivity, were gentle guides, signposts, which could return one to the Tao, the full flavor of the moment as it should be lived (Kaltenmark 69, p. 44). In principle by this means one could use time, to become refreshed, healed, and renewed, in order to conduct a more wholesome life of fulfilled moments (Girardot 90).

---

[3]David Pankenir points out that if o is substituted for a broken line and 1 for a full line, the hexagrams yield all of the integers from o to 63. He suggests that this might be indicative of a binary or dualistic kind of thinking among the traditional Chinese in contrast to the more singly directed kind of thinking in the West (Pankenir 88).

(a) Typical Hexagram

(b) Trigrams

(c) Yin Yang Symbol

FIG. 11

Alfred North Whitehead. For another picture of how the moment is fulfilled, but from a more analytical viewpoint, we turn to the West and again come back to Alfred North Whitehead. In contrast to the harmonious dualism characterizing the Chinese moment, Whitehead presents us with a penetrating and refined dissection of what makes up a moment in his organic metaphysics. It is a moment rich in subjective metaphors.

In developing his philosophic system he gave full expression to his conviction that the study of the world should be based on perceivable properties rather than detached mental abstractions about it (Whitehead 29, p. 64). For example, he criticized scientific materialism for mistaking mathematical physics for the concrete reality of nature. Thus a persistent motif that characterized much of his thought was the intimate interaction of the immediacy of sense and perception with nature in dynamic, processive interrelation:

> For us the glow of the sunset is as much a part of nature as are the molecules and electric waves by which the man of science would explain the phenomenon (Whitehead 20. p. 29).

While it is undoubtedly because of this approach that Whitehead freely uses subjective metaphors in presenting his system, this is intended to reflect the vibrant charge that he senses in all of nature, and not to suggest, for example, that inanimate objects actually possess consciousness. So it is that through his concept of "actual occasions" he invests the moment with an imaginative, complex structure of interactive components (Whitehead 29, p. 27ff).

In our earlier allusions to Whitehead we have noted how each actual occasion defines a particular domain of space–time. Accordingly, for him events define a finite temporal duration and spatial extent in their realization; instants and points possess no reality (Whitehead 19, p. 7; Hammerschmidt 47, p. 18). In its becoming present the actual occasion selectively draws from a host of "eternal objects" (properties, attributes) such as color, shape, number, etc. to arrive at its particular maturation (Whitehead 29, p. 32ff).

God presents the ideal configuration of eternal objects to use or prehend in this maturation (Whitehead 26, p. 156ff) In this role God thus influences, but does not determine, the resultant concrescence of the occasion (Thompson 71, p. 58–9). Therefore most actual occasions fall short of the ideal fulfillment. However, the degree to which this ideal pattern is achieved may be regarded as a measure of the value and grace characterizing the occasion.

Alfred North Whitehead
1861–1947

From "Dialogues of Alfred North Whitehead" by Lucien Price. Copyright © 1954
by Lucien Price. By permission of Little, Brown and Company

Depending on the process under consideration, a moment could consist of one or a nexus of actual occasions. In any case the moments can be considered as sacred in so far as God is always present offering them the potential for ideal realization. So that a moment (or actual occasion) comes to fruition and fades from existence, but some of its characteristics are passed on to the succeeding element in a continuing organic creative process (Hammerschmidt 47) interactive with God.

From a number of diverse sources we have seen how the moment in various ways is endowed with a sacred quality. The viewpoints are expressive of a primal need to sense the grace of each moment, to see it as precious, if not God–given. Let us now examine some scientific properties of the moment and its duration as seen by psychology and physics.

The Psychological Moment

If at a particular moment you realize that you are relishing the taste of your morning coffee and happen to be looking at the motion of the second hand of your kitchen clock, you can sense that the moment you experience had some duration; the second hand moved some while the moment came to full awareness. It takes some time for all of the signals—visual, auditory, tactile, olfactory—to be processed by the brain and synthesized to the consciousness of an experiential moment, a moment with a diffuse, inexact beginning or ending.

The diffuseness of the moment is a necessary feature of living, for, as mentioned earlier, if human moments were true instants, points in time, we would not be able to integrate the successive positions of a baseball into a smooth trajectory. We would not be able to enjoy the haunting, soothing measures of Mozart's clarinet concerto, because we could not assemble the group of notes, say in a measure, and experience their synthesis as part of a living moment. In returning the ball in a tennis game, the whole sweep of the racquet in your stroke is part of the moment, not just the instant the racquet strikes the ball.

All of this tells us that somehow the human conscious moment has some finite duration. This is something experimental psychologists have tried to measure using various tests based on some set of reasonable criteria and controls. As might be expected, it is very difficult, essentially impossible, to determine precisely the duration of what humans experience as the present, if only because of the variation among individuals. Also the results of a particular test often depend on the nature of the test, its purpose and method, as well as the type of equipment used.

However, as an example, one test involved trying to recognize eight letters presented four at a time in two successive 10 millisecond flashes to the subject. The interval between the flashes was varied. Recognizing all eight letters was possible when the interval between the two flashes of four letters was as short as about 0.7 to 1 second. In such studies and in others there seemed therefore to be an average time of about three quarters of a second which is required for a *complete* perceptual process (Whitrow 80, p. 72–3; Calebresi 30). However, depending on the extent of attention and degree of organization needed in the complete experience of the moment, more recent experiments indicate its duration can be as long as 2 seconds (Fraisse 69; Macar 80).

There are other ways to define such a minimum duration. For example, a measurement can be made of the rate at which moving picture frames can be decreased and still be seen as apparent movement. It averages around 17 frames a second, which is comparable to the minimum frequency of 16 to 18 cycles per second for auditory perception of a continuous sound instead of the "up and down" intensity variation of the sound waves. A similar frequency of approximately 18 tactile signals per second is the threshold rate beyond which the signals are experienced as vibrations as opposed to discrete members of a series (Whitrow 80, p. 74). Based on this degree of temporal discrimination in these different sense organs, Whitrow concludes that the approximate duration of the "mental moment," the interval between distinguishable perceptions, is about one twentieth of a second (Whitrow 80, p. 74). However, this conclusion is open to question since other tests find, for example, that the visual and auditory thresholds for distinguishing separate events are about one tenth and one hundredth of a second, respectively (Macar 92).

Nevertheless, both at the level of response to tests in experimental psychology (the results of which depend on the nature of the test), and at the level of daily conscious experience, our now, our present, appears to have some roughly measurable, finite duration. With such a property the present has often unfortunately been termed the "specious present" (James 1890, p. 635; see also Denbigh 81, pgs. 65–6), but might better have been called the conscious present or the psychological present (Whitrow 80, p. 74ff). The label was probably intended to convey the idea that the moment, which capsulizes the human present, is not an instant. Our present is more than one peck of the woodpecker (of course, even the peck is not a mathematical instant). It must have some duration, since our "now" involves the apparent "simultaneous presence in our awareness of events in distinct phases of presentation" (Whitrow 80, p. 74).

It should be evident that the human moment, the duration of the conscious present, has a complex structure. It is made up of components of our most recent past as registered in our immediate memory, but also gives the general flavor of the immediate future. In Whitehead's succinct words: "What we perceive as present is the vivid fringe of memory tinged with anticipation" (Whitehead 20, p. 72–3).

INCREMENTAL TIME IN THE PHYSICAL WORLD

This realization that the moment encompasses a finite duration undoubtedly has had some influence, conscious or unconscious, on how we look upon time in physical nature. In particular it suggests the question: Does time in the physical world come in increments, and space as well? Still other questions arise: Does the concept of a present make any sense when applied to the physical world? In particular what is meant by the present in discussions of the simultaneity of events in the theory of relativity?

Simultaneity. When we take a walk through the woods, the muted flight of a bird, the gentle rustling of the leaves, the capricious play of the sun's beams shining through the treetops, are all simultaneous impressions making up our present. From the viewpoint of relativity such events can be simultaneous when observed in our local frame of reference, our immediate surroundings using our own timepiece.

However, such familiar perceptions of simultaneity are challenged by relativity when, say, two people moving at a high velocity relative to each other observe the same events. As discussed in Chapter 3, two events that are seen as simultaneous in one frame of reference can in general be observed as one occurring after the other in another frame moving at an appropriate relative velocity.

Thus our notion of the present in the physical world and the manifold simultaneities that it encompasses must be qualified by what we know of relativistic effects. Certainly this is true when we try to think of the present in any cosmic sense. However, our "non–cosmic" local present, the present of our daily life, may indeed be experienced as being rather extensive in spacetime, in fact embracing the whole earth, at least approximately. For example, if you are on ham radio talking to a friend in Hong Kong, it takes less than seven hundredths of a second for her signal to reach you. On the other hand, if you try to imagine what might be happening "right now" on some planet orbiting some star in some galaxy millions of light years away, you must face the reality that you will never live long enough to know. There is no way of determining what "right now" is on that planet. This is again because so far there is no way to transmit information without transmitting energy along with it, and relativity informs us that energy cannot move faster than the speed of light.

All of this tells us that the simultaneity of two events is best ascertained when we and the events are in the same frame of reference, all moving at a single common velocity. For again, if the two events are observed by another experimenter in another frame moving at some high velocity relative to ours, she will in general not see them as simultaneous. Relativity then says that a physical "moment," judged in terms of simultaneous events only makes sense "locally."

Can Time and Space Be Quantized? While relativity and simultaneity considerations help elucidate an aspect of the physical moment, the central question of what duration this moment has, if any, (or in particular whether it is somehow quantized) obviously presents itself. In attempting to address this question it is undoubtedly arguable whether I can in the same chapter, the same context, discuss the human present concurrently with the possibility of time quantization in the physical world. Nevertheless, running the risk of transgressing all kinds of philosophic categories, I treat the two together because in general contemplation about what constitutes a moment and what is the finest division of time I believe it is natural to think of them in a similar context. Let us see why this might be so.

From the viewpoint of quantum theory we can think of dissecting our present into elemental microscopic events. Let us recall the behavior of the wave function, which gives the probability of obtaining a given result when a measurement is made. The process of measurement has been popularly termed the collapse of the wave function, the collapse to a single measured result. But a microscopic event under the influence of the macroscopic aggregate of its immediate surroundings essentially reacts no differently to it than to the imposed "surroundings" of a measuring device. Thus unbeknownst to us wave functions are collapsing all the time, each yielding a specific result out of all the possible ones of varying probability as predicted by its wave function. Our present is made up of a host of such collapses so that in the words of Reichenbach:

The present which separates the future from the past, is the moment
when that which was undetermined becomes determined, and
"becoming" means the same as "becoming determined"
(Reichenbach 56, p. 269).

With this in mind let us look at what might be meant by a "quantum
moment." As one example, a quantum moment might be seen as the brief
lifetime of a particle created by a high energy accelerator. Recall in
Chapter 4 we saw that the temporal duration of the particle and the
particle's energy have conjugate roles according to the Heisenberg
Uncertainty Principle. So that if the event is the production of a particle
by the accelerator, the uncertainty principle tells us that the shorter the
life–time of the particle the less precisely known is its energy and thus its
mass (using $E = mc^2$). It takes the measurement of many events (which
when plotted form a bell–shaped curve similar to that in Figure 2a) to
determine the most probable mass, which is taken to be the particle's
mass. In any case the brief temporal existence of such a particle could be
interpreted as an example of a quantum moment.

However, in the last few decades some theoretical physicists have
tried on occasion to go much further and explore the possibility that time
itself is quantized into what some have called chronons. The same
would be true of space. Since other quantities such as electric charge and
mass or energy are quantized in the microscopic world, why cannot time
and space, at least at some very submicroscopic level, be divided into
tiny quantized increments?

A significant attempt to address this question was made over ten
years ago by Nobel Laureate T. D. Lee, who challenged the time–
honored belief that continuous mathematical functions can accurately
represent physical phenomena (Lee 83). All of calculus is based on the
assumption of the continuity of such functions, the simplest case of
which would be a straight line in which all of the points are
infinitesimally close with no breaks in the line, however small. Lee
maintained that such a concept does not correspond to physical reality
and should not be used to describe that reality.

Consequently, on the assumption that only a finite number of
discrete observations can be made in a volume of physical space, he
undertook the program of reformulating, among other things, all of the
equations of classical and quantum mechanics in terms of what he called
a discrete (or discontinuous) mathematics. This entailed the

visualization of a kind of latticelike four dimensional space–time.[4] For him continuous mathematics only represents an approximation, which is just the opposite of what has been believed in the physical science community for the last 300 years.

Naturally his discrete mathematics must at least match the traditional continuous mathematics in its ability to predict physical phenomena. The hope was that it might do more than that and help us understand some phenomena that the latter mathematics fails to describe accurately. However, Lee has not pursued the theory beyond his initial reports on the subject (Lee 83).

Yet the possibility of space–time quantization is not dead. A lattice–like structure for space–time is used today in some calculations in quantum field theory (an extension of quantum theory applied to elementary particle physics). It has also come up more recently in another context, quantum gravity. Recall from Chapter 7 that such a theory is needed to describe the incredibly compactified situation at the earliest stage following the Big Bang known as the Planck era.[5] At this stage the universe, ordinarily described by general relativity, was thought to be so compressed that it was essentially a microscopic quantum object, requiring therefore a theory of quantum gravity for its description. As mentioned earlier, although there have been many attempts, such a theory has not yet been successfully formulated.

Nevertheless some theorists (e.g. Roger Penrose) tell us that a viable theory of quantum gravity may require time quantization. One might imagine why this might be so, because with such an enormous mass concentration, space–time would have such an incredible curvature that there may be some kind of equivalence of the quantization of mass and that of space–time. We saw in Chapter 7 that among the kinds of candidate theories that include quantum gravity in their formulation have been a variety of string theories. In these theories the ultimate element of matter is a string, its different frequencies of oscillation corresponding to different particles. So that

---

[4]For those who know some calculus, this means using summations of discrete elements instead of integrals. Lee held that it is the discrete mathematics (using summations) instead of continuous mathematics (using integrals) that truly represents physical phenomena.

[5]The Planck era, is characterized by a length of 10^{-33} centimeters. The corresponding characteristic time, the time it would take light to traverse that distance, is found by dividing 10^{-33} centimeters by the velocity of light (3 times 10^{10} centimeters per second), giving roughly 10^{-43} seconds.

the ultimate elementary particle is not conceived as a point but a tiny string. If such an ultimate object is not a point, then time and space may not be instants and points and be quantized in some way.

All of this is highly speculative. Indeed the various candidate theories (string theories, theories of everything, etc.) are themselves speculative because, as discussed in Chapter 7, there is so far no way to experimentally test any theory dealing with such early stages of the universe. So perhaps we have pursued the notion of incremental time in the physical world, in particular the microscopic world, as far as we can, given our current knowledge, which thus far reveals no definite evidence of time quantization. In any case, whatever the definition or duration of the physical moment, it is apparent that it is a coordinated assembly of such moments that comprises the humanly experienced moment.

AN EXPANDED PRESENT: BEING AND BECOMING

But the attempt to define the physical moment does help in formulating another challenging question: "Is there such a thing as a now, or a present in the physical world?" Whether or not there is time quantization at the microscopic level or some short duration for a physical moment, is there a now in nature as we observe it at the macroscopic level. As I look out at the gracious swaying of the high grass, the trembling of the maple leaves, and the whimsical flutter of a butterfly, are they parts of a natural present, independent of my consciousness? Many thinkers, scientists, and philosophers have concluded that this is not so, but I disagree.

Human consciousness has undoubtedly endowed time with a much richer content than it would otherwise have, but I believe that there is some kind of a primitive, non–conscious present in nature. May we not be somewhat arrogant in maintaining that only humans have access to the present? Maybe it reduces to a matter of semantics, or definition of the word "time," but I believe that time in some form must have existed before we evolved. Compared to the age of the universe, we are a very recent evolution.

There is some kind of "now" for the falling acorn when it strikes the ground, disturbs the grass, and crackles a leaf. There is some kind of "now" for the squirrel when she later discovers and absconds with it. The human now, the now of consciousness, is a marvelous orchestration of a myriad of concurrent mini–events, but I believe nature can say the same thing, even without consciousness. I tend to be sympathetic with

Whitehead's metaphysics on this point. His system gives a self–consistent basis for a moment in nature not necessarily dependent on human presence. Perhaps the principle difference between nature's now and the human now is that the latter is comprised of a more numerous, complex, and variegated assembly of mini–events.

Nature is being, just as we are, as part of it. Nature is becoming, just as we are, as part of it. The now is a wondrous confluence of being and becoming, for humans and nature. In the now, being becomes, and becoming is. The moment is a being–becoming.

But the moment, through its being aspect, haunts us with some apprehension of an abiding now, and indeed, may afford us access to the Eternal Now. It is in the moment that time and eternity, if not timelessness itself, find their interface and coalesce in vibrant wholeness. As Erwin Schrödinger sees it:

> For eternally and always there is only now, one and the same now; the present is the only thing that has no end (Schrödinger 83, p.22).

And even more specifically in the words of Soren Kierkegaard:

> The instant is that ambiguous moment in which time and eternity touch one another…, where time is constantly intersecting eternity and eternity constantly permeating time (Kierkegaard 57, p.80).

Whether the now is the same as in the eyes of Schrödinger and Kierkegaard or is continually different as in the Buddhist view, surely it is only by responding to the fullness of the now that the devout meditators of whatever religion see the gateway to a transcendent consciousness, affording them passage from the burden of time to some apprehension of timelessness, which we next discuss.

SUMMARY

The richness and power of the moment are only appreciated when the moment is accorded the sanctity it continually calls upon us to give it. In all of modern religious literature this is no more clearly and beautifully expressed than in the thought of Martin Buber as exemplified in his *I and Thou*. It is in this work that he cogently distinguishes between the moments lived in "I–It" relation, as most of us do, and the moments of grace lived in the "I–Thou" relation.

The uniqueness and primacy of the moment is a central feature of Buddhist religious philosophy, in particular its philosophy of time. Each moment is new, irreproducible in a world where the ultimate reality is regarded as change. Because each succeeding moment is completely different in the process of change, there is no abiding entity that can be called a self. So that non–self, the moment, and change self–consistently characterize the Buddhist metaphysical position.

In the Chinese tradition the quality and value of the moment can be revealed in terms of appropriate use of the hexagrams of the I Ching. The unique metaphysics of Alfred North Whitehead gives us an analysis of the complexity of the moment. Whitehead's "actual occasion," defining a finite temporal duration and spatial extent and being influenced but not determined by God, can also endow the moment with value and grace. Furthermore, studies in experimental psychology attest to a finite duration of the human moment.

In examining the concept of a moment in the physical world one must consider how the notion of simultaneity is significantly qualified by the theory of relativity. Theoretical physicists continue to occasionally take seriously the idea of time being quantized, which, according to some, may be a characteristic of any successful theory of quantum gravity. Whatever are the increments of time in the physical world, it is a coherent aggregation of such increments that constitutes a human moment.

Although the moment is possessed of a very special richness for conscious humans, I believe a now, a present, also exists in some more primitive form for the nature surrounding us.

12 TIMELESSNESS

There is a thing inherent and natural
Which existed before heaven and earth.
Motionless and fathomless,
It stands alone and never changes;
It pervades everywhere and never becomes exhausted.
It may be regarded as the Mother of the Universe.
—Tao te Ching, Chapter 25

With powerful simplicity this passage of the Tao te Ching (Chu Ta–kao 82, p. 44) describes an underlying timeless essence immanent in all of nature and throughout the universe, a grounding of eternity. Some perception of eternity, understood as either timelessness, the full cosmic sweep of time, or everlasting time, is a fundamental attribute of the ultimate deity in most of the religions throughout the world. It is a haunting, inarticulable sense of a Silent Other that gives wordless testimony to the presence of the ever–abiding god of these religions. But whether or not the religion embraces a god (Buddhism does not, aside from some worship of the Buddha himself), in any experience of union with an ultimate Reality, whether achieved by meditation, sudden enlightenment, or prolonged spiritual striving, there is an attendant timeless aura, a sense of having transcended time. This is true of the unitive experience of the great mystics of the Judeo–Christian and Islamic traditions, as well as the Hindus in attaining moksha or the Buddhists, nirvana. Access to some form of eternity has been reached.

ETERNITY AND TIMELESSNESS

Theologies of the major world religions are replete with a full spectrum of concepts of eternity, involving a manifold array of highly refined distinctions. The word "eternity" as defined in Webster's Third New International Dictionary can mean endless time, the totality of infinite time, or absolute timelessness. This definition suggests that eternity is to some degree a "generic" word and that the three meanings cited can imply a host of subtle ramifying explications.

Regardless of the plethora of possible theological distinctions concerning eternity, the essential notion of eternity as a consummate state of personal peace, fulfillment, and unity with God or Reality has been the subject of the most profound human yearning since the dawn of spiritual awareness. The fact that some form of transcendence of time is what seems to transpire in this unity, implies that a meaningful understanding of eternity may be found by examining its relation to time. One of the most penetrating studies of this relationship was that of Soren Kierkegaard. He saw the three modes of temporality, past, present, and future, not as parts of time but as horizons arising from a synthesis of eternity and time, i.e. "horizons of meaning and disclosure of life: there is a past today, not yesterday; likewise a future today, not tomorrow" (Manchester 93, pgs. 115 and 129). More specifically, for Kierkegaard time's connection with eternity is through the present, the moment:

> ...the moment is not properly an atom of time but an atom of eternity.
> It is the first reflection of eternity in time, its first attempt, as it were at
> stopping time (Kierkegaard 80, p. 86).

An especially engaging view of eternity and its interface with time is given in the recent work of Robert Neville (Neville 93). He argues that time cannot be understood without eternity and holds that "time's flow should be understood as eternity's child," that the flow of time encompassing past, present, and future is "set in the context of eternity" (Neville 93, pgs. xi, xiii). Thus for Neville:

> Eternity is the context in which dates are together with all three
> temporal modes. Eternity is not mere static nontemporal form; nor is
> it the present writ large. Eternity rather is the togetherness of the
> modes of time—past, present, and future—so that each can be its
> temporal self.

Underlying this position is his conviction that personal identity is both temporal and eternal, so that one's lived life in the fullness of its time consummates its own eternity, an eternity which is dependent in large part on moral responsibility (Neville 93, pgs. 117, 188–9).

Neville's thesis is incisive and compelling, in terms of a person's spiritual access to eternity. However, I believe that the concept of eternity, whether in a theological or spiritual context, can be enlarged to specifically include the notion of timelessness. God is eternal, but God is also complete, and a timeless aspect should be a part of that completeness. In a sense eternity, as discussed above, could be regarded as a kind of mediary between timelessness and time.

Timelessness need not be understood as a static entity, whose metaphor is some spatially rigid form. Timelessness is simply not time as we know it. Timelessness can have its own idiosyncratic, but ineffable, dimension of vibrant dynamism. But, it can reveal many subtle, camouflaged faces. So it is that a conception of timelessness as an absolute an irreducible background of reality has haunted the imagination of thinkers for millennia. Expressions of some concept of timelessness can be found not only in religious thought throughout the world, but also from what has been learned of the physical world. In the following sections we survey selected views of the nature of timelessness from religious traditions as well as physics with the hope of realizing some sense of its mystery.

SPIRITUAL EXPRESSIONS OF TIMELESSNESS

The variety of spiritual contexts and theological perceptions of timelessness among the religious traditions of the world is manifold. While timelessness per se is an aspect of the god that nucleates and empowers many religions, it is perceived from the viewpoint of the religion's own characteristic theological framework. Furthermore there is often a diversity of interpretations even within that framework.

A number of religions were influenced directly or indirectly by Greek conceptions of ideality and timelessness. As we have noted earlier, Plato in his *Timaeus* saw the universe as patterned after an eternal Living Being, who wished to fashion it as closely as possible to its pattern. The universe could not be endowed with the eternal perfection of the pattern but was made a moving image of it. In particular the Living Being made "that which we call time an eternal moving image of the eternity which remains forever at one." Time itself is a manifestation in dynamic form of a timeless, motionless Ideal.

These Platonic concepts found their way into the thought of St. Augustine, who was largely responsible for introducing the idea of timelessness into Christian theology. As noted earlier, it was Augustine, influenced by the neo–platonism of Plotinus, who saw God as outside of time, creating the universe with all of its inherent natural clocks marking off time. Although he cites God as the governor over time in an earlier book of his "Confessions," he fully elaborates the contrast between the eternality of God and the time of mankind in Book XI. More than being a governor over the course of time, God, in eternity and not in time, created time as well as heaven and earth:

> You are the Maker of all time....You must have made that time, for
> time could not elapse before you made it....you are before all time; and
> the "time," if such we may call it, when there was not time was not
> time at all (St. Augustine 61, p. 263).

Augustine chides the superficial thinker who wonders what God
was doing before the creation:

> But if there was no time before heaven and earth were created, how
> can any one ask what you were doing "then"? If there was no time,
> there was no "then" (St. Augustine 61, p. 263).

Though admittedly not as specific, I believe hints of timelessness can
also be extracted from the work of St. Thomas Aquinas, who, in contrast
to Augustine, was influenced by Aristotle. With his monumental and
meticulous "*Summa Theologica*," he provided Christian theology with a
sound philosophical basis. He held that faith and reason must be in
harmony, and science and theology should not be contradictory. From
this basic viewpoint, after extensive exposition, he maintained that God
created the world from nothing (*ex nihilo*); time and the world had a
beginning (Gilson 94, p. 152). In discussing certain aspects of eternity
Aquinas says: "For God is said to be before eternity, according as it is
shared by immaterial substances." He further pursues this idea:

> to reign beyond eternity can be taken to mean that if any other thing
> were conceived to exist forever, as the movement of the heavens
> according to some philosophers, then God would still reign
> beyond...(Aquinas 81, p. 41).

I believe that God considered as timeless is one valid interpretation of
these remarks.

However, it must be kept in mind that such suggestions of
timelessness were not as evident in the seminal theology of biblical
times. As noted in Chapter 6, time was a series of "times" (or events)
many of which were spiritually crucial "times" leading to the
culminating time of judgment and salvation. The eternality of God is
generally expressed as everlasting time or the encompassing of all time.
God's "time" is different from mankind's:

> For a thousand years in thy sight are but yesterday...
>
> Proverbs 90:4

> ...one day is with the Lord as a thousand years, and a thousand years as
> one day.   Peter II 3:8

Also in the Koran:

> The angels and the Spirit ascend unto Him in a Day,
> the measure whereof is fifty thousand years.
>
> Koran, Sura 70:4

Prevailing Christian theology has returned somewhat to this early view and sees eternity as accessed in the fullness of time, wherein eternity embraces all of time, past, present, and future. Nevertheless I hold timelessness has a place in the ongoing dialectic about the nature of God and eternity.[1]

In contrast to the arguability of timelessness in the Judeo–Christian–Islamic tradition, it is a more evident element in Eastern religious traditions. Timelessness, especially its transcendent nature, is most extensively and comprehensively developed in the Advaita Vedanta of the Brahmanical (Hindu) tradition. Indeed one can find no more powerful and awesome expression of the concept of timelessness than in the Vedantic literature. We saw in Chapter 6 that Brahman is the only Absolute Reality; only things are real that neither change nor cease to exist (Prabhavananda and Isherwood 70, pgs. 13, 68). The natural universe along with time are but inconstant manifestations of Brahman; they emerge from, and return to, Brahman.

One can then imagine a sweeping cosmic panorama of the living, natural universe, including time, undergoing the unceasing alternation of creation, life, and destruction. But beyond and outside of this tumultuous activity is Brahman in timeless, transcendent, and imperturbable majesty. Thus endless periodicity superimposed on a background of timelessness figures in a supremely coherent vista of the cosmos.

Humans have access to an apprehension of this timelessness through Atman (the Self), the ever–abiding spirit of Brahman in humankind. Atman not only provides a consciousness of the timeless Brahman, but also renders consciousness itself timeless. As Anindita Balslev has expressed it: "The philosophy of Advaita Vedanta stands as the culminating point of the Brahmamial understanding of consciousness as timeless" (Balslev 83, p. 113).

In very general terms the quality of timelessness found in Brahmanism bears some broad similarity to that evident in Taoism. Just

---

[1] I believe this will be increasingly true in the future with the gradual tendency to ecumenicity among some of the major religions as well as the growing interaction between science and religion.

as all things emerge from and return to the timeless Brahman, so also they emerge from and return to the Tao. However, with the Tao tradition there are no numerically specified periods as in the Hindu cosmology. The Tao cosmology is suffused with an aura of gentle, diffuse rhythm and natural serenity. But, as noted in Chapter 6, it is necessary to distinguish two aspects of the Tao, the *apparent* aspect manifested by the order of the universe, and the *absolute* aspect which is the Essence from which the order arises. It is the Absolute Tao that is the timeless grounding for the natural world. Thus the Tao te Ching describes the ultimate dependence of the natural world on the Absolute Tao, or Non–Being:

> In the Tao the only motion is returning.
> The only quality, weakness.
> For though Heaven and Earth and the
> Ten Thousand Creatures were produced by Being,
> Being was produced by Non–Being. (Welch 57, p. 68)

This emergence from and return to the Absolute Tao can be expressed in terms of the Yin–Yang principle, the Yang representing emergence, the Yin representing return. Conforming to this rhythm of the universe is the manifestation of wisdom for the Chinese (Kaltenmark 69, p. 46). However, the Taoist mystic wishes to go beyond adherence to the rhythm and seeks to escape from the determinism of life and death by transcending it (Kaltenmark 69, p. 46).

Just as the Taoist mystic finds access to the timeless essence of the Absolute Tao, and the Hindu identifies with the timeless Brahman on attaining moksha, so also does the Buddhist escape time on achieving nirvana. The Buddhist emphasis on the reality of the moment is consistent with the goal of nirvana. For it is in the experience of total, unrestrained being in the moment, that its mysterious quality of timelessness may come to one's full awareness. This awareness becomes an essential feature of the background in the Buddhist meditative path leading to release from the ensnaring time–bound suffering of the natural world, which is represented in most Buddhist sects by an endless cyclical cosmology. With this release the timeless glow of enlightenment, the salvation of nirvana, is won (Pande 93).

In sum I believe the examples cited in this brief survey of religious sources could serve as a starting point for arguing that a timeless quality can be associated with the religion's God or Reality.

Hints of Timelessness in the Natural World

What can physics and cosmology tell us about the reality of timelessness? From what was described in earlier chapters we know that according to the currently prevailing version of the Big Bang Theory (including some versions of inflation), as we look back in time, we come to the Planck regime. Remember this was when the mass–energy concentrations were so extreme that the whole universe was in the quantum realm, and time and space as we know them were undefined. The universe and time are supposed to have evolved from this realm.

Although there is thus far no way to really know what went on in the earliest stages of cosmic evolution in terms of any kind of experimental proof, most cosmologists seem to say that time emerged from the Big Bang. Somehow this event occurred and arose from some antecedent non–temporal grounding. Whether it was nothing, "no–thing," or whatever, it is generally thought to have been timeless. The notion of timelessness antecedent to the Big Bang is therefore an unavoidable suggestion when considering its initiatory stages.

The apparent possibility that there was no time as we know it antecedent to the Big Bang is consistent with St. Augustine's contention that there was no time "before" God created the world. As I have stressed earlier, since they arise from such disparate sources, neither the physical nor the religious description concerning the origin of the universe should necessarily be taken as grounds for mutual evidential support. However, the fact that in broad terms both sources are essentially saying that somehow time began, implying the notion of a timeless origin provokes the imagination. At the very least, the possibility of a concordance of the two sources may engender a sense of awe. For some it leaves a haunting apprehension of possible meaning and inspires a quest for meaning. I cannot claim to know what this meaning might be, but I do believe that there is meaning to be found. Furthermore, I believe that a catalyst in the search for this meaning is the full appreciation of a much closer link between the intuitive and the rational, the spiritual and the material, sources of knowledge than generally believed.

Another physical phenomenon that may suggest the reality of timelessness comes from an analysis of what happens, for example, when measurements are made on the polarizations of two photons simultaneously emitted in opposite directions (the EPR experiment). This was discussed in Chapter 4 where it was noted that when a polarization measurement was made on one photon, it was certain what the result of such a measurement on the other photon would be, even if separated by hundreds of miles. The interpretation given of this behavior was that the measurement on the first photon is in effect a measurement on the whole system, including both the photons. The system is described by a single wave function before as well as after the photons are emitted, so that when the measurement is made the *whole* wave function "collapses" to a given result. In any case this suggests some kind of underlying non–temporal and/or non–spatial grounding that maintains a communicative cohesion, however far dispersed, for the original system (Rosen 91).

A third hint of timelessness comes from a consideration of the photon itself. We saw in Chapter 3 dealing with the theory of relativity that as the velocity of light is approached, time approaches cessation. Thus the photon knows no time; light is essentially timeless. We are also aware of the creation myth of Genesis as well as creation myths of many other traditions, which speak of light as a concomitant feature of creation. Thus I feel it can be said that an atemporal or timeless God somehow provided a timeless object, the photon, as among the earliest ingredients of creation, as an indispensable means of communication for humankind, and for some, as a manifestation of God's presence. This manifestation has been reported in the visions of mystics and was attendant with the dramatic conversion of Paul on the road to Damascus. It is also often expressed in religious rituals, as well as with one's private spirituality, through the use of a candle. This quiet center of light somehow evokes an abiding sense of a timeless Presence.

A quality timelessness is to be found in the thought of Carl Jung concerning the characteristics of the unconscious. He introduced the concept of the "collective unconscious," made up of psychological patterns common to members of a whole culture or universally to all humans. In certain circumstances these patterns reveal themselves as what Jung calls "archetypes," symbols and images that appear universally in dreams, myths, and fairy tales (Columbia 83, p. 441).

The persistence and universality of the collective unconscious and archetypes, representing the deepest layers of the unconscious, possess an inherent timeless quality according to Maria von Franz (von Franz 81, p. 221). Another characteristic of the collective unconscious is what Jung calls synchronicity. In his work he cites many instances of simultaneous acts, emotions, or thoughts of persons separated by considerable distances. However, for synchronicity to have occurred there has to not only be coincidence of events in time, but also a connection between events via an archetypal meaning (von Franz 81, p. 223). These connections are "links with shared universal archetypes," and "seem to transcend ordinary space and time" (Halpern 90, p. 102).

It is as if by a fuller interaction and communication between the temporality of consciousness and the timeless qualities of the unconscious we might find, at least intuitively, a better understanding of the interface between time and timelessness. To achieve any such understanding is not a trivial matter, for as T. S. Eliot puts it: "But to apprehend the point of intersection of the timeless with time is an occupation for the saint" (Eliot 43, p. 44).

As we have seen, there are grounds for making a case for the reality of timelessness from religious sources as well as some suggestive evidence from the study of the physical world and of the unconscious. Is it possible that the spiritual insights and the experimental observations both may ultimately be addressing the same timeless essence, an essence we have yet to understand?[2]

Somehow toward the end of his life I feel that Einstein had a strong apprehension of such a timeless essence. Though he often stated that he did not believe in an anthropomorphic or personal God, he had a profound reverence for the beauty and order in a universe governed by Reason. And his apprehension of timelessness was quite apparent in the comment he made at the death of his dear and life–long friend, Michele Besso:

> And now he has preceded me briefly in bidding farewell to this strange world. This signifies nothing. For us who are convinced physicists, the distinction between past, present, and future is only an illusion, even if a stubborn one.

Summary

Some suggestions of timelessness can be extracted from the scriptures and theologies of many of the world's religions and is expressed as either an attribute of the religion's god or of a timeless underlying Essence. Plato spoke of the eternal Living Being; St. Augustine and St. Thomas Aquinas essentially expressed the idea of an Uncaused Causer; and the Hindus speak of the timeless Brahman. Transcending

---

[2]True to his irrepressible wit, even while serving in World War I before his tragic death in 1915, Rupert Brooke put it another way:
"But somewhere, beyond Space and Time
Is wetter water, slimier slime!" (Brooke 46, p. 35)

the vicissitudes of periodic nature and identifying with a timeless god or essence is the goal of the Eastern believer.

The possibility of timelessness seems to be suggested in the consideration of some aspects of the physical world. Most physicists believe that time and the natural universe emerged out of the big bang. This provokes the speculation that there may be some antecedent atemporal grounding for this emergence. An atemporal grounding is also a suggested possibility in contemplating explanations of the EPR experiment. The theory of relativity tells us that light itself has an atemporal character. A spiritual affirmation of the eternality of light is captured through its appearance in creation myths and visions of mystics as well as religious rituals.

There is a timeless quality to be found in Carl Jung's concept of the "collective unconscious" in terms of abiding universal archetypes, which provide the linkages necessary for occurrences of synchronicity. Perhaps a fuller interaction between the temporal conscious and the timeless aspects of the unconscious may lead to insights about the interface between time and timelessness. In any case I believe a case can be made for the reality of timelessness from religious traditions as well as suggestions of it from the observations of the natural world.

Part IV   WHAT WILL TIME TELL?

"Behind the curtain's mystic fold,
The glowing future lies unrolled."

—Francis Brette Harte

You are walking along a trail in the New Hampshire mountains. It is very foggy; you can barely see ten feet ahead. As you walk, you begin to notice a tall, dark, diffuse shape in the forefront. Continuing on, the shape becomes thinner at the bottom and, rising in a smooth, gradual arc, fills out between the middle and the top. You realize it is a tree. Moving closer you observe that the tree trunk becomes lighter. Finally, reaching the tree, you see it is a lone birch—with its endearing snow-white bark and small, gently tapering leaves, almost heart-shaped—a birch tree standing in mute testimony to the silence of the mist.

In much the same way the future seems to unfold its picture at first in broad, diffuse, ill-defined strokes, then gradually focuses to the rich, vibrant detail of the present, finally passing on to be submerged in the past. In pondering on the nature of time many thinkers will attest to the reality of the present, and even of the past, but what about the future?

In our examination of the thought of Husserl as interpreted by Merleau-Ponty, we saw that our future, at least in sketchy outline, is traced out by what is termed "lines of intentionality." How far ahead do these "lines" project? Certainly our future is shaped in part by our past and present, but how much so?

In the following chapters we will discuss some thoughtful speculations about time in the future in terms of such time–related subjects as astronomic predictions for the Earth, stars, and galaxies; the SETI program; the propagation of consciousness; interpretations of death; and the question of the reality of the future.

13 Time in the Cosmic Future

"The wave of the future is coming
and there is no fighting it."

—Anne Morrow Lindbergh

What mysterious and wondrous power did the year 2000 possess that, as it approached, it began to lurk ever more frequently at the edges of our consciousness? It somehow seemed to stir in the subterrains of our psyches an inarticulable melange of apprehension, awe, and challenge. With progressive certainty it loomed and perhaps more than any other aspect of our collective existence evoked in us the sense of the future relentlessly streaming toward us.

Can we in some way have been viscerally intuiting the possibility of a revolution in some areas of human concern as profound as that which occurred in the physical sciences in 1900? Such a revolution seems almost indispensable in view of the host of formidable problems facing humankind. These include not only global warming, ozone depletion, over population with its attendant food shortage, and the AIDS epidemic, but also the bewildering question of intelligently distilling, assimilating, and acting on the staggering accumulation of information in virtually every category of human endeavor.

Hopefully somehow developing the ability to deal with these extremely pressing problems facing us in our immediate future may prepare and temper us for even greater future challenges. In contemplating what some of the longer range challenges might be one cannot avoid wondering what the very long range future might bring in terms of the projected fate of the earth, the sun, and the universe. Let us see what some of the predictions are for the future of our cosmos.

Cosmic Predictions: The First 6 Billion Years

Most of us believe that human consciousness evolved. It is a consciousness, which, out of its own inherent curiosity, and much more, out of the driving need for its own survival and propagation, instinctively presses to learn evermore about its material home. Like a child exploring every nook and cranny of a new house, we persist in probing the farthest reaches of our cosmic cocoon, the edges of the universe, and the edges of divisibility in the microscopic domain. One of the disconcerting things we have learned in this probing is that on a cosmic time scale we inhabit what seems to be a very hostile environment.

Asteroids, Comets, and Meteorites. On March 22, 1989, asteroid 1989FC crossed the Earth's orbit where only six hours earlier the Earth had been (Broad 91). Asteroid 1993KA missed collision with the Earth on May 20, 1993 by 140,000 kilometers, less than half the distance to the Moon. On astronomic scales these are considered "near misses." But at 7:30 A.M. on June 30, 1908, in the great taiga forests of Siberia (Morrison 90) there was a "direct hit." Actually it was not a direct hit as such; it was worse. The asteroid exploded about 6 km above the ground releasing a searing shock wave that flattened thousands of square miles of trees, a shock detected as far away as London. It was the most serious collision with an extraterrestrial object in the last century (Morrison 90). The awesome power of such collisions was observed with the impact of the 21 fragments of the comet Shoemaker–Levy 9 on Jupiter in July, 1994.

Most asteroids are observed to move for at least part of their orbit in the region of the solar system between Mars and Jupiter, but many have orbits that can carry them far out of this region. 1989FC and 1993KA were large enough to be detectable, but it is estimated that the 1908 missile was no more than 100 meters in diameter, too small to be detected from any significant distance. Recently a considerable number of small meteorites have been detected *after* they have entered and exploded in the earth's atmosphere. Over a 17 year period military satellites observed an average of 8 such events per year. Analysis indicates that the actual bombardment rate may be 10 times greater, 80 per year (Broad 94).

Estimates vary by as much as a factor of ten, but theoretical astronomers calculate that collisions with objects 100 meters in diameter can occur with a frequency of once in a hundred to a few hundred years. Asteroids of 1km diameter are estimated to strike at intervals in the hundreds of thousands of years, those 10 km in diameter at intervals of tens of millions of years (Morrison 90). Accumulating evidence seems to indicate that it was an asteroid of roughly the latter size which impacted on the Yucatan peninsula 65 million years ago and may have caused the extinction of the dinosaurs along with roughly half of all other animal species.

While we may find some conditional consolation in the fact that collisions with larger asteroids or comets are less probable, we are still dealing with essentially statistical probabilities. Such collisions can in principle occur at any time; it is not a question of if, but when. To put it at a more personal level, some authorities calculate that the statistical risk of death over a 50-year period from an asteroid impact is three times greater than that from an airplane crash (Chapman and Morrison 91).

Actually the most dangerous collisions may be from the smaller objects producing collisions comparable in results to an A–bomb explosion. Such missiles not only occur more frequently than larger ones, but also are as yet undetectable from a sufficient distance to provide some time to seek safety. On the other hand the larger, asteroids and comets may be less of a threat, since they are detectable and less frequent. Already scientists and engineers are considering ways in which a rocket or even a small A-bomb could nudge such an object away from its destructive path.

By the early 90's some 200 asteroids of the size of 1989FC or larger in orbits approaching the Earth were being tracked (Beardsley 91). However, there may be thousands more. Congress is taking the threat quite seriously and considering ways to support the detection effort. Although NASA is presently spending about one million dollars for Earth-based searches, many think that a space-based search for these dangerous objects would be the most effective.

As far as the nature of our cosmic environment is concerned, on scales of hundreds to millions of years it is asteroids, comets, and like objects that hang over us somewhat like astronomic "swords of Damocles." On the other hand the incredibly rapid development and diversity of sophisticated technology especially in the last fifty years may truly have a deeper purpose, that of our own physical survival.

Till the Sun Dies. If our progeny somehow manage to survive the "asteroid attack," another danger looms on the distant horizon. In some six billion years the hydrogen at the core of the sun will have all "burned," i.e. combined to form helium. This will upset the equilibrium that existed between outward pressure due to hydrogen "burning" and the inward pressure of gravity. So that when the core's nuclear fuel is exhausted, the sun will compress and produce a heating that will burn the hydrogen in the outer layers at a prodigious rate (Pagels 85, p. 55). As a result of intricate processes of energy exchange, this will result in an enormous ballooning of the sun's surface (Pagels 85, p. 56). The expansion will cool the gases and the sun will gradually turn red.

What is known as a "red giant" will have been born. It will ultimately swell to envelop Mercury and probably Venus, and the Earth will be uninhabitable.[1] We, that is our progeny if they are still around, will have to move. Of course the time scale involved, billions of years, is so large that this eventuality is hardly an immediate concern. However, it may happen in the nearer future that a very large asteroid or comet (whose trajectory, though detectable, is unalterable with the technology then available) may be headed on a collision course with the Earth. Again our descendants would have to move. Since such a body, clearly capable of annihilating life on Earth would probably be detectable from a considerable distance, there would be some time available for departure.

In any event it seems obvious that human space flight and space colonization may some day become an absolute necessity. It is in principle within our present technological capacity to travel to Mars and to some of the large asteroids beyond. This may become a reality when humankind attains enough political, economic, and social maturity for a worldwide cooperative effort. That is, when aggressive nationalism and weapons are relegated to the history books, and weapons technology is converted to space exploration.

Physicist James Trefil predicts that within the next 500 hundred years we could colonize as far out as the asteroid belt. Valuable minerals could be mined on Mars and the larger asteroids. In the not-so-near term, say within 30 million years, Trefil speculates that humans, or some evolute thereof, could be colonizing other parts of our galaxy on a selective basis (Trefil 87). This would obviously require large self-supporting space ships in which communities could live for generations.

When space exploration and colonization do become a significant part of a coherent world enterprise, we will find ourselves on "neo-colonial" time. Depending on how far we probe, it could take decades, centuries, and millenia to conduct travel or even to get responses via electromagnetic signals from our colonies or

---

[1]Some astrophysicists calculate that the sun will be a red giant in 7.5 billion years and the Earth uninhabitable in 1.5 billion years (Browne 94).

extraterrestrial neighbors—just as in the colonial times of the 16th and 17th centuries it took months and years. To reach out beyond the distance feasible for human travel we must turn to electromagnetic radiation, which can proceed at the speed of light. In this case we have access to a much larger horizon of communication. How such communication will be accomplished is at the heart of the increasing efforts in the Search for Extraterrestrial Intelligence (SETI).

SETI

Thinkers throughout history have expressed an almost visceral sense that we many not be alone in the universe. About 2,000 years ago, the great Roman poet Lucretius wrote: "There are other worlds in other parts of the universe with races of different men and different animals" (Drake and Sobel 92, p. 21). In 1830, German mathematician Karl Gauss suggested growing a wheat field in Siberia in the shape of a right triangle. Three forests of pine trees in the shape of squares based on each of the three sides of the triangle, as in Figure 12, would demonstrate to extraterrestrials our knowledge of the Pythagorean Theorem (Drake and Sobel 92, pgs. 170–1). Czech astronomer Joseph von Littrow proposed a system of ditches in the Sahara desert, forming an array of geometric shapes, which would be filled with kerosene and ignited. In 1900, the French Academy of Sciences was so convinced that Martians existed that it offered a prize of 100,000 francs to the first person to communicate with beings *other* than those on Mars.

More recently the question of whether life of any kind exists on Mars was essentially answered by the two Viking landings in 1976, which found no conclusive evidence for even microscopic life. Although some life may have existed in earlier stages of its evolution, these two missions have confirmed that the Martian surface and atmosphere are now in fact quite uncongenial to life.

While hope for extraterrestrial life in our solar system seems meager, astronomers have detected organic molecules (assemblies of atoms consisting generally of carbon joined with various combinations of hydrogen, oxygen, or nitrogen) in surprising quantities throughout our galaxy. Some 150 varieties of these building blocks of life permeate the Milky Way. Among them is ethyl alcohol, or vodka. There is enough vodka near the center of our galaxy, according to the late Heinz Pagels, to fill 10,000 goblets the size of Earth (Pagels 85, p. 45) (somehow my imagination prompts me to observe that this could have been a powerful motivation for the Soviet space effort). When a certain species of these

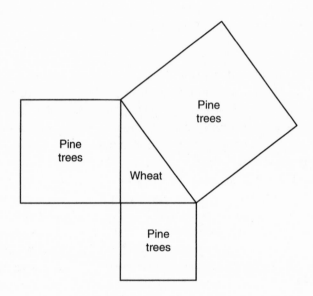

FIG. 12–A wheat field and pine forests illustrating the
Pythagorean Theorem

molecules, such as methane, combine under the right conditions, amino acids form—the beginning of a chain of events that can lead to the basic process of self–replication. Biologist Gerald Sauson says that once self–replication occurs, the rest of the progressive picture is easy, at least relatively: cells, chromosomes, multicells, sex, intelligence (Sauson 87).

So even if there is no other life in our solar system, could extraterrestrial intelligence (ETI) exist elsewhere in our galaxy or beyond? Serious attempts to answer this question have become progressively more sophisticated since the discoveries made in the 1930s by Karl Jansky of Bell Laboratories, whose work helped open the field of radio astronomy.

Modern efforts in the search for extraterrestrial intelligence (SETI) were begun by astronomer Frank Drake in 1959–60. Called Project Ozma (after a princess in "The Wizard of Oz"), the giant radio telescope at the National Radio Astronomy Observatory (NRAO) in Greenbank, W.Va., was used to study two nearby solar-like stars (Drake and Sobel 92, p. 27ff).

To scan the necessary electromagnetic frequency range, however, Drake had only a receiver with a single narrow-frequency channel a minuscule 100 Hz (100 cycles per second) wide. Given the vastness of the universe, the SETI enterprise was like looking for a needle in a cosmic haystack.

Succeeding efforts began to add many more receiver channels, all simultaneously monitored. Of course the greater the number of such channels, the greater is the chance of detecting a meaningful signal. Currently in the United States there are some four major SETI projects each using separately monitored frequency channels numbering in the tens of millions with plans to increase to hundreds of millions.[2] In terms of sheer number of channels the most comprehensive of these programs (Naeye 92) is one which has been led by Paul Horowitz since 1983, now called Project META, which achieved an increase from 8.4 to 160 million channels in 1994.

On the other hand the most comprehensive in terms of diversity of approach was the NASA program entitled the High Resolution Microwave Survey (HRMS). Its comprehensiveness was evident in its dual approach which amounts to two separate programs each originally planned to last through the year 2002. The first, known as the all-sky survey, swept all directions of the heavens, while the second concurrent

---

[2]Other searches are in progress in Australia, France, and Russia.

study, called the targeted search, unique to the HRMS program, focused on some 1,000 solar-like stars within 100 light years of the Earth (Naeye 92).

On October 12, 1992, the 500th anniversary of Columbus' arrival in the New World, Dr. Jill Tarter and her colleagues closed the switches of the electronics and computer systems collating the data from some of the largest radio telescopes in the world. Unfortunately Congress withdrew funding for the project a year later. However, recent private funding has become available at least for the targeted search, appropriately named Project Phoenix, which will observe in the 1 to 3 gigahertz frequency range (a gigahertz is 10^9 cycles per second) (Wilford 94).

This microwave region of the electromagnetic spectrum has been chosen in most searches in part because it contains a well-known emission frequency of the hydrogen atom, a likely frequency for extraterrestrials to use since hydrogen is the most plentiful atom in the universe. This region was also chosen because of the lack of interfering radiation from Earthbound radio and satellite transmitters. This "hole" in the spectrum will probably be filled in a decade or so as the world-wide communication explosion proceeds, lending a special urgency to the present SETI efforts. After that space–based searches may become necessary, perhaps encompassing other regions of the electromagnetic spectrum, such as the infrared and optical.

Why has nothing thus far been seen? Some scientists have tried to calculate our chances of observing an extraterrestrial intelligence (ETI), say within our lifetime—an exercise that may illustrate why we have not thus far heard from any cosmic neighbors. The calculation basically consists of multiplying a series of probabilities together. A simple example would be calculating the decreasing probability of getting consecutive heads when the number of successive coin tosses is increased (the probability for heads on one toss is $1/2$; for two consecutive heads, $1/2 \times 1/2$ or $1/4$; and for three, $1/2 \times 1/2 \times 1/2$ or $1/8$; etc.).

Because of the practical limitations imposed by the velocity of light, most calculations are confined to our galaxy. Also, most SETI estimators first multiply the number of stars in the galaxy by $1/2$, because of the high percentage of binary stars (two partners orbiting each other), for the most part considered unsuitable gravitational environments for the existence of liveable planets. Next, we multiply the number of remaining stars by the probability of their having planetary systems. The string of winnowing multiplications goes on: of stars with planets, which might have suitable environments for life? Of these, which might actually support some biological systems? Of these, which might have intelligent life? Of these, which would have the ability and desire to communicate?[3]

Of course such calculations must be taken with a "grain of salt" because most of these probabilities are little more than enlightened guesses. Nevertheless they help illustrate the scope of the problem. However, these probabilities only deal with the "spatial" part of the problem. A drastic further winnowing occurs when time durations are considered.

As was discussed in Chapter 3 a star like the sun has an effective radiant life-time of some 10 billion years. An ETI on some viable planet of such a star could have evolved a billion years ago, or a billion years hence. We have only been looking for ETI for roughly 40 years; in fact we have only possessed the technological capacity for communication via radio astronomy for somewhat more than 60 years. Suppose that a technologically sophisticated alien culture lasted 10 times as long before extinction from disease, asteroids, nuclear holocaust, etc. This is like comparing a year to 20 seconds. If we were to hear from an ETI 1,000 light years away, it could be long extinct by the time it received a response from us. Thus time plays an equally important role along with space in acting as a powerful barrier for any signals that might have emanated from a galactic neighbor.

It is nevertheless meaningful to contemplate what it might mean to us if we received some extraterrestrial news. Their temporal evolution and consequent concept of time might be significantly different from ours and as such could furnish a burst of enlightenment and resultant technology. Indeed the mere occurrence of such an ETI signal would electrify the world. All of humankind would be awestruck. A collective groundswell of our global oneness would be sensed; the world as one "we" would be in dialogue with an alien civilization "they." Our sense of time and space at an instinctive level would be immediately and dramatically expanded. Our cognizance of who we are and what is our relation to the universe would forever be transformed, and our view of the destiny of consciousness would unfold to embrace the whole cosmos.

A message from an ETI 100 light years away would immediately connect us in the present with their past events 100 years ago. If we

---

[3]This is a simplified description of what professionals call the Drake Equation for finding the probable number of communicating civilizations in our galaxy.

respond, our present would be connected to their future 100 years from now. The receipt of a message, even though per force from the past, would irrevocably alter our future. In no more powerful way might the past direct our future.

The possibility of such an expanded view of the universe and its spatio–temporality raises the profound question of how the reception of an extraterrestrial message might affect the world's religions and their temporal development. The Judeo-Christian–Muslim tradition began as an essentially tribal faith in a god of sacrifice. With the early Israelite prophets such as Amos there was growth to a national religion worshipping a god of history. The later prophets, Isaiah and Ezekiel, saw God as not just having an effect on Israel and its neighbors but as a universal God encompassing and governing the whole world. This was also Paul's vision for Christianity in the inexhaustible efforts of his ministry, as it was for Mohammed.

Most modern religions now maintain that God's dominion embraces the universe. However, depending on the ETI message, the nature of this dominion will undoubtedly change and the religious world may have to reassess its theologies and be prepared to accommodate anything from a more profound understanding of altruism to an awesome onslaught of exquisite rationality, not to mention unimagined technology. A new more focused theology of the universe and the meaning of salvation may await development. Our "parochialness" would dissolve and our sense of who and/or what God is would reach a far greater fullness.

Nevertheless so far we have received nothing from an ETI. Thus for the present it seems wise to follow a balanced approach. On one hand, we must accept the possibility that we really may be alone. In that case, we may have to shoulder a profound responsibility, a responsibility for nothing less than the self-consciousness of the universe, or at least that part with which we can communicate, given the finiteness of our lives and the velocity of light (Fagg 88). On the other hand, we must also accept the reality of the primal apprehension in most of us that someone must be out there. Not to look would be to be to try to stifle something within us that will not die (Fagg 88).

Cosmic Predictions: Trillions of Years and Beyond

Considerations of the SETI program have helped provide a fitting context for the vista that the 21st century opens for us and particularly for an expanded, more cosmic view of time in the future. But far beyond the death of the sun is an almost unimaginable scope of time yet to be. The extent of this scope may depend on whether the universe is open, closed, or in between. This question was discussed in Chapter 7, where it was indicated that most theoretical cosmologists currently believe that the universe is exactly in between being open and closed, and as such will continue to expand indefinitely but at an ever decreasing rate.

Even if the universe is closed, it appears to be close enough to the critical density of mass that the mutual gravitational attraction of the galactic clusters will take a very long time to reverse the expansion. Therefore many of the very long range cosmic predictions will be applicable regardless of whether the universe is open, closed, or in between. However, in order to describe the complete list of predictions we will assume for simplicity that the universe is either open or in between so that the expansion continues indefinitely. Reasonable predictions based on this assumption and on known cosmological data indicate that the stars will exhaust their nuclear fuel and stop shining in about 10^{14} years (remember the present time is very roughly 10^{10} years; so that 10^{14} years is ten thousand times the present age of the universe) (Dyson 79). In 10^{17} years the stars will have lost their planets by interstellar collisions, which will be preliminary to the escape of some stars due to galactic collisions and the collapse of the galaxies to black holes by 10^{18} years.

The next step in the open universe story depends on the validity of a successful grand unified theory, GUT, discussed in Chapter 7. In part because the original GUT predicted too short a life time for the proton, the theories have undergone revisions and now can predict half-lives for the proton of as long as 10^{36} years. That is, one half of the protons now present will have ultimately decayed into positrons, electrons, neutrinos, and photons in that time. Because the half-life is so long, decay events should be extremely rare and their detection involves massive quantities of water (i.e. H_2O, to provide lots of hydrogen atoms; at the center of each is a proton), elaborate and sensitive particle detectors, and associated electronic equipment. The watch for a genuine proton decay has been conducted for several years by a number of groups of experimental physicists, with present results indicating that the half-life is greater than 10^{32} years. Therefore the current versions of GUTs appear to be consistent with experiment thus far, but the situation could change when a value is available for the proton half-life, and especially if it is concluded that it cannot be observed to decay at all.

If we set aside the uncertain status of the proton's mortality, the final stage of the disintegration scenario is considered to be the decay of the black holes. Stephen Hawking has shown, in part through the use of the Heisenberg Uncertainty Principle and the quantum behavior of the vacuum (see Chapter 4), that such decay should be expected (Hawking 88, p. 105ff). Thus the universe would ultimately end as a diffuse gas of electrons, positrons, neutrinos, and photons cooling to even lower temperatures as the expansion continues and the cosmological clock ticks on.

All of this presents a rather grim picture for our long–term cosmic future, but some thinkers feel that the prospects are more sanguine. That is, in addition to reasonable scientific extrapolations as to the future of the universe based on known data, some cosmologists have attempted to estimate how some form of intelligent life might be propagated into the indefinite future. For example, Robert Jastrow, who calls contemporary humans "living fossils" (Jastrow 80), portrays a progressive development and interaction between us and the computers we build. As the sophistication of the computers increases and our interaction with them becomes more intimate, they will ultimately be able to exist and reproduce on their own, forming a more lasting silicon-based society as we carbon-based humans gradually die out.

Although by their nature such predictive efforts are speculative, some are based on comprehensive thought and serious calculations. Among the most fascinating scenarios of our future in an open universe is that suggested by Freeman Dyson (Dyson 79). He prefers the prospect of the progressive cooling of the open universe rather than the torrid implosion ending the closed universe because, as he puts it, he would rather "freeze than fry."

Probably the most fundamental of the assumptions that Dyson makes in his calculations is that consciousness is based on structure, not on matter. For example, any similarity between the human brain and a computer lies in their structure, i.e., the peculiar arrangement and interlinking of the components; it does not depend so much on the material of which the components are made. In the brain the arrangement and interaction are of the carbon-based molecules; in the computer they are of the silicon-based minicomponents. Thus his calculations envision our ultimate evolution into a more lasting form of embodiment than blood, flesh, and bone. Now that genetic engineering is becoming a viable technology, Dyson feels it is reasonable to conjecture that we could redesign ourselves to be progressively more adaptable to the ever cooler and more rarified environment characterizing an indefinitely expanding universe. He considers our ability to evolve into beings capable of existing in extremely rarefied surroundings as comparable to our evolutionary ancestors emerging from water to air half a billion years ago (Dyson 88).

In fact, Dyson visualizes as one possibility a kind of "sentient black cloud" that has all of the memory, thought capacity, and communication ability of the human brain without its material frailties and thus could more easily adapt to the ever colder environment. Since the rate of metabolism of energy is proportional to the square of the temperature, cold environments are essentially more hospitable to complex forms of life than those that are hot. Life is an ordered form of matter and low temperature is conducive to order (Dyson 88). Also by undergoing carefully chosen periodic hibernations, such intelligent beings would use less and less energy to operate and to communicate with other beings. Because of the ever-decreasing use of energy, these beings could exist into the indefinite future, according to Dyson. Although it is a moot question whether any beings could survive without protons, Dyson sees no reason even then to declare the situation hopeless (Dyson 88).

THE TEMPORAL EXPANSION OF CONSCIOUSNESS

Several years ago I attended a science and religion conference at which Freeman Dyson, among other notable scholars, gave a lecture. Shortly thereafter it happened that I sat next to him at one of the meals given for conference participants. During our conversation I, with some trepidation, asked him if he had ever thought about the question: if the universe is so delicately balanced between being open and closed as predicted by the recent inflationary universe theories, would this not leave open the possibility for consciousness, human or otherwise, to influence the outcome? I was gratified that he took the question quite seriously despite its highly speculative nature. He answered that he did believe that this was a possibility. His answer was consistent with his ideas mentioned earlier about how conscious beings might be propagated indefinitely into the future. Even though he published his study of how this propagation might occur in the context of an open universe shortly before the inflation concept came on the scene, it would undoubtedly be applicable with little alteration for the in–between universe predicted by inflation.

In his masterful book "Perfect Symmetry," the late Heinz Pagels poses a similar question concerning the influence of humans or their derivatives on the future of the universe: "Is it possible that life, or whatever it might become, can alter the program of the cosmic computer (universe), changing the course of its destiny?" (Pagels 85, p. 360)

The notion of an open ended growth of consciousness with time deliberately and irreversibly permeating the universe also finds a congenial parallel with the thought of Teilhard de Chardin. Recall that Teilhard saw the cosmos as evolving irreversibly along a "favored axis" to ever greater states of complexity and holism. The crucial stage of this evolution resulting in human consciousness is described with vivid eloquence:

> It is perfectly possible that in the general spectrum of Life the line ending in Man was originally no more than one psychic radiation among others. But it happened, for some reason of hazard, position or structure, that this sole ray among the millions contrived to pass the critical barrier separating the Unreflective from the Reflective (human consciousness)...until finally, by means of the human brain...the breaking of the dikes, followed by what is now in progress, the flooding of Thought over the entire surface of the biosphere (Teilhard de Chardin 68, p. 222).

Is it not conceivable that in an entirely analogous vein, Thought is even now restlessly probing, progressively more ready to break through and spread its sensitive tendrils through the solar system, the galaxy, and beyond? And may not there be other extrasolar or extragalactic sources involved in the breakthrough? This momentous process of cosmic becoming perforce will bring with it a more panoramic perception of time perhaps congenial with that delineated by the cosmologic gauge of time (discussed in Chapter 9). Time will be perceived in a way that encompasses cosmic being and becoming on a vaster scale than ever before realized.

The brain is an organ with spatial properties; it occupies space; its different components are spatially arranged and connected to form a functional whole. But consciousness and in particular the mind, the perceptive thinking aspect of consciousness, is essentially temporal in nature. The life of the mind is a succession of becoming moments creatively evolving primarily from a harmonious confluence of the impact of the immediate past and the thrust of intentionality of the present jointly engaging in the immediate future. So also is there an inarticulable apprehension of the temporal advance of some form of collective or universal consciousness whether in the vein visualized by Carl Jung, Teilhard de Chardin, or otherwise. Inherent in this universal

Pierre Teilhard de Chardin
1881-1955

Courtesy of Philippe Halsman

consciousness may be some kind of coherence of being and becoming that characterizes a cosmic concept of time.

These speculative thoughts suggest that our concept of time may in some respects be evolving to ever greater degrees of sophistication embracing ever larger domains accessible to consciousness. This idea bears some rough, general similarity to the thought of J. T. Fraser who sees time as having a natural history or evolution, just as other entities including ourselves. He proposes what he calls the "principle of temporal levels," based on the idea that at each significant level or stage in the universe's evolution to ever more complex phenomena, a distinct and unique temporality or kind of time was manifested. The most primitive level is that embodied by the photon with its essentially atemporal character (as discussed in Chapter 12). Some four or five succeeding levels evolve following roughly the evolution of the universe: elementary particles with mass (protons, electrons, etc.), astronomic bodies (galaxies, stars, etc.), primordial life, humans, and even the society of humans. He further postulates that these temporalities "co-exist in a hierarchically nested, dynamic unity," which is still developing and openended. As each temporality has evolved from the previous, from which it received its grounding, it continues to exist in interaction with its forebears in such a nested hierarchy (Fraser 81, pgs. 19ff, 28–9).

As thought–provoking and ingenious as his metaphysical structure of time is, I disagree that our concept of time can so neatly and specifically be categorized into such temporal levels. On the other hand I do think that the evolution of life and consciousness has endowed time with more expanded and richer content and meaning. Furthermore I believe this expanded concept of time can continue and help define an openended irreversible radiation of consciousness, not to mention some form of spirituality, throughout the universe. In short I find myself in accord with K. G. Denbigh who speculates: "...it is attractive to conjecture that there occurs a steady increase of the total of conscious activity within the cosmos, a process of spiritualization in the time direction of conscious awareness" (Denbigh 81, p. 170).

A New Eschatology

In Chapter 6 we discussed some facets of eschatology, the theology of the End Time with its characteristics of judgment and redemption. Essentially the eschatology of a given religion constitutes the final scene of its cosmology. A religion's cosmology and eschatology are principally based on the way the leaders and scripture writers interpreted the spiritual relationship of men and women to each other and to the external and physical world as they comprehended it at that time, and especially to the god or gods who created and governed them and the world.

How the external world, in particular the political world, at the time can influence scripture writers is apparent in the apocalyptic literature of the Judeo–Christian tradition, prototypical examples of which are the Books of Daniel in the Old Testament and Revelation in the New Testament. Although there are other apocalyptic passages both in the Old and New Testaments, e.g., Isaiah 24-27 and Mark 13, Daniel and Revelation essentially represent a mature embodiment of this type of scripture. The purpose in these cases was to give courage to the faithful in the face of suppression and persecution. In Daniel it was designed to provide solace and inspiration for the Jews whose worship and law were being interdicted by Antiochus Epiphanes IV, Seleucid ruler of the Syrian empire, a segment of the earlier empire of Alexander the Great (Laymon 71, p. 437). It was at this time in the second century B.C. that Judas Maccabaeus led the revolt against Antiochus's attempts to force Greek deities and culture on the Jews. Revelation was written, according to biblical scholars (Laymon 71, p. 947) to reinforce the faith of Christians in the first century A.D. who were facing the threat of persecution if they did not yield to the practice of Roman emperor worship.

However, these examples of apocalyptic scripture also included portrayals of the physical world as it was viewed and understood in that era. They were spiritually inspired, judgmental responses to the world around them in terms of, and in a context of, a comprehensive world view that included the Earth and the heavens, that is, the entire natural world they observed. Examples of such literature, but of a more cyclical character, can also be found in the East. The Puranas, which represent the natural culmination of Brahmanical scriptures, describe the characteristics of the four yugas that comprise a mahayuga. We are thought to be living in the last, the Kali Yuga, which will end in its own apocalypse, the total dissolution of all moral values and the ultimate ubiquity of unbridled bestiality. However, the world will then be resolved into Brahman and another quartet of yugas, a new mahayuga, will emerge from Brahman. This form of what might be termed "periodic eschatology" is set forth in the framework of a sweeping transcendent cosmology which was probably derived from the observations of early Vedic astronomy (Balslev 83, p. 146).

Again, common to all of these eschatologies is an encompassing world view that included the physical cosmos as it was viewed at the time. Given what has been learned of this cosmos in this century, I suggest that the time may soon come for us to join in intuiting and formulating, in part through a consensus of spiritual insight, a new eschatology. Would it not be possible someday to develop a global, ecumenical eschatology that includes as a cosmic setting the present facts of physical cosmology as we know them, e.g. that includes the fact that the universe will expand for an indefinitely long time? Can we consider an eschatology based not only on a theology of justice and righteousness, but additionally on a theology of spiritual challenge, where benevolent courage and ingenuity assume equal roles with equity and goodness, a unifying theology embracing the immanent wisdom of Buddha, the transcendent perception of Shankara, the quietude and humility of Lao Tzu, the love and grace of Jesus, and the courage and insight of Moses and Mohammed? Perhaps such an ecumenical theology could provide an eschatology of openended spiritual challenge, whose judgmental feature is based on how diligently we conduct our search for meaning and on how well we care for and revere the consciousness, the living present, and the perpetuity of time, which God or Reality has provided. Personal salvation could come to those who, with unqualified faith and love, have given themselves to this effort using their full "God–given" ability, however minimal or limited.

All of this is admittedly somewhat visionary, and requires a more thorough development than is appropriate here. Nevertheless it needs to be said. It is an idea long–expressed in many forms, but one whose time may have come and that may constitute a "vital tick of the internal clock" of the universe's spiritual consciousness. Only with the persistent, continued pursuit of scientific knowledge fueled by, and coupled with, an abiding spiritual search for meaning may we hope to deal with the future that time relentlessly brings to us. In the words of theologian Karl Schmitz–Moormann:

> The process of becoming in its totality, not in its details, presents itself
> as a world that is on its way to God. But this way is not made of nicely
> stretched rails, but found by groping ahead laboriously (Schmitz–
> Moormann 92).

SUMMARY

As we approach the 21st century the awareness of what kind of universe we are in, particularly in terms of its future, assumes an increasing importance. The first cosmic challenge that the world as a whole will have to meet is that of an asteroid or comet collision. It is not a question of if, but when this will occur with an object large enough to inflict catastrophic destruction. Next on the cosmic time scale is the exhaustion of the sun's nuclear fuel, its swelling to become a red giant star and rendering the Earth uninhabitable. This event in our future immediately brings to mind the ultimate need for space colonization.

As one step toward helping educate ourselves more fully about some of the problems involved in such an enterprise, particularly with respect to communication, the recently initiated SETI programs could prove extremely useful. The discovery of an ETI would drastically affect our perception of who we are and what is our place in the universe. It would immediately at an instinctive level alter our sense of time and space and could seriously test the theologies of the world's religions.

Cosmic predictions on an even vaster scale tell us that the stars will stop shining and lose their planets, the galaxies will collapse to black holes, and much later the proton may decay as well as the black holes. In the face of this bleak prospect Freeman Dyson suggests a more sanguine future in which we evolve into beings better able to cope with the ever expanding and cooling environment.

This suggests the expansion of consciousness, and the consequent possibility of its influence, throughout the universe. Associated with this could be a much more sophisticated and comprehensive concept of time. Of equal importance could be the ultimate development of an ecumenical theology and eschatology in accord with the facts of science which would spiritually arm us to deal with time's future.

14 A Time to Die

Who the living would explain
He must enter death's domain.

—Christian Morgenstern

Life is a balancing act
Between Never and Always.

—L. W. F.

Time and the Fear of Death

It was early in the morning of a summer's day in 1970. I was attending a week–long physics conference at Brandeis University where each participant was accommodated with a dormitory room. Just as I emerged from sleep and with no warning at all, the reality of my own ultimate death presented itself as my first conscious thought. With a cold shudder I realized that then there would be no me; time and the world would proceed with my total absence. So that now I know that for me the moment is to come after which there is no moment.

No other fact of life impresses on us a sense of time more powerfully than the raw ultimacy of our own death. Indeed Martin Heidegger maintains that we perceive time only because we must die. The idea of death is only terrifying when one tries to grasp the notion of one's own nonexistence or nonbeing (Heidegger 62). The awareness of time and of death are peculiar to humankind, so that as we become more cognizant that we must die, we become as afraid of time as we are of death (Hartocollis 83, p. 227). With death in the background, however distant, we nevertheless seem to live our days on the one hand behaving as if we will live forever and on the other cherishing an occasional moment realizing how precious and transient it is. Indeed many who read this or other books about time do so with a visceral motive based on some amalgamation of the fear of death and the hope for immortality.

Contemplation about time, life, and death may initially evoke some apparent contradictions, but they are contradictions that many see as resolvable. As I sit and reflect on the vibrance of a given moment, it has sometimes occurred to me that, except for having become somewhat used to the habit of living, there is no fundamental reason why I should expect the next moment to come. I cannot hold on to that priceless "now." I yearn for its permanence and fear change, for it could bring adversity or death. But I soon see that the only true permanence is death. So the contradiction is that we yearn for permanence, but the only permanence available is the death that we fear.

However if we think about the fear of death another contradiction arises. On the one hand the fear of death is a realistically justified fear, in large part because it is often preceded by a painful process of dying. The intensity of this experience undoubtedly generates severe apprehension of death itself, despite the fact that at the moment of death there is a release from the travail of dying. On the other hand the fear of death has its positive aspect. It helps generate in us a collectively accepted concept of time along with its value and usefulness, without which much constructive human work and accomplishment would be impossible. In fact why should we fear death so much? We emerge from the "dark" at birth and return to it at death, in between lies our life experience (Mann 55). We have no fear of the "dark" before birth, why after death:

> There was a time when we were not; this gives us no concern—why then should it trouble us that a time will come when we shall cease to be?
>
> William Hazlitt
> (quoted from Enright 87, p. 31)

So it is that we sprout from the ground of eternity, flower, whither, die, and return to it, with only our spirit to fertilize its texture.

Yet it is far from trivial to reason away the fear of death. Ernest Becker has characterized this fear as "one of the great rediscoveries of modern thought: that of all things that move man, one of the principal ones is his terror of death." The power of this fear is easily seen in our attitude toward heroism, which he claims is "first and foremost a reflex of the terror of death" (Becker 73, p. 11). We feel unqualified admiration for those who perform valorous acts in the face of their own extinction: "it moves us deeply in our hearts because we have doubts about how brave we ourselves would be" (Becker 73, pgs. 11–12). This profound respect for the hero has been with us since the dawn of our evolution

(Becker 73, p. 12), and it is universally revealed in a host of myths characterizing early cultures throughout the world.

Nevertheless the stark reality that our internal clocks relentlessly are ticking their way to our ultimate death forces us to seek some kind of wholesome, realistic attitude toward it. We must realize that death is part and parcel of life and needs to be regarded as just as integral a part of life as birth. Indeed many people see that as we age, we gradually somehow prepare our hearts for this final moment; and through either realizing we have fulfilled our role in life or just shear weariness, we can perhaps regard death as a consolation, a final rest:

> With courage seek the kingdom of the dead
> The path before you lies,
> It is not hard to find, nor tread,
> No rocks to climb, no lanes to thread;
> But broad, and straight, and even still,
> And even gently slopes downhill;
> You cannot miss it, though you shut your eyes.
>
> Leonidas of Tarentum
(quoted from Enright 87, p. 51)

Or in a lighter vein:

> It is said we start to die at age twenty–three;
> By the time it actually happens
> We should be pretty good at it.
>
> Mary Skipp

Near Death Experiences

However, for many there is a more specific source of consolation in the face of death from the reports of those who have undergone a near death experience (NDE). These reports seem to fall into three general categories: 1) those resuscitated after being pronounced clinically dead, 2) those very close to death as a result of an accident, and 3) those who have seen and heard the last stages of the dying of someone else (Moody 76, p. 16). The experiences apparently happen to people in all walks of life independent of sex, religion, social status, or education. Although the specifics of each person's NDE are unique and no two people report exactly the same events, there do seem to be a number of common general features characteristic of many of these episodes. These features can perhaps best be described in a "typical" experience recounted by Dr. Raymond Moody:

> A man is dying and, as he reaches the point of greatest physical distress, he hears himself pronounced dead by his doctor. He begins to

hear an uncomfortable noise, a loud ringing or buzzing, and at the same time feels himself moving very rapidly through a long dark tunnel. After this, he suddenly finds himself outside of his own physical body, but still in the immediate physical environment, and he sees his own body from a distance, as though he is a spectator. He watches the resuscitation attempt from this unusual vantage point and is in a state of emotional upheaval.

After a while, he collects himself and becomes more accustomed to his odd condition. He notices that he still has a "body," but one of a very different nature and with very different powers from the physical body he has left behind. Soon other things begin to happen. Others come to meet and to help him. He glimpses the spirits of relatives and friends who have already died, and a loving warm spirit of a kind he has never encountered before—a being of light—appears before him. This being asks him a question, nonverbally, to make him evaluate his life and helps him along by showing him a panoramic, instantaneous playback of the major events of his life. At some point he finds himself approaching some sort of barrier or border, apparently representing the limit between earthly life and the next life. Yet, he finds that he must go back to the earth, that the time for his death has not yet come. At this point he resists, for by now he is taken up with his experiences in the afterlife and does not want to return. He is overwhelmed by intense feelings of joy, love, and peace. Despite his attitude, though, he somehow reunites with his physical body and lives (Moody 76, p. 21ff).

Among the outstanding features of the above episode as well as most NDE's is the out of body experience, the long dark tunnel, the "being of light," and the panoramic review of the major events of the subject's life. Also only visual and auditory sensations generally seem to be involved, no olfactory or tactile sensations. The "being of light" is actually experienced as a spiritual being exuding irresistible warmth and love, and requiring unequivocally honest response.

However, the most remarkable time–related aspect of such experience is the sweeping review of the principal events of one's life (Moody 76, p. 64; Moody 77, p. 101). This is a truly astonishing phenomenon. The human mind and its instrument, the brain, seem to have the capacity to compress an abridged version of a lifetime into an incredibly short time duration. Furthermore there is an instantaneous unerring selection of the most dramatic life events for the contents of this abstracted biography. This is a cogent exhibition of the temporal versatility of the human mind and its material home, the brain, as well as an indication of the time–related frontiers that may have yet to be explored by human consciousness.

Those who have survived an NDE generally report feeling far more integrated and emotionally stable than before, and on a firm psychic grounding. Their ability to love without reservation and to appreciate the richness and vitality of life is essentially complete (Moody 76, p. 88ff). With this new capacity to live in the here and now there is no longer a fear of time or of death. Conversely, for those who have recovered from an NDE caused by suicide the experience is reported to be extremely painful both emotionally and spiritually, and most maintain that they will never try it again (Moody 77, p. 43ff).

In any case these accounts reveal that for many death seems to be a passage to a spiritual realm to which the living have no access. It is this ending time, this passage afforded by death to continued life in another world, that has been an essential element in the beliefs and ritual practices of religions beginning with many of the earliest cultures.

A prototypical example is the elaborate preparations made for the royalty and noblemen of Egypt in the Dynastic period starting about 3100 B.C. In the "Egyptian Book of the Dead," the myth of Isis and Osiris symbolizes the renewal and continuum of life beyond. This scripture provides the means by which the dead can overcome any kind of obstacle to the ultimate renewal of life. These obstacles range from the threat of crocodiles and serpents to other malevolent gods and goddesses of the underworld (Budge 89, p. 153). Prescriptions are given on everything from how to avoid eating filthy matter and drinking foul water to preventing one's soul from being taken from one's body. All of this is prelude to coming forth on the earth in any form the soul chooses, often a bird or a serpent (Budge 89, pgs. 283, 285).

Although the elaborate and painstaking Egyptian preparations for the passage of the dead to an afterlife undoubtedly represent an ultimate in such rituals in the ancient world, they are clearly indicative of the firm belief in immortality, and in either an everlasting perpetuation of time or an eternity transcending time. Such beliefs in one form or another characterize most of the major world religions to this day. Let us briefly survey how death and its temporal aspects are dealt with by some of these religions.

DEATH IN THE WEST

Through a major part of the biblical period, almost until its very end, the prospect of death for the Israelites could be said to be rather grim. After death the body disintegrates to the dust of which it was once made, and the breath (ruah) diffuses into the air, or returns to God. If there was to be any propagation of religious or cultural values and spiritual continuity it would occur primarily through one's progeny or via the

Israelite nation as a whole (Bowker 91, p. 50). Even for the righteous, essentially nothing is promised for having led a good life. What one could expect after death was Sheol, a murky realm beneath the earth, which is described with telling pathos in the Book of Job:

> Are not the days of my life few?
> Let me alone, that I may find a little comfort before
> I go whence I shall not return,
> to the land of gloom and deep darkness,
> the land of gloom and chaos, where light is as darkness.

> Job 10:20–22

Sheol was not considered to be oblivion but a miserable separation from the living and from God. Thus the entrance into this somber domain was to be postponed for as long as possible. However, God could make very occasional exceptions and grant afterlife, as was done with Enoch and Elijah (Bowker 91, p. 54).

It is not until near the end of the biblical period that the expectation of an afterlife appears in the scriptures, e.g., in Daniel, Isaiah 24-27, and with modifications in non–canonical literature such as Maccabees II. In this era God was thought to be in control of Sheol, and resurrection was considered to occur. The seeds for the belief in resurrection were germinated in the early rabbinic period during the Babylonian exile. Except for the Sadducees, this belief was in flower, especially for the Pharisees and Essenes, by the time of Jesus and ultimately became one of the fundamental tenets of Judaism (Anderson 66, pgs. 551–2; Bowker 91, p. 70).

But, it was with Christianity that the belief in resurrection reached its ultimate level. For it was not just one of the basic doctrines, but constituted the central underpinning of Christianity. In a word, the resurrection of Jesus is the very cornerstone of the Christian faith. Furthermore resurrection was considered not simply a resumption of life as before, but a new life of eternal deliverance and triumph over time and death (Kee *et al.* 65, p. 53). The essential spiritual force provided by the ministry of Jesus, that injected life into this central Christian doctrine, was unqualified faith. This was faith that there was for each individual a more direct access to God provided by Jesus. This access was considered a vital and supervening completion to the traditional adherence of the Jews to the Torah as interpreted by a priest or rabbi (Bowker 91, p. 83).

However, according to the theologian John Bowker the Christian understanding of death is found, not in the Crucifixion, but in the

Eucharist. It is the power of the Eucharist, instituted by the Last Supper, that makes possible the involvement of others in the meaning of Jesus' death: "For as often as you eat this bread and drink the cup, you proclaim the Lord's death until he comes" I Corinthians 11:26. The propagation of this understanding of Christ's death and of the faith in his resurrection was the essential mission in Paul's incredible ministry, without which there would probably be no Christianity as we know it today. It was Paul, who on many occasions in his teachings, more fully developed the universal nature of resurrection as an experience available to all:

We were buried therefore with him
    by baptism into death
So that as Christ was raised from the dead
    by the glory of the Father,
We too might walk in newness of life.
                              Romans 6:4

Paul elaborated by contrasting Adam, and the ordinary death experience, with Christ wherein death can be overcome by association with him via baptism and the Eucharist:

For as by a man came death,
    by a man has come also
    the resurrection of the dead.
For as in Adam all die, so also
    in Christ shall all be made alive.
                      I Corinthians 15:21-22

However, the generally hopeful message of Paul concerning resurrection is balanced and qualified by the ominous words of warning in Revelation. Although there may be resurrection for all, it is on God's Day that all will be judged; the evil will suffer the "lake of fire" while the righteous will be blessed with eternal life in the "New Jerusalem."

The judgmental character of God is also an especially vital component of Islamic eschatology. The majesty and power of God's Day of Judgment is an emphatic theme that threads through the compelling verses of the Koran. The ubiquitous power of God is evident in the belief that death occurs only with God's permission: "Nor can a soul die, except by God's leave" (Sura 3:145). Furthermore, while the Islamic literature is quite specific in its portrayal of an interim phase in death, i.e., the period in the grave, there are no rituals as with the Egyptians to facilitate the transition to final judgment. Indeed any such procedure would be regarded as an interference with God's action (Bowker 91, p. 126).

But death itself is not generally considered a punishment; what punishment is justified lies ahead. The Koran is replete with dramatic descriptions rich in metaphor portraying resurrection and judgment. Typical is the description in Sura 69:13ff:

> Then, when one blast
> is sounded on the Trumpet,
> And the earth is moved,
> And its mountains,
> And they are crushed
> to powder at one stroke
> On that Day shall the
> (Great) Event come to pass,
> And the sky will be
> rent asunder....
> That Day shall ye be
> Brought to Judgment.
> Not an act of yours
> That ye hide will be hidden.

With few exceptions judgment in the Koran is a rather black and white matter. There is a clear division between those who enter the Garden, enjoying its rewards, and those who are condemned to the Fire; and although God has the power to change one's status, the judgment is essentially final (Bowker 91, p. 105). If one heeds the warning of the prophets (and Isa, Jesus, is considered one) one may find salvation through good works, but they must be works in cooperation with, and according to the will of, God (Bowker 91, p. 111). Indeed time itself is used by God for a purpose. That purpose is judgment for the sake of which time was first created (Goodman 93, p. 162).

The rather austere one-time judgment of one's deeds and works characteristic of these Western religions is modified and in general is exercised over a continuous and indefinitely long time period in the major Eastern religions.

DEATH IN THE EAST

The rich diversity of beliefs embraced by Hinduism, as we have seen, accommodates many paths to the goal of salvation. Of the vast body of sacred literature that express these beliefs, undoubtedly the most universally accepted by Hindus is the Bhagavad Gita, the scriptural jewel of the epic Mahabharata. A central theme in the Gita is dharma, the rule of righteousness, the duty to do what one ought to do (Hopkins 71, p. 73; Bowker 91, p. 131). In particular dharma is applied to coping with death. In the Gita the dialogue between the warrior Arjuna and his charioteer and mentor, who is later revealed to be the god Krishna, is used as a literary vehicle to express its message of faithful execution of dharma. The scene is a battlefield where the kinsmen of a large royal family are lined up in opposition, ready for battle, to decide who gains the family kingdom. Arjuna is struck with guilt and paralyzing indecision over the prospect of slaying his kinsmen. Would it not be better for him to be slain instead?

Krishna becomes his teacher, urges him to fight, and gradually persuades him that, though the body may be slain, the inner self is not. One should take action and perform one's duty with faith and without concern for the karmic consequences. He stresses to Arjuna that it is not the actions themselves that are the problem, but our attachment to the fruits of the actions. In the discourse he first reveals his identity as the god Krishna, but later as the supreme Atman, the Self, the spiritual manifestation of Brahman in man and woman (Deutsch 68, p. 120).

Thus in the performance of one's duty with devoted detachment even in the face of the bodily death of oneself or others, one is creating the karma leading to the realization of one's highest indestructible self and its identity with Atman. The Gita is therefore a powerful metaphor addressing the struggle of life, offering the hope of salvation through faith and dutiful action.

The law of karma, that one is responsible for one's actions and must expect to experience their consequences, is an abiding constraint on the path of the soul as it progresses through many physical lives in striving for salvation. It is this progress of the soul through time that is the spiritually supreme consideration. The cyclical chain of one's physical births and deaths have little relative importance compared to this devoted course, struggling and groping for the Self, wherein one is finally released from this cycle:

> From the world of Brahma downwards, all worlds are reborn,
> O Arjuna; but having come to Me, O son of Kunti, there is no rebirth.
>   Bhagavad Gita VIII:16

Brahma (not the same as Brahman), Vishnu, and Shiva (or Rudra) are the creator, preserver, and destroyer, respectively, of the natural world in the Hindu cosmology. In this cosmic metaphor for one's chain of births and deaths the three gods driving the cosmic cycle are successive manifestations of the supreme Brahman. However, in the flexible and variegated Brahmanical tradition Vishnu can actually assume all three of the above roles. At a later stage in the drama of the

Gita, Krishna reveals himself as a manifestation of Vishnu, and declares:

> Time[1] am I, the world destroyer, matured, come forth to subdue the worlds here. Even without thee, all the warriors arrayed in the opposing armies shall cease to be.
>
> Bhagavad Gita XI:32

One therefore must ultimately come to terms with the process of Time. One may dread it because of death or love it because of birth, but ultimately one must extract oneself from the emotional involvement with Time. This is the necessary precondition for the achievement of moksha, unity with Atman (Self), the spirit of Brahman (Bowker 91, p. 139).

Again it is the reality of the self that is a crucial issue distinguishing Hinduism from Buddhism. This issue in turn impacts on the attendant views of time and death. Throughout the Buddha's ministry he stressed the central message, that nothing is permanent, not even a self or a soul (Bowker 91, p. 172). As was discussed in Chapters 6 and 11, most Buddhist schools believe that there is no underlying abiding essence that can constitute a self. What appears to be the self is an organized composite of five skandhas, or aggregates, perhaps better understood as principally psychological components. They are sensations, perceptions, impulses or volitions, consciousness, and matter.

This difficult concept can perhaps be understood from the story of King Milinda's questions to the great Buddhist sage Nagasena concerning the reality of a self. Nagasena cited the example of a chariot which is an aggregate of axles, wheels, yoke, and boards. While the chariot has properties which are more than the sum of its parts, it does not exist apart from its parts or aggregates, and the chariot is not endowed with some independent existence beyond its appearance as a chariot comprised of aggregates (Keith 74, p. 77). It is similarly true for the living individual. One's sense of self is actually an illusion glimpsed in one living moment in a sequence of moments, each of them different from the previous (Bowker 91, p. 173).

So while the Buddhists believe in karma and in the samsaric cycle of birth and deaths generally similar to the Hindus, it is not a real self that struggles along the karmic path through this chain of lives. So what does pass on? For them the aggregate of five skandhas presents a

---

[1]Here Vishnu assumes the role of Kala the Vedic god of time.

different appearance with each rebirth so that what is actually transmitted is the karmic consequence of the action of the previous individual comprised of a set of skandhas (Bowker 91, p. 174).

Nevertheless death is very important, for it is at this moment that the individual can see, via his/her consciousness, the karmic fruits of his/her life at its conclusion and realize what is indicated as a karmic task in a future life (Bowker 91, p. 174). There is perhaps a no more compelling expression of the significance of death in Buddhism than found in the Tibetan Book of the Dead. Here in contrast to the general denial and evasion of the subject found in the West (although this is gradually changing), the emotional and spiritual condition of the dying person is of utmost concern to those left behind. Through the use of the incantations and readings of the text, the living can assist the dying and immediately dead to make the transition from the life that is terminating to a higher karmic state in the next, or even to enlightenment.

Specifically the Tibetan Book of the Dead is concerned with the "bardo," the transition state after death and before a new existence. "Bar" means in between and "do" means island, so that "bardo" means gap (Freemantle and Trungpa 75, pgs. 1, 10). That is, like a small island in a stream, bardo is a stepping stone from the karmic accumulation of one life to the opportunity in another. If one ritual incantation is seen to fail, then another is tried until there is satisfaction that the subject is launched on a suitable spiritual path (Freemantle and Trungpa 75, e.g. p. 39).

But again it is the ultimate goal of all Buddhists, Tibetan or otherwise, to resolve, and be released from, the karmic struggle in the chain of rebirths to achieve nirvana. This may be done in life or at death. In any case one is then freed from attachment to desire, grasping, passion, and transcends time.

The general capacity of the Hindus and Buddhists to view death with some degree of detachment as a perfectly natural event in the course of the living cosmos is shared by the Taoists. The Taoist master Chuang Tzu was particularly expressive about the place of death in the cosmic scheme of things. He approached the problem of life and death with equal serenity of mind. Scholar Max Kaltenmark notes that for Chuang Tzu: "Life and Death are merely two aspects of the same reality, and change from one to the other is as natural as the succession of day and night, waking and sleeping" (Kaltenmark 69, pgs. 80–1). Life and death are simply transformations from one form to another, such as the change of silkworms to moths. In fact the earliest almanacs maintained that sparrows become oysters in the fall, and changed back to sparrows in the spring. Similarly the notion of permutational interchange of forms is an underlying theme in the I Ching (Kaltenmark 69, pgs. 81–2). The idea of a series of transformations from one creature to another is also prevalent in the writing of Lieh Tzu as well as Chuang Tzu. Death is simply a part of this natural process. So that there is a chain of transformations that results in a human, who ultimately "goes back into the great weaving machine: thus all creatures issue from the Loom and return to the Loom" (The Chuang Tzu and The Lieh Tzu as quoted in Kaltenmark 69, p. 82).

TIME, IMMORTALITY, AND THE NECESSITY OF DEATH

Indeed as part of nature and its immutable laws we are destined to return to the Loom, "doomed to the Loom." Putting it bluntly, we are biodegradable, and are just as much subject as anything else to the Second Law of Thermodynamics, the basis for the thermodynamic gauge of time, discussed in Chapter 9. There it was shown how we are essentially the ultimate example of a far–from–equilibrium system still subject to the Second Law. Such systems are "open" systems, surviving by the exchange of matter and energy with the environment. Animals and humans live by the intake and discharge of matter and energy as a vital part of the processing mechanism for cell reproduction. But only so many cycles of such reproduction are accorded each creature. Ultimately we, with all of living nature, totally disintegrate to thermal equilibrium, victims of the Second Law of Thermodynamics. The equilibrium state of life is death.

Thus at death we are "planted" to become the seed for generations to come (Campbell 88, p. 216). Our biological clocks run down and we cannot indefinitely "borrow" from our natural surroundings without giving something back:

> ...nature, almost envious of the good she has given us, tells us often and gives us notice that she cannot for long allow us that scrap of matter she has lent....she has need for it for other forms, she claims it back for other works.
>
> Jacques–Bénigne Bossuet
> (quoted from Enright 87, p. 6)

Moreover, if we think about it, however difficult it may be to accept, death is absolutely necessary. If we kept on living, given the metabolism, immune system, etc. with which we were born, we would probably not be able to adapt ultimately to the rigors of a changing environment. The vigor and versatility of young and new generations are needed for this adaptation. The evolution of sex with greater opportunity of diversity makes this possible, in contrast to the cloning reproduction process of microbes which in principle can continue indefinitely (Bhargava 92). Thus death affords the opportunity for necessary changes in evolution. Indeed there can be no life without death. Death is the means by which erroneous mutations are discouraged leaving room for more virile, productive mutations to propagate. But for the death of a host of creatures we would not be alive today.

While we should generously accept this gift from this legion of forbears, we must also accept that our turn to repay the gift will come. It seems best to consider our death as a gift of loving sacrifice for the further productive evolution of our universe and its consciousness.

Our life is an endeavor and an opportunity to beneficially affect our world and its evolution. It is true that our lifetime is to a billion years on the cosmic scale as three seconds is to a year. Thus our life is but a moment, albeit a vital one, in the prodigious evolving that is cosmic time, a heartbeat in the life of the universe.

The surety of our death then makes us realize that we are participators in a colossal process. But regardless of how minuscule is our role in this process, the remarkable thing is that we nevertheless *care*. We care for our family and friends; we care for our houses and gardens; we care for what we create, be it a bridge or a book; we care even though we are ninety and will die the next day. And particularly with death in the offing we care with the need to know that our life had meaning and value. With this wondrous bequeathal of instinctive caring we make our mark on the scroll of cosmic history and weave our vital thread in the tapestry of the great Loom. Religious and theological convictions aside, certainly at the minimum I believe our immortality is assured through the beneficent influence of our life, however small, on future generations, spreading out among our progeny like a wavelet on the waters until it merges with the universe, its consciousness, and their Creator.

SUMMARY

The ultimate certainty of our own death, probably more than any other fact of life, impresses on us a consciousness of time. We yearn for permanence when the only permanence is death. While death may instill fear, in large part due to anxiety about the pain of the dying process, it can be considered as a stimulus for constructive activity with the time we have available. The fact that we did not exist before birth may be helpful in bearing the thought of our non–existence after death.

However, perhaps a more substantive consolation in facing death may be afforded by the many sanguine reports of near-death experiences. In these cases the individual involved is left with a profoundly salutary love of life and with no fear of death.

The attitude toward death and belief in an afterlife underwent a gradual evolution in the Judeo-Christian-Muslim tradition. Although the early Israelites believed in Sheol, a dolorous domain whose entry is to be postponed for as long as possible, by the end of the biblical period the concept of resurrection grew to be an accepted doctrine in Judaism. Indeed the resurrection of Christ is at the very core of the Christian faith, and it was primarily Paul who proclaimed the belief that resurrection through acceptance of Christ was available to all. Nevertheless following resurrection was judgment, as dramatically described in Revelation as well as in Daniel for the Jews. The distinction between the good and the bad in the judgment after resurrection is an especially powerful theme found throughout the Koran.

In the East judgment seems to be a much longer process continually coming into play in the struggle with karma through an indefinite chain of rebirths. The goal of this struggle is enlightenment, moksha for the Hindus and nirvana for the Buddhists. An essential difference between these two religions hinges on the question of what is transmitted through the series of rebirths, a self or some aggregate of karmic consequence. This generally qualified more benign attitude toward death is shared by the Taoists who regard it as a perfectly natural component of life.

In terms of hard physics we will all become victims of the Second Law of Thermodynamics, and therefore will decay ultimately to a state of thermal equilibrium, blending with our surroundings. However, our death is vital to provide opportunity for our progeny in their youth and vigor to sustain constructive mutations and adapt to an ever changing environment. It is the remarkable instinct of caring that endows our life efforts, however minuscule, with a meaning that I believe propagates through time down through the ever spreading generations and melds with the cosmic Consciousness.

15 How Real the Future?

"We make the future real by reacting to our anticipation of it."
—J. P. Dupuy

HUMANS AND THE FUTURE

From the earliest times of recorded thought philosophers have given abundant testimony to the special reality of the present. The singular vividness of this present, this "here and now," carries with it access to a visceral sense of reality. But what about the past? Can it be said to possess some reality because at one time it was present? Does the fact that the future cannot even claim this support render its reality even more questionable? In a word is there any sense in which the past, and especially the future, can lay claim to reality?

For a capsulized treatment of the case for the reality of the present relative to the past and future, let us start by returning to St. Augustine. He posed the question: "Of these three divisions of time (past, present, future) then, how can two, the past and future, *be*, when the past no longer is, and the future is not yet?" Although he finally concludes that "it is abundantly clear that neither the future nor the past exist," he makes a qualification by suggesting that there may be what he calls a present of past, a present of present, and a present of future things, that is:

> The present of past things is the memory
> The present of present things is direct perception
> The present of future things is expectation.
>
> (Augustine 61, p. 269)

This is Augustine's way of expressing the idea that the present may possess some realistic content of the past and, of particular concern in this chapter, the future. Philosophers often speak in terms of "orders of reality"; for example some claim that time is a higher order of reality than motion, or vice versa. So can the future be accorded an order of reality, perhaps below that of the present, but nevertheless meaningful?

As a beginning in an approach to this question we have only to reflect on some general attitudes of behavior in humans, which indicate that at least for them the future seems to be accorded some degree of reality. With the gift of consciousness humans can exercise and envision a much richer and intimately correlated view of the past, present, and future. While most of us carry with us a past loaded not only with fond memories but also with regrets, mistakes, and tragedies, our present is imbued with meaning by the future to which we look forward. Despite regrets, limitations, and infirmities it is hope, however meager, that vitalizes our present with value and significance. Indeed the meaning of our present is often judged by means of our capacity to transcend the immediate "now" and invoke the envisioned, or hoped for, future as a purpose or reason for the present. In any case we arrive at the present hopeful that what we know equips us for the fulfillment of a future that radiates our living present with meaning (Sherover 75, p. 455). This hope is empowered by our instinctive knowledge that our future action is the only action that remains under our control (Peirce 75, p. 387).

Thus we are future oriented creatures impregnating our present with meaning by the vista we see ahead. Our experience of time follows "lines of intentionality" as expressed in the thought of Husserl and Merleau–Ponty discussed in earlier chapters. The future, comprised of our expectation and the relentless becoming of the world around us, in some sense comes at us and we deal with its imminence by means of a host of decisions, large and small, guided by the underlying thrust of intent. In this process we select from an assembly of possibilities, and we "anoint one with acceptance as anticipation" which vivifies our present (Sherover 75, p. 459). But driving this process, coursing through the subterrains of our psyches is our intent, or what Heidegger calls anticipatory resoluteness. If you are driving a car to visit your parents for Thanksgiving, your "now" while driving the car finds its significance in the anticipated celebration of the holiday (Sherover 75, p. 457).

Accordingly the future is not just an event or a set of events, but, in the view of George Santayana, is the remainder of a transformation, or of a becoming. He further maintains that the "psyche is magnificently confident not only that a future will be forthcoming, but that its paces will be familiar" (Santayana 75, p. 415). Just as the lines of protention or intentionality of Merleau–Ponty feel out the general style of the future, certainly the near future, for Santayana the general character of the future is spelled out like the rest of a half–spoken sentence (Santayana 75, p. 415).

Indeed, pressing the simile of a sentence a little further, when we speak a sentence, the immediate future is bound up in its presentation in terms of the effect intended. This is true in face of the fact that when a sentence, in particular a short sentence, is spoken, it is experienced as a whole, as a moment in a conversation. Furthermore in analyzing this moment of expression we see that it is an example that helps illustrate two fundamental properties of experienced time discussed earlier, duration and succession. Surely the statement of the short sentence requires some temporal duration, and certainly there is a succession of separate words in the sentence.

If we examine these two characteristics of time, particularly in the case of humanly experienced time, we realize they are both necessary. Time as a mere succession of discrete events does not tell the whole story. Groups of events comprising an experienced moment must exhibit some duration as described in Chapter 11. On the other hand duration alone without succession would amount to some form of eternity. Thus both succession and duration characterize an experienced "now," which by virtue of these very properties unavoidably incorporates at least some features of the immediate past and future into the realized present.

Human time then is a concurrent synergy of succession and duration involving the coexistence of selected components of the past and future along with the present (Kummel 81, p. 35ff). As Friedrich Kummel expresses it, time is characterized by a

> relation of temporal coexistence between past, future, and present, a relation which can be conceived not only as one of succession but as one of conjoint existence, too. We are thus in a position to describe time as enduring insofar as the past does not wholly disappear and the future is in some way always already present" (Kummel 81, p. 36ff).

In essence Kummel holds that only when both succession and duration involving the correlation of past, present, and future are taken together can the nature of time be fully described. Indeed some coexistence of past, present, and future may be considered as a condition for the real continuity of time. Therefore Kummel concludes that human time is not just a transitory present, but it is an interrelation and coexistence of future, past, and present, so that reality cannot be necessarily considered the exclusive characteristic of the present (Kummel 81, p. 44ff).

Another significant aspect of Kummel's thought pertaining to the reality of the future is how even parts of a human's past have future aspects. Men and women relate freely to both their past and future and in so doing color and affect their present. In particular some components of the past project into the future in the sense that, whether consciously or unconsciously, much of a person's past has yet to be fully digested, understood, and interpreted. This process of assimilation then becomes part of our future. Furthermore, because of the enduring effect of past events, part of our future will be realized through the need to make up for past mistakes. This desire to "set things right" brings the past into the present and the future (Kummel 81, p. 53).

Nevertheless whatever element of reality the past contributes to the future as thus far discussed, the two are clearly different regardless of their real or unreal aspects. In terms of everyday living the past, irrevocably formed, has some claim to reality particularly in terms of our memory, which can be called on in any of our present moments. Moreover, though the past is non–existent in the present, at least at one time it enjoyed the reality of being. On the other hand the future like the progressive defocussing of a telescope image, becomes increasingly more diffuse and ill–defined the further we project into our temporal possibilities yet unrealized. Even so, although it possesses no being in the present, again it is endowed with some degree of reality by the momentum of intent, an intent shaped in the past, vivid in the present, demanding realization in the future by means of an incessant chain of decisions and consequent actions or inactions, some trivial and some of significant import.

For humans it is this intent that vitalizes and gives meaning to duration. And it is duration that serves as a kind of propagator for the continuance of time. Thus we seem to have the experience of being and participating in a world that we objectively observe to be progressing from before to after while simultaneously subjectively feeling the future somehow coming at us (at least in terms of the decisions required of us), passing through us, and receding into the archives of remembrance.

If we turn to a consideration of the future from the subjective viewpoint of one spiritually committed to a given religion, it is surely some apprehension of the "eternal now" that serves as a continuing source of support for one's faith in a future salvation. The hope for salvation and the concomitant respect and fear of judgment provide the religious person with a fixed view of a spiritual future that is as real for them as anything they can touch. It is this belief in ultimate judgment and in the possibility of enlightenment or salvation that motivates the spiritual striving of the believer and supports the reality of this goal as an embodiment of the future. This observation is congenial with the thought of Kierkegaard who held that in a sense the future even becomes identified with eternity itself (Kierkegaard 57, p. 80).

Nevertheless the spiritual striving is also continually catalyzed by the abiding sustenance derived from a response to the eternal now. In its basic essentials this spiritual process of sensing eternity in both the present and the future is common to the believer whether Judeo–Christian–Muslim, Hindu, Taoist, or, with some qualifications, Buddhist. Surely these religious vistas of a salvational future enlarge the scope of the human view of the future in general, and add to it a completing, more spiritually cosmic dimension.

The Future and the Physical World

The setting for the humanly experienced eternal now nourishing the potentialities for the future is provided by the physical space of our environs. Both change and at least relative permanence characterize the natural world around us. Though based ultimately on a bustle of microscopic activity, much of the physical world (e.g. rocks, earth, tree stumps, etc.) stands in quasi–stationary witness to the remainder that is in visible motion (birds, swaying trees, etc.). The collective impact of these natural phenomena provides a basis for the notion of duration (Kummel 81), as well as a basis for some degree of reality for the future in the physical world.

How is this so? Certainly a central underlying quality of duration in the physical world is that of ongoingness, motional inertia, or momentum. An understanding of the nature of motional inertia was given us by Newton who, in addition to the famous classical law of the gravitational attraction between two bodies, enunciated three laws of motion. The first of these, often called the law of inertia, states that a body either at rest or moving at uniform velocity will continue to do so unless acted on by an external force. We see the majestic power of this law in the motion of all astronomic bodies. Though the stars and galaxies are gravitationally interacting with each other, mutually altering each others' courses gradually, they largely proceed by their inertial momentum. It is calculations based on Newton's law of gravitational interaction and on his laws of motion that yield the cosmic predictions for the future described in Chapter 13. Indeed these predictions tell us that sooner or later the earth may suffer an impact with an asteroid or comet, which helps in a very real way to support the feeling (not to mention the philosophical viewpoint) that the future is coming at us.

But the law of inertia also applies in the microscopic world of the quantum as well as the macroscopic world of the everyday living. This integrated persistence of motion and vibrant rest rumbles on with ponderous, irresistible momentum seeming to guarantee some kind of a future, though certainly not the totally deterministic future characteristic of late 19th century philosophy. The guarantee that it will be close to what we observe in the present becomes less and less valid the further we project into the future. The myriad of possibilities for what will be nature's future are being incessantly selected at the quantum level "under our noses" at this moment. Countless numbers of quantum systems, interacting with each other, are mutually reciprocating the roles of 'measured' and 'measurer' like the observer and observed discussed in the quantum theory of Chapter 4. Events interact, each taking the measure of the other, waves functions collapse, probabilities reduce to one result in continual restlessness, groping their way and integrating to choose nature's future.

Thus even the physical world possesses in its present some degree of reality of the future. This reality is essentially described by the predictive power of what we presently know of the laws of nature. Generally the briefer the projection into the future and the larger the physical system, the more accurate is the prediction. Accordingly, near–term astronomic events are the most certain, with the picture of nature becoming progressively more blurred as we consider smaller and smaller systems[1] and project further and further into the future.

Thus there is a difference between the future as realized by inanimate matter and by living creatures, in particular humans. Both share the general property of the immediate future being more clearly focussed than that to come later. But with animals, and especially humans, the future becomes determined as the present in a much larger theater of choices and potentialities by the thrust of will and intent with a virtually infinite variety of nuances attendant with the becoming.

In any case whether in the physical world, the domain of human sense experience, or the spiritual world, the case for the reality of the future that we have explored seems to have some philosophical validity.

---

[1]This is based on the very general assumption that the smaller the system the more easily and likely it will be affected by neighboring systems or its environment.

However, the philosophical issue is by no means settled. In considerable part it seems to depend on what we mean by reality. If we rigorously mean reality as exclusively the present instantaneous moment of being, then one may argue that there is little room for future content. On the other hand, if we allow for the impetus of intent, the reach for salvation, and the momentum of nature, all in a more durational present, imbedded in this present is at least an approximate guidance to the future, giving it some measure of reality.

Summary

Humans, at least most modern humans, are by and large future oriented creatures. Anticipation and intent impregnate our present along with the haunting warnings and remnant yearnings from our past. This intent fueled by expectation is experienced in our present, giving it meaning, and is thus the basis for according some degree of reality to the future. The two characteristics of time, duration and succession, collaborate, according to Kummel, in a way that accommodates some coalescence of past, present, and future in the humanly experienced moment. Although the past is different from the future in that it once could claim the reality of the present, it is part of the human future, among other things, in terms of unfulfilled desires.

The reverent experience of the eternal "now" is certainly an abiding source of support for the believer in any religion in his or her search for future enlightenment and salvation. Faith in the attainability of this goal endows the present and the future with a completing value provided by the hope or anticipation of redemption.

In the physical world the future is real particularly in terms of the dynamic inertia of all of its manifold motions; things in motion tend to continue in motion. Our projections, our predictions, are made possible by the laws of physics. The predictability is in general more valid the larger the system and the briefer the projection into the future. This dynamic inertia characteristic of all physical systems, from cosmic to quantum, then provides some kind of future, though not with the richness of choices and potentialities possible for animals and humans. Although it is an abiding philosophical issue, there is some basis for arguing that the future should possess some degree of reality.

Part V TIME

Time is at the crossing point between consciousness and matter.
—Raimundo Panikkar

In the preceding four Parts of this book we have examined a number of characteristics of time primarily from two viewpoints –modern physics and major world religions. This approach was taken because it was judged to reflect in the most penetrating way the fundamental subjective–objective duality that inevitably seems to arise in any serious attempt at a study of time.

We set a context for this bilateral approach by first discussing relativity, quantum theory, and electromagnetism in order to understand the temporal aspects of the cosmologic, macroscopic, and microscopic domains which play a role in delineating and enclosing us in a kind of cosmic cocoon. Then the spiritual aspect of our cocoon's temporality was described in terms of principal religious world views.

With these temporal properties of our cosmic cocoon in mind, we next investigated problems dealing with several aspects of time and time–related phenomena. These included such problems as: whether time began, its relation to motion and space, its irrevocable becoming, the concept of the moment, and the notion of timelessness. Finally, some characteristics of the future were treated in terms of the cosmic future, the issue of death, and the question of the reality of the future.

Throughout the discussion of these topics dual aspects of time have appeared in a variety of forms. In the next chapter I shall describe how all of these forms of temporal duality can essentially be embraced by, or related to, the subjective–objective duality with which the book began. This will be followed by a discussion of possible ways the components of this duality can be reconciled. Then I will advance some speculations as to how time may be regarded as a conceptual unity. In the final chapter I will conclude with an attempt to address the perennially challenging question: "What is Time?"

16 TIME: A DUALITY OR UNITY?

It is impossible to meditate on time and the mystery of the creative passage of nature without an overwhelming emotion at the limitation of human intelligence.

—Alfred North Whitehead

We have the task of not only of making clear that the fundamental problem of philosophy is to provide us with an integral theory of time, but also of facilitating its solution.

—Franz Von Baader

One of the fundamental problems inherent in any attempt to comprehend anything as elusive as time is that we are so inextricably and intimately interrelated with it in the natural universe. Time, along with ourselves, is *in* nature; nature is not in time. That is, the prevailing current opinion, whether physical, philosophic, or religious, seems to be that time does not exist "out there" beyond the universe, transcendently and imperturbably flowing on and on. It is one of the characteristics of the universe, and as such is part of the universe just as we ourselves are.

The whole situation appears to be an example of an axiomatic principle that can be applied to many areas of study. It goes something like this: Complete knowledge of a system cannot be acquired if the observer is part of the system. We cannot get outside the universe to determine fully its nature or the nature of time and our deep enmeshment with it. Accordingly, despite the fact that we can claim considerable objectivity in science, we cannot really claim absolute objectivity in any view of time, or indeed in anything else. It is therefore far better, instead of uselessly straining for absolute objectivity, to use the objectivity that is available in conjunction with what one hopes is an enlightened subjectivity in approaching a problem.

Utilizing accessible objectivity and subjectivity to address the problem of time brings us right back to the first chapter of this book where this dual approach was introduced. I attempted to simplify as well as accentuate this approach by choosing to jointly examine time largely from the viewpoints of modern physics and major world religions, the "hardest" of sciences and "softest" of humanities, respectively. I did this because I felt that these two disciplines most incisively represent the objective–subjective duality. In so doing we have seen a variety of time relevant dualities emerge in the development of the subject. Let us review these dualities and see how they may be considered in some respects as special cases, forms, or related aspects of the more general objective–subjective, or kindred rational–intuitive, duality.

TIME AS A DUALITY

We are humans with consciousness and consciousness of consciousness, and consequently with a special access to an experience of the present. Because of the nature of this consciousness we tend to think of the outside world as an objectively separate, essentially non–conscious entity. Thus when we think about ourselves and our relation to this world, some sense of duality in our view of time seems unavoidable. Versions of this dualism in varying degrees of specificity have found their way into the thinking of philosophers and sages for millennia. Even in cases where it is not specifically mentioned, evidence of its presence in the ponderings of these thinkers appears inevitably.

Among the dualities we have discussed, Martin Buber's companion concepts of I-Thou and I-It have been found especially relevant at several points in the text in clarifying the temporal nature of the subjective–objective dualism. Again, in the I-Thou experience spirituality, intuition, and instinct are in full flower. Whether the relation is with a person, a tree, a poem, or God, one is enveloped in the here and now, with free and complete grace. The vibrant present and the benign flow of indistinguishable living moments is seen with a total subjectivity. On the other hand, the I-It experience connotes a role of observer or witness of the living present. It entails a distancing from, and objectification of, whatever or whomever the experiencer is relating to. Rational analysis and logical thinking generally come into play here.

It is true that the lawyer working on a complex case, the biologist testing in the laboratory, or the physicist devising a theory, do not exclusively operate in the rational I–It mode and at least occasionally may experience an I-Thou episode during their labors. Likewise it is unusual that even the most consumed mystic can continually exist only in the I-Thou mode. Thus, both modes exist for everyone in the temporal experience of themselves and their observation of the world, and the I-Thou and I-It states find a congenial association with the twin temporalities, subjective and objective.

Another duality was discussed in Chapter 9 where we introduced McTaggart's two modes of temporal advance called the A and B series (McTaggart 27, vol. 2, p. 9ff). Recall, the A series is comprised of the experience of past, present, and future, while in the B series time ordering is effected through the cognizance of before and after. The A series expresses a more dynamic and subjective context for the serial advancing of time, because it is characterized by the continually evolving, personally experienced now, separating the past from the future. The B series more often finds application in a more objective and relatively static context, because past events can be made sequential as to before and after by the memory or records, and future events made so by rational anticipation or prediction.

It is particularly through the peculiarly human experience of the present that the A series could be considered as an aspect of subjectively viewed time, while the simple idea of before–after temporal order suggests that the B series is more often objective in nature. Therefore I believe that, again in the case of this A and B dyad, it can be argued (with some qualifications) that it is an expression of some particular aspects of the subjective–objective temporal dualism.

Still another couplet of basic temporal concepts is that of succession and duration, which have been used on several occasions in our descriptions of the characteristics of time. It is undoubtedly true that succession and duration jointly in varying measure may reasonably constitute aspects of both the subjective as well as the objective view of time. Nevertheless I maintain that the general connotation of succession, certainly in the sense of mathematical sequence, finds a generally more relevant application in describing the characteristics of the objective aspect of time as opposed to the subjective. In contrast I feel that the idea of duration realizes its full development in the human experience of time and thus is a clear constituent in any valid elucidation of subjectively conceived time. Therefore, while succession and duration do not represent a clearly delineated example of an objective–subjective duality, they are a duality consisting of two essential properties of time that are absolutely necessary for a full understanding of the objective–subjective duality.

Next we consider the contrasting views of time seeming to pass from past to future as opposed to future to past. Clearly the view that time is passing from the future to the past is an essentially human impression. It is the response of human consciousness to temporal phenomena in terms of the continual chain of decisions, large and small, required of us, even in the most primitive of living. On the other hand, while it is true that time observed as passing from past to future cannot be so apparently categorized as being exclusively identified with either the subjective or objective viewpoint, nevertheless some thinkers have argued forcefully that it is predominantly an objective conception (Sherover 89). It is certainly consistent with any objective observation of the temporal behavior of the external world.

Finally let us consider the thought of Mircea Eliade which was first discussed in Chapter 6. Recall that in analyzing the beliefs and religious behavior of many ancient peoples throughout the world, he conceived of them subscribing to two different temporalities, which he called sacred and profane time. The former occurred when the cosmogonic creation event, generally brought about by a mythical hero, was ritually re-enacted, usually each year. For these people the world was literally reborn in this celebration; all past mistakes and miseries were erased, and time started all over again. Such hallowed events constituted what these cultures considered real time, sacred time (Eliade 71, pgs. 20–2). Given its pregnant and highly charged spiritual context, this time could be considered an extreme example of subjectively viewed time.

This was in contrast to the time in between the celebrations, profane time, that was spent in day–to–day living. During this time undoubtedly all of the rational thought that could be mustered was brought to bear in effectively performing necessary daily tasks. Given the elementary analysis required in accomplishing these chores, it seems reasonable that much of Eliade's profane time could be correlated with, and be included as an aspect of, the general category of objective time. On the other hand, a subjective experience and view of time must have been a part of everyday living as well. Therefore it appears that Eliade's sacred and profane time together represent both a significantly diluted yet highly polarized example of the subjective–objective duality, the polarity being due to the intense, once–yearly subjective experience of sacred time.

In any case we have now surveyed five different and specific ways that time has been seen as some kind of a duality throughout this book: I-Thou and I-It, A and B series, succession and duration, past to future and future to past, sacred and profane. Undoubtedly there are others. All are illustrative of the manifold ways in which time exhibits, or can be described in terms of, a duality in some form. Admittedly, the arguments

I have made for the ways by which these five couplets are versions of, are subsumed by, or help define, the general subjective–objective duality have involved some generalizations and imprecisions.

Nevertheless, I believe that, in the main, the way I have presented the five dualities in terms of their relation to the subjective–objective duality is approximately valid. It is out of place here to develop the extensive discourse involving the rigorous philosophical analysis that would be necessary to elucidate in full detail the inevitable qualifications, refinements, and nuances implicit in what I have said. Such a protracted philosophical digression would be inconsistent with the principal purpose of this book, which is to look at the scope of what the joint viewpoints of modern physics and major world religions can tell us about not only the subjective–objective temporal dualism but also about what basis there is for a unified view of time. It is to explore this latter possibility that we now direct our thought and speculation.

TIME AS A UNITY

As a first step in our search for clues of some unity underlying the subjective–objective duality, let us ask a couple of questions. Since both elements of this duality are addressing time, is there some more holistic viewpoint that would embrace the two and provide some degree of integration? Can this viewpoint somehow relate or connect the components of this duality, at least partially depolarize them, or provide some threads of implicit unity?

Complementarity. One such approach that suggests itself is through the application of a generalization of Bohr's Principle of Complementarity. This principle, as discussed in Chapter 4, was conceived by Bohr to reconcile the particle–wave duality in quantum theory. However, as indicated earlier, it has been generalized by many thinkers and applied to a variety of dichotomies in other fields (see Barbour 74, p. 55ff).

There are certain fundamental criteria that an entity that presents itself to us as a duality must fulfill in order for us to apply the complementarity principle to it. First, we must be certain that it is indeed a single phenomenon or entity that we are observing. Second, the phenomenon or entity must appear differently to the two modes of observation. Third, the two modes must be independent and mutually exclusive. That is, one mode cannot be reduced to the other or subsumed by the other. Neither mode gives a complete description; both modes are necessary for completeness. This implies, of course, that the two modes are limited; but it also hints that from some more transcendent viewpoint, apparently unavailable to us, a complete picture may be achievable in one sweeping observation.

Just as Bohr endeavored to attain some degree of unity in the wave–particle duality through the use of complementarity, it may be useful to attempt the application of a more generalized version of the principle to the duality existing between the subjective and objective views of time. I believe that it is feasible with appropriate qualifications to make a case for the above criteria for complementarity being satisfied. That is, it should be possible to determine the extent to which 1) one phenomenon really is being observed, 2) neither mode of observation is complete, and 3) one cannot be reduced to, or subsumed by, the other, at least not completely.

The generalized complementarity principle finds an interesting and beautiful comparison with the Chinese yin–yang principle discussed in Chapter 11. For the Chinese these two complementary realities are the basis of operation for all things in the world. Recall that yin represents the passive, feminine, and intuitive aspect of things, while yang corresponds to the active, masculine, and rational aspect of things. Therefore, the notion of complementarity is instinctive and deep–seated in China and is not new. Indeed Bohr became aware of this after a visit to China and found so much beauty in, and identity with, the yin–yang principle that he incorporated the yin–yang symbol in his coat–of–arms and often used it to represent complementarity. For time comparisons, yin would obviously be associated with intuitive (subjective) time and yang with rational (objective) time. Then by its very nature the principle tells us that the subjective and objective modes are in continual mutual interplay in characterizing evolving time.

At first sight it may seem contradictory to claim on the one hand that there may be some validity to the application of generalized complementarity to objective and subjective time concepts as a duality, and on the other to maintain that the viewpoints of physics and religion (the primary representatives of objectivity and subjectivity in this book) give roughly similar perceptions of several aspects of time. These include especially the question of whether time began, the irreversible evolving nature of time, its relation to space, and the notion of timelessness.

In the first place this application of complementarity is much more general with some attendant diffuseness in definition; that is, here the two aspects cannot be defined with logic as rigorous as in the case of the wave–particle dualism. Second, just because two modes of observation give complementary and mutually exclusive views of a phenomenon does not mean that they cannot at least say some of the same things about it. For example, light, whether conceived of as a wave or as a photon, carries energy.

Another possible path to temporal unity is suggested in the thought of David Park. In his "Image of Eternity" he posits two kinds of time which he calls Time 1 and Time 2 (Park 80). In essence Time 1 is the time of physical theory that is represented in the equations of physics and registered on a clock dial. Time 2 is the time of human consciousness, with its access to a living present. Thus he also sees time as characterized by some form of objective–subjective duality, but he speculates that there may be some connection between the two components of the duality which might be realized through a deeper understanding of the human brain. His suggestion may have some merit, particularly if we extend it to consider what has been learned in recent decades about the interactive operation of the left and right hemispheres of the brain. Generally the left hemisphere performs more analytic and rational tasks while the right handles more intuitive and instinctive responses. This seems at least partially consistent with evidence which indicates that the left brain is dominant in distinguishing the temporal order of two closely timed events, while the right brain possesses a better sense of time duration as well as velocity and acceleration (Levi 84). This is a fertile area for continuing active study in experimental psychology, and additional interesting results should be forthcoming.

However, the foregoing speculations as to how the subjective and objective views of time may be integrated thus far seem somewhat incomplete or unsatisfying. Perhaps if we reexamine the nature of each of these views a little more carefully, we may find some clues as to whether one view should be considered dominant or primary, or at least understand more clearly their relationship. To this end let us look at the two perceptions separately by considering the case for each. Perhaps we can best do this by means of a little story.

Longfellow and Einstein. One sunny afternoon Henry Wadsworth Longfellow and Albert Einstein chance to meet in heaven. They soon become engaged in conversation, and after a while Einstein invites Longfellow into his celestial study. It isn't long before they begin to focus on the subject of time. The discussion becomes quite lively, with Einstein scribbling equations on the blackboard and Longfellow remonstrating vigorously with his arms.

They stop for a moment, Einstein fondles his pipe, then says, "Mr. Longfellow, let me ask you this. Is not the intuitive, spiritual view of time to a considerable extent a matter of individual and unique personal experience that would never be identical in a total or absolute sense to the experience of others, though it may bear some similarity? A fundamental criterion for any rational, and in particular any scientific, endeavor is that the method's logic and/or observation be clearly specified and be such that it can be performed by anyone properly equipped (methodologically and/or with instruments). Furthermore, the results of such logic and/or observation should be capable of being reproduced by anyone using the same methods. Therefore, is it not true that we can only find a universally agreed upon concept of time, independent of individual human bias, through a rational, scientific approach?"

Longfellow sits quietly, deep in thought. Einstein draws on his pipe once more and continues. "Cannot a physical concept of time describe the temporal behavior of each of the atoms that contribute to the material composition of our bodies? Indeed, does not a physical concept of time also describe the temporal behavior of an incredibly vast array of natural phenomena throughout a universe, whose size makes us seem exceedingly insignificant? How could we have revealed the remarkable temporal behavior described by the relativity and quantum theories without objective study and rational analysis? In short how can we say that we can ever fully understand something as enigmatic as time if we do not utilize all of the objective analysis available to us?"

Feeling rather satisfied with himself, Einstein ceases his questions. After a prolonged moment Longfellow shakes himself from his contemplation and finally speaks, "Well professor, I must admit that what you have said is indeed impressive, but it still does not tell the whole story. Is not virtually all of rational, objective, or measured time somehow rendered static, abstracted, idealized, or spatialized? The physical time we rationally think about and measure is recorded on a clock dial or on one of those new-fangled digital readouts; or recorded in terms of some fixed array of molecules in the memory bank at a location in our brain or in one of those terrifying computers that are around nowadays; or set down on a piece of paper in some mathematical equation or plotted on a graph. All these are spatial or static in one way or another. The living present that we subjectively and spiritually experience is for most of us the truest and deepest reality we know, and the only way to capture the holistic essence of time. An acorn falling from an oak tree can have its time of fall recorded, its trajectory of fall analyzed, and its impact on the earth measured. But to one in the living 'now' its reality is expressed as a living event in a dynamic and vibrant universe."

Longfellow hesitates for a moment, gives his beard a thoughtful tug and continues. "Perhaps your contemporary, Alfred North Whitehead, is right when he faults physical scientists for not using human senses in a much more direct fashion to describe adequately the nature around us. Are not rational time and physical time then an extrapolation from this experienced time and find their value in all of the fascinating and practically useful detailing in terms of abstract equations and physical models? Can our notion of time derived from intuition and spirituality therefore be likened to the trunk and roots of a tree, while our rational and physical views correspond to its branches and leaves?"[1]

Longfellow pauses, then suggests, "Professor Einstein why don't you put down your chalk, give the blackboard a rest, and sit down for a minute. Let me read you something I wrote many years ago:

> What is time? The shadow of the dial, the striking of the clock, the running of the sand, day and night, summer and winter, months, years, centuries—these are but arbitrary and outward signs, the measures of Time, not Time itself. Time is the life of the soul."

Longfellow feels he has made his point and can say no more. Both men sit in silent thought for several minutes, Longfellow gently stroking his beard and Einstein quietly puffing his pipe. Finally Einstein slowly sets down his pipe, picks up his violin, and begins to play....

Perhaps this episode may illustrate that the question of which view of time is the most fundamental and real is rather unsettled and may continue indefinitely to engage the thought of philosophers, physicists, biologists, psychologists, and religious scholars. However, now that some of the advantages and strengths of each perception of time have been specified, let us further explore how they may possibly be integrated, and not regarded as irreconcilable polar opposites. In other words, can these apparently different viewpoints be looked upon in a way that reveals some evidence for an underlying unity, perhaps more unity than the generalized complementarity principle can provide?

---

[1]This analogy is due to F. Capra (Capra 77).

Universal Temporal Ordering. I believe that to extract evidence from what has thus far been said for time possessing an underlying unity, we must accept the position that it is a universal property of all nature. There is clear evidence that there was a long time duration experienced by the universe in general, and this planet in particular, before we ever arrived on the scene. Then we finally do arrive on the scene and begin to think about it. We sense its moment–to–moment passage in our living, we observe and assess its cumulative effects in our lives and on our environment. Indeed this temporal passage is seen by many as "a window of opportunity" for a spiritual access to God, an opportunity for unity with, and for an understanding of, God, i.e. an opportunity for salvation.

We also examine time by performing what we call time measurements, that is, by comparing the physical process under study with another regularly paced repetitive process, e.g. periodicity of the sun or the oscillations of radiation emitted by a cesium atom. Perforce in recording these measurements we must use spatial or static representations. This is a valid procedure as long as we do not become so emotionally enamored of spatial metaphors that we begin to obscure the inherent dynamism of time.

But regardless of whether we mentally experience the continual chain of moments in our lives or observe the number of seconds in the fall of an apple, we sense that both our mental processes and the apple's motion are somehow embraced in a common temporal framework. All of the cyclical, repetitive, and oscillatory phenomena continuously operating in our bodies, and especially in our brain, delicately and precisely synchronize to somehow produce the miracle of consciousness, a consciousness of temporal order in full harmony with the temporal order of the changes we observe in the external world. This idea, and the coherence it brings, is clearly expressed by Kenneth Denbigh in his incisive work, "Three Concepts of Time":

> Furthermore both sorts of events, mental and physical, define *the same* temporal order, since experienced "presents" can be placed in a one to one correspondence with sets of external events. The concept of time thus provides a common ground (Denbigh 81, p. 153).

He expresses this thought even more cogently earlier in his book:

> It seems that *all* experienced events can be accommodated within a *single* temporal order, and this is a very remarkable empirical fact, one of the most striking simplicities in nature which have ever been discovered. There appear to be no events which cannot be so accommodated. In other words, *particular* sequences, such as deaths of

kings and queens, stages in the growth of a tree, the movements of the stars, etc., do not require separate temporal orders of their own (Denbigh 81, p. 21).

It is this characteristic of nature that all phenomena, mental and physical, are encompassed in a single universal temporal sequence[2] that may provide us with a starting point in our search for temporal unity. This unity is further suggested by the general similarities that have been described in religious and physical perceptions of such aspects of time as the question of its beginning, its irreversible progressive character, its relation to space, and the notion of timelessness.

These similarities in temporal perception along with the existence of a universal order may give us a glimmer of realization that there is indeed an underlying unity and that the subjective and objective approaches are ways, perhaps complementary ways, of perceiving aspects of that unity. It is from this starting point that we next approach the daunting question: "What is Time?"

SUMMARY

If we accept the prevailing conviction that time is in nature and not the converse, then absolute objectivity appears impossible. We are then forced to utilize jointly the available objectivity in conjunction with hopefully sensible subjectivity in investigating the problem of time. This fundamental subjective–objective duality in the perception of time was seen to be informed by at least five specific and different dualities that have been discussed at various stages in the book: I-Thou and I-It, A and B series, succession and duration, past to future and future to past, sacred and profane time. The dualities are versions of, aspects of, or help define, the general subjective–objective duality.

As a first attempt at a reconciliation of the subjective and objective views of time, a generalization of Bohr's Complementarity Principle as well as the yin–yang principle was suggested. It seemed reasonable that these principles might find application to the subjective–objective duality in providing some degree of unity by virtue of their broad conceptual frameworks. Another suggested path toward a unified view of time would be through a deeper understanding of the human brain. In particular this might be true of a thorough study of the temporal aspects of the right and left brain as essentially representing the intuitive and rational modes of the brain, respectively.

---

[2]At least at the macroscopic level and in a given frame of reference according to the theory of relativity.

The case for each of the two perceptions of time was presented. From Longfellow's viewpoint, objective time has a static quality and almost always suffers from a tendency to spatialize time. Only the human intuitive experience of time can capture its holistic dynamism. On the other hand Einstein maintained that only rational and analytical study can reveal a concept of time that is free from individual bias. Using the scientific method, our temporal scope extends from the microscopic to the cosmologic domain, and the relativity and quantum theories have afforded us concepts of time never before envisioned.

Without claiming either the subjective or objective position as ascendent, it was suggested that a basis for some underlying unity might be found through the fact that each is subjected to a common time ordering. In Kenneth Denbigh's opinion this universal commonality is one of the greatest discoveries about nature. This common temporal ordering along with the similarities that have been discussed regarding several aspects of time provide a basis in the search for an understanding of time as a unity.

17 WHAT IS TIME?

But it is not *in* time itself that everything comes to be and passes away, rather time itself is the *becoming*, this coming–to–be and passing away, the actual existent abstraction, *Chronos*,...

—G. W. F. Hegel

What, then, is time? I know well enough what it is, provided nobody asks me....

—St. Augustine

Although St. Augustine's remark may seem slightly trivial or facetious, it is probably true that most people probably do feel that they know what time is, provided nobody asks them. Despite the 27 different definitions of time to be found in Webster's Dictionary, most people seem to speak and act as if they instinctively know what time is. Actually there appears to be some anthropological and linguistic basis for this statement.

In a recent fascinating study by Hoyt Alverson, the time–relevant expressions of people speaking four very disparate, entirely independent languages in widely separated parts of the world were analyzed and categorized (Alverson 94, pgs. 67–91). The four he chose were American English, Mandarin, Hindi–Urdu, and Sesotho.[1] He collected time–relevant idioms, aphorisms, cliches, figures of speech, fragments of proverbs, and other frequently used expressions of time. These expressions were then sorted into five general categories:

1) Time as used, particularized, or valued (e.g. save time, waste time, time is ripe, allot time, borrowed time)

2) Effects of time (e.g. time–worn, time heals, time reveals, father time)

---

[1] Alverson deliberately chose Sesotho because there is little writing in this society. It is spoken in the tiny Kingdom of Lesotho, one of the several small "enclave" nations surrounded by South Africa.

3) Time and motion (e.g. time marches on, flow of time, time stood still)

4) Time as a course (e.g. a long time, once upon a time, time and time again)

5) Ascertaining or measuring time (e.g. keep time, mind time, tell time, gain time) (Alverson 94).

For each of the four languages there were numerous expressions that fell into each of the five categories. Though there are understandable idiosyncrasies peculiar to each language, this definitive study reveals convincing evidence for a remarkable uniformity among humans around the globe in their response to change, motion, and process in themselves and their environment. Common to these diverse cultures, there seems to be an archetypical, instinctive sense about what time is. In discussing this commonality Alverson invokes the thought of Merleau–Ponty by suggesting it arises from a fundamental bio–cultural grounding (Alverson 92).

Thus men and women among a full spectrum of cultures appear to be aware of a temporal ordering that is common to both themselves (their bodies and minds) and the surrounding natural world, as discussed in the previous chapter. However, if anyone in any of these cultures begins to philosophize or theorize about time, and try to say what time is, the written or verbal results are undoubtedly as varied and legion as the stars in the sky. This certainly seems to be true among the philosophers of time. Recall Whitrow's observation that very generally many philosophers seem to fall into two opposing camps: those who would eliminate time as a reality altogether, and those who find it a fundamental and irreducible property of the world (Whitrow 80, pgs. 1, 370). Obviously there is an entire spectrum of thought in between these two extreme positions. This despite the fact that certainly in their daily lives these philosophers, regardless of their writings, conduct themselves as if there were a reality called time, again in large part due to this universal temporal ordering common to themselves, their neighbors, and their world.

Conversely, the fact that we can sense, talk about, and at least nebulously identify something we call time implies a remarkable degree of order in the world (Rosen 91), some form of ordered relationization of the motions of the world. For me it is this relational ordering of events that is central to addressing the question: "What is Time?" While, as we have noted in several instances, time and motion are intimately related, they are not the same. Aristotle said that time is the measure of

A commonality in human time: as skiers come down a relatively steep slope which had an initially smooth surface, bumps (called moguls) begin to form. The geometric patterning of the moguls is a remarkable testimony to the uniformity of human timing.

motion, but it is through the relativization of motions that time can be the measurer. Whether we are observing a deer's flight across a field and into the woods or are watching an apple at rest on the ground underneath a tree, the time duration involved is measured either through the relation to the temporal awareness made possible by the ongoing synchronized and pulsating motions comprising the life of our mind and body, or by the relation to some other motion, or assembly of motions, such as a clock.

Thus while it is certainly true that there can be no time without motion, the time that something remains at rest can still be measured because of its relation to something that is undergoing some form of motion; that is, motion is still involved. But again, time is not the same as motion. Time is a coherent orchestration of motions and the events they produce which collectively give rise to becoming. In a word, events are realized becomings and time is becoming. It is measured by comparison to another uniformly repetitive becoming.

At what threshold level in the physical world time may have meaning remains a moot question. As indicated in Chapters 8 and 9, I have posed the question: How many moving particles does it take for their collective interaction and relation to cohere to yield what we would call time, at least in some primitive form?

Posing this question reflects my belief that time has some reality independent of human existence. Again, there was a long time, much evolution, a vast multiplicity of becomings, before we emerged in this world. Thus I feel that at some level in the natural world time begins to have meaning as a symphony of interactive motions. Perhaps as soon as there are enough particles in motion so that some relating, irreversible ordering of their motions and the events (realized becomings) they produce is possible and meaningful, then there may be time.

Time develops its meaning in its ability to embrace and be descriptive of larger and larger complexes of dynamic matter. It is becoming, but also the coherent ordering of an assembly of becomings, including human becoming. The past is becoming because it is always being added to, the present because it is always new, the future because the configuration of its potentialities is always being rearranged through the loss of those that have been chosen to become the present.

For me time is an example of something that is greater than the sum of its parts. In this respect I find time analogous to consciousness. Consciousness may be perceived as a miraculous integration of an incredible complexity of phenomena in the brain, but it even transcends this description, and thus is greater, greater by far, than the sum of its parts. Perhaps time cannot make so lofty a claim; nevertheless, I see time as greater than the sum of its parts, the parts being the motions and the successive becomings they bring about. These motions and events in their relation and irreversible succession cohere to exhibit the property we call time. As such it is empirically real as the process of becoming that characterizes the world (Sherover 75, p. 166).

Indeed time and mind, with its consciousness, somehow go hand and hand. The brain occupies space and is describable in considerable part in spatial terms. However, mind and consciousness localize in no particular space, and so are essentially temporal in nature.

Therefore the domain of time as a meaningful descriptive and universal property of our world extends from primitive material phenomena to the human mind, and even to the ensemble of minds, often called the collective consciousness. Indeed it extends further; from a spiritual perspective it projects beyond the human mind to merge and interface with the timeless eternity of the God or whatever Reality that generated and sustains this universe. It is with a spiritual perspective that the full scope, richness, and dynamism of time that is available to us can be perceived, and its timeless grounding sensed.

It is because of my conviction of the value of this spiritual perspective that I have attempted this synthesis of physical and religious time views. This attempt was in significant part due to the words of Sir Arthur Eddington, quoted in Chapter 1 but repeated here: "In any attempt to bridge the domains of experience belonging to the spiritual and physical sides of our nature, time occupies the key position" (Eddington 28, p. 91).

It is as if we ourselves, through a much more intimate integration of our spiritual and physical selves, might be able to sense time as the fluid link between the two, and thus concurrently see time as a unity. That is, no longer under the illusion that time is something we can grasp and inspect, by allowing ourselves to ride free in its becoming, we might identify with it and its vibrant, holistic, ever–changing nature and even sense the haunting apprehension of a timeless background presence. Realizing that we are somehow linked by time to our ancestors and will be to our progeny, perhaps we may even extend our perception to see time as some kind of cohesive connection with the rest of the universe and indeed to its earliest emergence, via that awesome limiting medium, the velocity of light (Fagg 85, p. 174).

With the universe, God or Nature has opened up, perhaps out of what may seem to be a point of nothing, a vast system of space, time, and matter for us to *be* and *become* in. Time has been granted us to understand our being in it and our true relation to its Origin. For man and woman it is especially time with its intrinsic vitality that is the means, the divine link, by which an interaction with God or Nature can be known. It is the telescope through which whatever may be Divine can be seen (Fagg 85, p. 174).

Modern physics has revealed the wondrous subtleties of time in the natural world, especially the arresting insights provided by the relativity and quantum theories. However, the central thrust of this book is that a more complete comprehension of time can only be achieved by incorporating a spiritual perspective with the physical view in a harmonious union of faith and reason. I believe that in so doing support has been found for seeing time as a unity, an holistic becoming, the subjective and objective perceptions of which are but different manifestations.

Years ago in the jungle of French Equatorial Africa, Albert Schweitzer, during his extensive pondering about life and its spiritual meaning, fervently sought a succinct expression that capsulized his thought. One day at sunset he was rewarded by a flash of inspiration with these words which are a beautiful distillation of his long contemplation: "Reverence for life" (Schweitzer 53, p. 124).

Though I may not have adequately answered the question, "What is Time?", I am convinced that unless there is a concomitant "Reverence for time," we will not have exhausted all possible means of understanding it.

BIBLIOGRAPHY

CHAPTER 1

Barbour 97 — I. Barbour, "Religion and Science" (Harper San Francisco, New York, 1997).

Barbour 90 — I. Barbour, "Religion in an Age of Science" (Harper Collins Publishers, New York, 1990).

Capra 77 — F. Capra, "The Tao of Physics" (Bantam Books, New York, 1977).

Davies 83 — P. Davies, "God and the New Physics" (Simon and Schuster, New York, 1983).

Denbigh 81 — K. G. Denbigh, "Three Concepts of Time" (Springer-Verlag, New York, 1981).

Eddington 28 — A. Eddington, "The Nature of the Physical World" (Cambridge University Press, Cambridge, 1928).

Eddington 29 — A. Eddington, "Science and the Unseen World" (Macmillan, New York, 1929).

Eddington 35 — A. Eddington, "New Pathways in Science" (Macmillan, New York, 1935).

Einstein 54 — A. Einstein, "Ideas and Opinions" (Crown Publishers, New York, 1954).

Heisenberg 71 — W. Heisenberg, "Physics and Beyond" (Harper and Row, New York, 1971).

Heisenberg 74 — W. Heisenberg, "Across the Frontiers" (Harper and Row, New York, 1974).

Jastrow 80 — R. Jastrow, "God and the Astronomers" (Warner Books, New York, 1980).

Jones 86 — R. Jones, "Science and Mysticism" (Bucknell University Press, Lewisburg, PA, 1986).

Park 80 — D. Park, "Image of Eternity" (University of Massachusetts Press, Amherst, 1980).

Peacocke 81 — A. Peacocke, editor, "The Sciences and Theology in the Twentieth Century" (University of Notre Dame Press, Notre Dame, IN, 1981).

Peacocke 90

A. Peacocke, "Theology for a Scientific Age" (Basil Blackwell, New York, 1990).

Polkinghorne 98

J. Polkinghorne, "Belief in God in an Age of Science" (Yale University Press, 1998).

Russell et al. 88

R. J. Russell, W. R. Stoeger, and G. V. Coyne, editors, "Physics, Philosophy, and Theology" (University of Notre Dame Press, Notre Dame, IN, 1988).

Russell et al. 93

R. J., Russell, N. Murphy, and C. J. Isham, editors, "Quantum Cosmology and the Laws of Nature" (Vatican Observatory Publications, Vatican, and Center for Theology and the Natural Sciences, Berkeley, 1993).

Schrödinger 47

E. S. Schrödinger, "What Is Life?" (Cambridge University Press, Cambridge, 1947).

Schrödinger 51

E. S. Schrödinger, "Science and Humanism" (Cambridge University Press, Cambridge, 1951).

Schrödinger 58

E. S. Schrödinger, "Mind and Matter" (Cambridge University Press, Cambridge, 1958).

Schrödinger 64

E. S. Schrödinger, "My View of the World" (Cambridge University Press, Cambridge, 1964).

Whitrow 80

G. J. Whitrow, "The Natural Philosophy of Time" (Clarendon Press, Oxford, 1980).

Wilbur 84

K. Wilbur, "Quantum Questions" (Shambhala, Boston, 1984).

Chapter 2

Aristotle 83

Aristotle, "The Physics, Book IV," (Oxford University Press, New York, 1983).

Augustine 61

St. Augustine, "Confessions," R. S. Pine-Coffin, translator (Penguin Books, Baltimore, 1961).

Benjamin 81

A. C. Benjamin, "Ideas of Time in the History of Philosophy," in "The Voices of Time," editor J. T. Fraser (University of Massachusetts Press, Amherst, 1981).

Bergson 10

H. Bergson, "Time and Free Will" (Macmillan, New York, 1910).

Bergson 65

H. Bergson, "Duration and Simultaneity" (Bobbs-Merrill Co., New York, 1965).

Heidegger 77

M. Heidegger, "On Time and Being" (Harper and Row, New York, 1977).

Mellert 75

R. B. Mellert, "What is Process Theology" (Paulist Press, New York, 1975).

Merleau-Ponty 62   M. Merleau-Ponty, "Phenomenology of Per-
                      ception" (Humanities Press, Atlantic
                      Highlands, NJ, 1962).

Roque 90   A. Roque, "Irreversibility or Eternal Return"
                      Smithsonian Lecture, November, 1990.

Sherover 75   C. M. Sherover, "The Human Experience of Time"
                      (New York University Press, New York, 1975).

Sherover 89   C. M. Sherover, "Concept of Time in Western
                      Thought" Smithsonian Lecture, June, 1989.

Thompson 71   K. Thompson, "Whitehead's Philosophy of
                      Religion" (Mouton and Co., The Hague, 1971).

Wassermann 92   C. W. Wassermann, "The Philosophy of Alfred
                      North Whitehead," lecture, conference of
                      European Society for the Study of Science and
                      Theology on "Origins, Time, and Complexity,"
                      Mondo Migliore, Italy, 1992.

Whitehead 19   A. N. Whitehead, "An Enquiry Concerning
                      Principles of Natural Knowledge" (Cambridge
                      University Press, London, 1919).

Whitehead 26   A. N. Whitehead, "Religion in the Making"
                      (Macmillan, New York, 1926).

Whitehead 29   A. N. Whitehead, "Process and Reality" (Harper
                      and Row, New York, 1929).

CHAPTER 3

Abramowicz 93   M. A. Abramowicz, "Black Holes and the
                      Centrifugal Force Paradox," Scientific American,
                      (March 1993), p. 74.

Denbigh 81   K. G. Denbigh, "Three Concepts of Time"
                      (Springer-Verlag, New York, 1981), quoting
                      C. D. Broad.

Einstein 20   A. Einstein, "The Special and General Theory"
                      (Metheun, London, 1920).

Feynman et al. 65   R. P. Feynman, R. B. Leighton, and M. Sands, "The
                      Feynman Lectures on Physics," Chaps. 15-16
                      (Addison-Wesley, New York, 1965).

Fraser 81   J. T. Fraser, editor, "The Voices of Time"
                      (University of Massachusetts Press, Amherst,
                      1981).

French 68   A. P. French, "Special Relativity" (W. W. Norton,
                      New York, 1968).

Harrison 85   E. Harrison, "Masks of the Universe" (Macmillan,
                      New York, 1985).

Michelson and Morley 1887   A. A. Michelson and E. W. Morley, Siliman Journal, Vol. 34 (1887), pp. 333-427.

Newton 1686   I. Newton, "Philosphiae Naturalis Principia Mathematica," 1686, as quoted in E. Marsh, "Science of Mechanics" (London, Open Court Publishing Co., 1907).

Pagels 85   H. Pagels, "Perfect Symmetry" (Simon and Schuster, New York, 1985).

Resnick 68   R. Resnick, "Introduction to Special Relativity" (Wiley, New York, 1968).

Taylor and Wheeler 66   E. F. Taylor and J. A. Wheeler, "Spacetime Physics" (W. H. Freeman and Co., San Francisco, 1966).

Wheeler 82   J. A. Wheeler, "Physics and Austerity: Law without Law" (University of Texas, Austin, 1982).

CHAPTER 4

Anandan 90   "Quantum Coherence," J. S. Anandan, editor (World Scientific, Singapore, 1990).

Aspect et al. 82   A. Aspect, J. Dalibard, and G. Roger, Physical Review Letters, Vol. 49 (1982), p. 1804.

Bell 64   J. S. Bell, "On the Einstein-Podolsky-Rosen Paradox," Physics Vol. 1 (1964), p. 195.

Bohm 80   D. Bohm, "Wholeness and the Implicate Order" (Routledge and Kegan Paul, London, 1980).

Bohm et al. 87   D. Bohm, B. J. Hiley, and P. N. Kaloyerou, Physics Reports, Vol. 144 (1987), p. 323ff, and p. 349ff.

Davies 88   P. Davies, "Time Asymmetry and Quantum Mechanics" in "The Nature of Time," editors R. Flood and M. Lockwood (Basil Blackwell, Inc., Cambridge, MA, 1988), p. 99.

Einstein et al. 35   A. Einstein, B. Podolsky, and N. Rosen, Physical Review, Vol. 47 (1935), p. 777.

Greenberger 94   D. Greenberger, Chairman, conference on "Fundamental Aspects of Quantum Theroy," Baltimore, June, 1994, proceedings to be published.

Hawking 88   S. W. Hawking, "A Brief History of Time" (Bantam Books, New York, 1988).

Herbert 85   N. Herbert, "Quantum Reality" (Anchor Press/Doubleday, Garden City, NY, 1985).

Kafatos 89   M. Kafatos, editor, "Bell's Theorem, Quantum Theory, and Conceptions of the Universe" (Kluwer Academic Publishers, Boston, 1989).

Pagels 82   H. Pagels, "The Cosmic Code" (Bantam Books, New York, 1982).

Peat 90   F. D. Peat, "Einstein's Moon" (Contemporary Books, Inc., Chicago, 1990).

Rosen 91   J. Rosen "Time, c, and Nonlocality: A glimpse beneath the surface," submitted for publication; J. Rosen, "The Capricious Cosmos" (Macmillan, New York, 1991).

Weidner and Sells 65   R. T. Weidner and R. L. Sells, Elementary Modern Physics (Allyn and Bacon, Inc., Boston, 1965).

Wheeler 76   J. A. Wheeler, "Genesis and Observership," Princeton University Report, 1976.

Wheeler 94   J. A. Wheeler, "At Home in the Universe" (American Institute of Physics Press, Woodbury, NY, 1994).

CHAPTER 5

Coe 69   L. Coe, "The Nature of Time," American Journal of Physics, Vol. 37 (1969), p. 810.

Feynman 85   R. P. Feynman, " Q. E. D." (Princeton University Press, Princeton, 1985).

Fraser 87   J. T. Fraser, "Time, the Familiar Stranger" (University of Massachusetts Press, Amherst, 1987).

Itano and Ramsey 93   W. Itano and N. Ramsey, "Accurate Measurement of Time," Scientific American, July, 1993, p. 56.

Kleppner 91   D. Kleppner, in "Physics Today," Vol. 44, No. 12, (1991), p. 9.

Manchester 92   R. Manchester, "Probing with Pulsars," lecture, Texas/Particles, Strings, and Cosmology Symposium, Berkeley, CA, 1992.

Morris 85   R. Morris, "Time's Arrows" (Simon and Schuster, New York, 1985).

Park 89   D. Park, private communication, 1989.

Richtmeyer and Kennard 47   F. K. Richtmeyer and E. H. Kennard "Introduction to Modern Physics " (McGraw-Hill, New York, 1947).

Wheeler and Feynman 45   J. A. Wheeler and R. P. Feynman, Reviews of Modern Physics, Vol. 17 (1945), p. 157.

CHAPTER 6

Balslev 83   A. N. Balslev, "A Study of Time in Indian Philosophy" (Otto Harrassowitz, Wiesbaden, 1983).

Balslev 90
A. N. Balslev, "Cosmology and Hindu Thought," Zygon, Vol. 25 (1990), p. 47.

Brown 77
R. Brown, "The Birth of the Messiah" (Doubleday, New York, 1977).

Conze 67
E. Conze, "Buddhist Thought in India" (University of Michigan Press, Ann Arbor, 1967).

Chung-yuan 75
C. Chung-yuan, translator "Tao: A New Way of Thinking" (Harper and Row, New York, 1975).

Delling 65
G. Delling in "Theological Dictionary of the New Testament," Vol. 3, R. Kittel, editor (William B. Erdmans Publishing Co., Grand Rapids, MI, 1965).

Eliade 71
M. Eliade, "Myth of the Eternal Return" (Princeton University Press, Princeton, 1971).

Fitzgerald 42
E. Fitzgerald, "The Rubaiyat of Omar Khayyam" (Walter J. Black, New York, 1942).

Girardot 90
N. Girardot, " Healing Time: Traditional Chinese Concepts of Time," Smithsonian Lecture, November, 1990.

Goodman 93
L. E. Goodman, "Time in Islam," in "Religion and Time," editors A. N. Balslev and J. N. Mohanty (E. J. Brill, New York, 1993).

Harrison 85
E. Harrison, "Masks of the Universe," (Macmillan, New York, 1985).

Hopkins 71
T. J. Hopkins, "The Hindu Religious Tradition" (Dickenson Publishing Co., Belmont, CA, 1971).

Hourani 75
G. F. Hourani, "Essays on Islamic Philosophy and Science" (State University of New York Press, Albany, 1975).

Nikhilananda 63
S. Nikhilananda, "The Upanishads" (Harper and Row, New York, 1963).

Panikkar 78
R. Panikkar, "Time and Sacrifice - The Sacrifice of Time and the Ritual of Modernity," in "The Study of Time III" editors J. T. Fraser, N. Lawrence, and D. Park (Springer-Verlag, New York, 1978).

Pannenberg 91
W. Pannenberg, "Systematic Theology, Volume 1," translator G. W. Bromiley (William B. Erdmans, Grand Rapids, MI, 1991).

Peters 93
T. Peters, "The Trinity in the Beyond Time" in "Quantum Cosmology and the Laws of Nature," editors, R. J. Russell, N. Murphy, and C. J. Isham (Vatican Observatory Publications, Vatican City State, 1993).

Reyna 71

R. Reyna, "Introduction to Indian Philosophy" (Tate McGraw-Hill, Bombay, 1971).

Torrance 69

T. F. Torrance, "Space, Time, and Resurrection" (Oxford University Press, New York, 1969).

von Rad 65

G. von Rad, "The Message of the Prophets" (Harper and Row, New York, 1965).

Welch 57

H. Welch, "Taoism, The Parting of the Way" (Beacon Press, Boston, 1957).

Yeide 90

H. Yeide, "The Seeds of Linear Temporality in Biblical Tradition," Smithsonian Lecture, 1990.

CHAPTER 7

Augustine 61

St. Augustine, "Confessions," R. S. Pine-Coffin, translator (Penguin Books, Baltimore, 1961).

Barrow and Tipler 86

J. D. Barrow and F. J. Tipler, "The Anthropic Cosmological Principle" (Oxford University Press, New York, 1986).

Barrow 91

J. D. Barrow, "Theories of Everything," (Clarendon Press, Oxford, 1991).

Burwasser 88

D. Burwasser, commentary, conference of Institute on Religion in an Age of Science on "Cosmology and the Meaning of Human Existence," Star Island, NH, 1988.

Campbell 88

J. Campbell, "The Power of Myth," (Doubleday, New York, 1988).

Dicus et al. 83

D. A. Dicus, J. R. LeTaw, D. C. Teplitz, and V. L. Teplitz, Scientific American, Vol. 248, March, 1983, p. 91.

Fagg 85

L. W. Fagg, "Two Faces of Time," (Quest Books, Theosophical Publishing House, Wheaton, IL, 1985).

Guth 86

A. H. Guth, Bulletin of the American Physical Society, invited paper, Vol. 31 (1986), p. 807.

Guth and Steinhardt 84

A. Guth and P. Steinhardt, "The Inflationary Universe," Scientific American, May, 1984.

Halliwell 91

J. Halliwell, "Quantum Cosmology and the Creation of the Universe," Scientific American, December, 1991.

Halliwell 92

J. Halliwell, "Quantum Cosmology and Time Asymmetry," in Proceedings of NATO workshop, "Physical Origins of Time Asymmetry," editors J. Halliwell, J. Perez-Mercades, and W. Zurek (Cambridge University Press, Cambridge, 1992).

Harrison 85   E. Harrison "Masks of the Universe," (Macmillan, New York, 1985).

Hartle and Hawking 83   J. B. Hartle and S. W. Hawking, "A Wave Function of the Universe," Physical Review D, Vol. 28 (1983), p. 2960.

Hawking 88   S. W. Hawking, "A Brief History of Time" (Bantam Books, New York, 1988).

Hawking et al. 93   S. W. Hawking, R. Laflamme, and G. W. Lyons, Physical Review D, Vol. 47 (1993), p. 5342.

Linde 84   A. Linde, "Quantum Creation of the Inflationary Universe," Il Nuovo Cimento, Vol. 39 (1984), p. 401.

Linde 87   A. Linde, "Particle Physics and Inflationary Cosmology," Physics Today, September, 1987.

Linde et al. 94   A. Linde, D. Linde, and A. Mezhlumian, Physical Review D, Vol. 49 (1994), p. 1783.

Long 63   C. H. Long "Alpha: The Myths of Creation" (George Braziller, New York, 1963).

Pagels 85   H. Pagels, "Perfect Symmetry" (Simon and Schuster, New York, 1985).

Peebles 92   J. Peebles, "Status of the Big Bang Model," lecture, Texas/Particles, Strings, and Cosmology Symposium, Berkeley, CA, 1992.

Physics Today 92   Physics Today, p. 17, June, 1992.

Salami and Friaca 92   R. R. Salami and A. C. S. Friaca, "Cosmic Time and Individual Time in Yoruba Thought and Life," contributed paper, conference of International Society for the Study of Time on "Time and Life," Cerisy-la-Salle, France, 1992.

Smoot et al. 92   G. F. Smoot, et al., "Structure in the COBE Differential Microwave Radiometer First-Year Maps," Astrophysical Journal Letters, Vol. 396 (1992), p. L1.

Turner 91   M. Turner, invited paper, Nuclear Physics Division Meeting of the American Physical Society, Champaign, IL, October, 1991.

Vilenkin 84   A. Vilenkin, "Quantum Creation of Universes," Physical Review D, Vol. 30 (1984), p. 509.

Weinberg 77   S. Weinberg, "The First Three Minutes" (Bantam Books, New York, 1977).

Wheeler 76   J. A. Wheeler "Genesis and Observership," Princeton University Report, Princeton, NJ, 1976.

Zeh 89   H. D. Zeh, "The Physical Basis for the Direction of Time" (Springer-Verlag, New York, 1989).

CHAPTER 8

Aristotle 83   Aristotle, "The Physics, Book IV," (Oxford University Press, New York, 1983).

Augustine 61   St. Augustine, "Confessions," R. S. Pine-Coffin, translator (Penguin Books, Baltimore, 1961).

Benjamin 81   A. C. Benjamin, "Ideas of Time in the History of Philosophy," in "The Voices of Time," editor J. T. Fraser (University of Massachusetts Press, Amherst, 1981).

Browne 93   M. W. Browne, "Migrating Birds Set Compasses by Sunlight and Stars," New York Times, Sept. 28, 1993.

Coveney and Highfield 91   P. Coveney and R. Highfield, "The Arrow of Time," (Fawcett Columbine, div. of Random House, New York, 1991).

Denbigh 81   K. G. Denbigh, "Three Concepts of Time" (Springer-Verlag, New York, 1981).

Lobban 60   M. C. Lobban, "The Entrainment of Circadian Rhythms in Man," in "Cold Spring Harbor Symp. 25, Biological Clocks," 1960.

Menaker 89   M. Menaker, lecture at "Cycle and Arrows" conference, University of Virginia, April, 1989.

Prigogine 80   I. Prigogine, "From Being to Becoming," (W. H. Freeman and Co., San Francisco, 1980.

Schlegel 68   R. Schlegel, "Time and the Physical World," (Dover Publications, New York, 1968).

Whitrow 80   G. J. Whitrow, "The Natural Philosophy of Time," (Oxford University Press, New York, 1980).

CHAPTER 9

Arecchi 92   F. T. Arecchi, "A critical approach to complexity and self organization," lecture, conference of European Society for the Study of Science and Theology on "Origins, Time, and Complexity," Mondo Migliore, Italy, 1992.

Balslev 90   A. N. Balslev, "Cosmology and Hindu Thought," Zygon, Vol. 25 (1990), p. 47.

Buber 58   M. Buber, "I and Thou," R. G. Smith, translator (Charles Scribner's Sons, New York, 1958).

Coveney and Highfield 90   P. Coveney and J. Highfield, "The Arrow of Time" (Fawcett Columbine, New York, 1990).

Denbigh 81

K. G. Denbigh, "Three Concepts of Time" (Springer-Verlag, New York, 1981).

Fadner 92

W. Fadner, "Time's Arrow in Quantum Mechanics," Bulletin of the American Physical Society, Vol. 37, p. 965 (1992).

Gleick 87

J. Gleick, "Chaos" (Viking Penguin Inc., New York, 1987).

Hawking 88

S. W. Hawking, "A Brief History of Time" (Bantam, New York, 1988).

Hawking et al. 93

S. W. Hawking, R. Laflamme, and G. W. Lyons, "Origin of Time Asymmetry," Physical Review D, Vol. 47 (1993), p. 5342.

Jones 86

R. H. Jones, "Science and Mysticism" (Associated Universities Presses, Cranbury, N.J., 1986).

Kadanoff 83

L. P. Kadanoff, Physics Today, Vol. 36, p. 46 (1983).

Layzer 75

D. Layzer, "The Arrow of Time," Scientific American, Vol. 256, p. 56 (1975).

McTaggart 27

J. M. E. McTaggart, "The Nature of Existence" (Cambridge University Press, Cambridge, 1927)

Morris 85

R. Morris, "Time's Arrows" (Simon and Schuster, New York, 1985).

Pagels 85

H. Pagels, "Perfect Symmetry" (Simon and Schuster, New York, 1985).

Park 80

D. Park, "Image of Eternity" (University of Massachusetts Press, Amherst, 1980).

Penrose 89

R. Penrose, "The Emperor's New Mind" (Oxford University Press, Oxford, 1989).

Piaget 81

J. Piaget, "Time Perception in Children," in "The Voices of Time," editor J. T. Fraser (University of Massachusetts Press, Amherst, 1981).

Prigogine 80

I. Prigogine, "From Being to Becoming" (Freeman, San Francisco, 1980).

Prigogine and Stengers 84

I. Prigogine and I. Stengers, "Order Out of Chaos" (Heinemann, London, 1984).

Puddefoot 92

J. Puddefoot, "The Notion of Complexity," lecture, conference of European Society for the Study of Science and Theology on "Origins, Time, and Complexity," Mondo Migliore, Italy, 1992.

Teilhard de Chardin 68

P. Teilhard de Chardin, "Turmoil or Genesis?" originally published in "L'Anthropologie," Paris, 1947. Translated in "Science and Religion," editor I. Barbour (Harper and Row, New York, 1968).

Verstraeten 91   G. Verstraeten, "Some Critical Remarks Concerning Prigogine's Conception of Temporal Irreversibility," Philosophy of Science, Vol. 58, p. 639 (1991).

Whitehead 19   A. N. Whitehead, "An Enquiry Concerning the Principles of Natural Knowledge" (Cambridge University Press, London, 1919).

Whitrow 80   G. J. Whitrow, "The Natural Philosophy of Time" (Oxford University Press, Oxford, 1980).

Zeh 89   H. D. Zeh, "The Physical Basis of the Direction of Time" (Springer-Verlag, New York, 1989).

Zermelo 1896   E. Zermelo, Annalen Phys. Vol. 57 (1896), p. 485.

CHAPTER 10

Alexander 20   S. Alexander, "Space, Time, and Deity," Vol. 1, (Humanities Press, Atlantic Highlands, NJ, 1920).

Benjamin 81   A. C. Benjamin, "Ideas of Time in the History of Philosophy," in "The Voices of Time," editor J. T. Fraser (University of Massachusetts Press, Amherst, 1981).

Capek 81   M. Capek, "Time in Relativity Theory: Arguments for a Philosophy of Becoming," in "The Voices of Time," editor J. T. Fraser (University of Massachusetts Press, Amherst, MA, 1981).

Capra 77   F. Capra, "The Tao of Physics," (Bantam, New York, 1977).

Cohen et al. 55   J. Cohen, C. E. Hansel, and J. D. Sylvester, "Interdependence in judgments of space, time, and movement," Acta Psychologica, Vol. 11, p. 750 (1955).

Denbigh 81   H. G. Denbigh, "Three Concepts of Time" (Springer-Verlag, New York, 1981).

Eliot 35   C. N. E. Eliot, "Japanese Buddhism" (Edward Arnold and Co., London, 1935).

Finklestein 89   D. Finklestein, "Quantum Net Dynamics," International Journal of Theoretical Physics, Vol. 28, p. 441 (1989).

Finklestein and Hallidy 91   D. Finklestein and W. H. Hallidy, "An Algebraic Language for Quantum-Spacetime Topology," International Journal of Theoretical Physics, Vol. 30, p. 463 (1991).

Govinda 69   Lama Anagarika Govinda, "Foundations of Tibetan Mysticism" (Samuel Weiser, Inc., York Beach, ME, 1969).

Hamilton 1837 — W. R. Hamilton, "Theory of Conjugate Functions on Algebraic Couples, with a Preliminary and Elementary Essay on Algebra as the Science of Pure Time," Transactions of the Royal Irish Academy, Vol.17 (1837), p. 293-422.

Helson and King 31 — H. Helson and S. M. King, "An example of psychologic relativity," Journal of Experimental Psychology, Vol. 14, p. 202 (1931).

Piaget 81 — J. Piaget, "Time Perception in Children," in "The Voices of Time," editor J. T. Fraser (University of Massachusetts Press, Amherst, MA, 1981).

Rosen 93 — J. Rosen, "The Physics of Einstein's Special Theory of Relativity," lecture, Smithsonian Institution, January, 1993.

Suzuki 38 — D. T. Suzuki in Introduction to B. L. Suzuki "Mahayana Buddhism" (The Buddhist Lodge, London, p. xxvii, 1938).

Suzuki 68 — D. T. Suzuki, "The Essence of Buddhism" (Hozoken, Tokyo, 1968).

Toben and Wolf 83 — R. Toben and F. A. Wolf, "Space, Time, and Beyond" (Bantam Books, New York, 1983).

Whitehead 20 — A. N. Whitehead, "The Concept of Nature" (Cambridge University Press, London, 1920).

Whitrow 80 — G. J. Whitrow, "The Natural Philosophy of Time" (Clarendon Press, Oxford, 1980).

CHAPTER 11

Balslev 83 — A. Balslev, "A Study of Time in Indian Philosophy" (Otto Harrassowitz, Wiesbaden, 1983).

Buber 57 — M. Buber, "Distance and Relation," William Alanson White Memorial Lecture, Psychiatry, Vol. 20 (1957), p. 97.

Buber 58 — M. Buber, "I and Thou," R. G. Smith, translator (Charles Scribner's Sons, New York, 1958).

Buber 60 — M. Buber, "The Origin and Meaning of Hasidism," M. Friedman, translator (Horizon Press, New York, 1960).

Calebresi 30 — R. Calebresi, "La Determinazione del Presente Psichico" (Bempored, Florence, 1930).

Denbigh 81 — K. G. Denbigh, "Three Concepts of Time" (Springer-Verlag, New York, 1981).

Fagg 85 — L. W. Fagg, "Two Faces of Time" (Quest Books, Theosophical Publishing House, Wheaton, IL, 1985).

Fraisse 69

P. Fraisse, "The Psychology of Time" (Eyre and Spottiswoode, London, 1969).

Girardot 90

N. Girardot, "Healing Time: Traditional Chinese Concepts of Time," Smithsonian Lecture, November, 1990.

Hammerschmidt 47

W. W. Hammerschmidt, "Whitehead's Philosophy of Time" (Russell and Russell, New York, 1947).

James 1890

W. James, "The Principles of Psychology" (reprinted Dover Publications, New York, 1950).

Kaltenmark 69

M. Kaltenmark, "Lao Tzu and Taoism," R. Greaves, translator (Stanford University Press, Stanford, 1969).

Kawamura 92

L. Kawamura, lecture, conference of Institute on Religion in an Age of Science on "Global Ecology and Human Destiny," Star Island, NH, 1992.

Kierkegaard 57

S. Kierkegaard, "The Concept of Dread," translator W. Lowrie (Princeton Universtiy Press, Princeton, 1957).

Lee 83

T. D. Lee, "Time as a Dynamical Variable and Discrete Mechanics," Bulletin of the American Pysical Society, Vol. 28, 1983, p. 700; "Can Time be a Discrete Dynamical Variable?" Physics Letters, Vol. 122B, 1983, p. 217.

Legge 63

J. Legge, translator, "The I Ching" (Dover Publications, Inc., New York, 1963).

Macar 80

F. Macar, "Le Temps-Perspectives and Physiologiques" (Pierre Mardagy, Brussels, 1980).

Macar 92

F. Macar, private communication, 1992.

Mellert 75

R. B. Mellert, "What is Process Theology" (Paulist Press, New York, 1975).

Pankenir 88

D. Pankenir, lecture, conference of Institute on Religion in an Age of Science on "Cosmology and the Meaning of Human Existence," Star Island, NH, 1988.

Reichenbach 56

H. Reichenbach, "The Direction of Time" (University of California Press, Berkeley, 1956).

Schrödinger 83

E. Schrödinger, "My View of the World" (Ox Bow Press, Woodridge, CT, 1983).

Thompson 71

K. Thompson, "Whitehead's Philosophy of Religion" (Mouton and Co., The Hague, 1971).

Whitehead 19

A. N. Whitehead, "An Enquiry Concerning the Principles of Natural Knowledge" (Cambridge University Press, London, 1919).

Whitehead 20   A. N. Whitehead, "The Concept of Nature"
                      (Cambridge University Press, London, 1920).

Whitehead 26   A. N. Whitehead, "Religion in the Making"
                      (Macmillan Co., New York, 1926).

Whitehead 29   A. N. Whitehead, "Process and Reality"
                      (Cambridge University Press, London, 1929).

Whitrow 80   G. J. Whitrow, "The Natural Philosophy of Time"
                      (Oxford University Press, New York, 1980).

CHAPTER 12

Aquinas 81   St. Thomas Aquinas, "Summa Theologica,
                      Vol. I," English translation (Christian Classics,
                      Westminster, MD, 1981).

Augustine 61   St. Augustine, "Confessions," R. S. Pine-Coffin,
                      translator (Penguin Books, Baltimore, 1961).

Balslev 83   A. Balslev, "A Study of Time in Indian
                      Philosophy" (Otto Harrassowitz, Wiesbaden, 1983).

Brooke 46   R. Brooke, "The Poetical Works of Rupert
                      Brooke," edited by Geoffrey Keynes (Faber and
                      Faber, London, 1946.

Chu Ta-kao 82   Chu Ta-kao, translator, "Tao te Ching" (Mandala
                      Books, Boston, 1982).

Columbia 83   "The Concise Columbia Encyclopedia" (Columbia
                      University Press, New York, 1983).

Eliot 43   T. S. Eliot, "Four Quartets" (Harcourt Brace
                      Jovanovich, Orlando, 1943).

Gilson 94   E. Gilson, "The Christian Philosophy of
                      St. Thomas Aquinas" (University of Notre Dame
                      Press, Notre Dame, IN, 1994).

Halpern 90   P. Halpern, "Time Journeys" (McGraw-Hill, New
                      York, 1990).

Kaltenmark 69   M. Kaltenmark, "Lao Tzu and Taoism,"
                      R. Greaves, translator (Stanford University Press,
                      Stanford, 1969).

Kierkegaard 80   S. Kierkegaard, "Concept of Anxiety" (Princeton
                      University Press, Princeton, 1980).

Manchester 93   P. Manchester, "Time in Christianity" in "Religion
                      and Time," editors A. N. Balslev and
                      J. N. Mohanty (E. J. Brill, Leiden and New York,
                      1993).

Neville 93   R. C. Neville, "Eternity and Time's Flow" (State
                      University of New York Press, Albany, 1993).

Pande 93

G. C. Pande, " Time in Buddhism" in "Religion and Time," editors A. N. Balslev and J. N. Mohanty (E. J. Brill, Leiden and New York, 1993).

Prabhavananda and Isherwood 70

Swami Prabhavananda and C. Isherwood, translators, "Crest-Jewel of Discrimination" (New American Library, Mentor Books, New York, 1970).

Rosen 91

J. Rosen, private communication, 1991.

von Franz 81

M. von Franz, "Time and Synchronicity in Analytic Psychology," in "The Voices of Time," editor J. T. Fraser (University of Massachusetts Press, Amherst, 1981).

Welch 57

H. Welch, "Taoism, The Parting of the Way" (Beacon Press, Boston, 1957).

CHAPTER 13

Balslev 83

A. N. Balslev, "A Study of Time in Indian Philosophy," (Otto Harrassowitz, Wiesbaden, 1983).

Beardsley 91

T. Beardsley, Scientific American, November, 1991, p. 30.

Broad 91

W. J. Broad, New York Times, June 18, 1991, p. C1.

Broad 94

W. J. Broad, New York Times, January 15, 1994, p. C1.

Browne 94

M. W. Browne, New York Times, September 20, 1994, p. C1.

Chapman and Morrison 91

C. R. Chapman and D. Morrison, quoted in New York Times, June 18, 1991, p. C1.

Denbigh 81

K. G. Denbigh, "Three Concepts of Time," (Springer-Verlag, New York, 1981).

Drake and Sobel 92

F. Drake and D. Sobel, "Is Anyone out There?" (Delacorte Press, New York, 1992).

Dyson 79

F. J. Dyson, "Time without End: Physics and Biology in and Open Universe," Reviews of Modern Physics, Vol. 51, July, 1979, p. 447.

Dyson 88

F. J. Dyson, "Will Man Survive in the Cosmos?" The Washington Post, April 3, 1988.

Fagg 88

L. W. Fagg, "The Universe: Seeking Life in the Cosmic Haystack," The Washington Post, August 21, 1988.

Fraser 81

J. T. Fraser, "The Genesis and Evolution of Time," (University of Massachusetts Press, Amherst, 1981).

Hawking 88	S. W. Hawking, "A Brief History of Time," (Bantam Books, New York, 1988).
Jastrow 80	R. Jastrow, "Until the Sun Dies," lecture, conference of Institute on Religion in an Age of Science on "Change, Aging, and the Passage of Time," Star Island, NH, 1980.
Laymon 71	C. M. Laymon, editor, "The Interpreter's One-Volume Commentary on the Bible," (Abingdon Press, New York, 1971), p. 437.
Morrison 90	D. Morrison, Sky and Telescope, March, 1990, p. 261.
Naeye 92	R. Naeye, Sky and Telescope, November, 1992, p. 507.
Pagels 85	H. Pagels, "Perfect Symmetry" (Simon and Schuster, New York, 1985).
Sauson 87	G. Sauson, lecture at Seminar: "Is There Life in Outer Space?" Smithsonian Institution, Feb. 1987.
Schmitz-Moormann 92	K. Schmitz-Moormann, "Evolution and Redemption," lecture, conference on Cosmos and Creation, Loyola College, Baltimore, 1992.
Teilhard de Chardin 68	P. Teilhard de Chardin, "Turmoil or Genesis?" in "Science and Religion," editor I. Barbour (Harper and Row, New York, 1968).
Trefil 87	J. Trefil, lecture at Seminar: "Is There Life in Outer Space?" Smithsonian Institution, Feb. 1987.
Wilford 94	J. N. Wilford, New York Times, January 25, 1994, p. C5.

CHAPTER 14

Anderson 66	B. W. Anderson, "Understanding the Old Testament" (Prentice-Hall, Inc., Englewood Cliffs, NJ, 1966).
Becker 73	E. Becker, "The Denial of Death" (Free Press, Macmillan, New York, 1973).
Bhargava 92	P. M. Bhargava, commentary, conference of International Society for the Study of Time on "Time and Life," Cerisy-la-Salle, France, 1992.
Bowker 91	J. Bowker, "The Meanings of Death" (Cambridge University Press, Cambridge, 1991).
Budge 89	E. A. W. Budge, "The Book of the Dead" (Clays Ltd. (Arkana), London, 1989).
Campbell 88	J. Campbell, "The Power of Myth," (Doubleday, New York, 1988).

Deutsch 68

E. Deutsch, translator, "The Bhagavad Gita" (Holt, Rinehart, and Winston, New York, 1968).

Enright 87

D. J. Enright, editor, "The Oxford Book of Death" (Oxford University Press, New York, 1987).

Goodman 93

L. E. Goodman, "Time in Islam," in "Religion and Time," editors A. N. Balslev and J. N. Mohanty (E. J. Brill, New York, 1993).

Freemantle and Trungpa 75

F. Freemantle and C. Trungpa, "The Tibetan Book of the Dead" (Shambhala Publications, Inc., Berkeley, CA, 1975).

Halpern 90

P. Halpern, "Time Journeys" (McGraw-Hill, New York, 1990).

Hartocollis 83

P. Hartocollis, "Time and Timelessness" (International Universities Press, New York, 1983).

Heidegger 62

M. Heidegger, "Being and Time," translators J. Macquarrie and E. Robinson (Harper and Row, New York, 1962).

Hopkins 71

T. J. Hopkins, "The Hindu Religious Tradition" (Dickenson Publishing Co., Encino, CA, 1971).

Kaltenmark 69

M. Kaltenmark, "Lao Tzu and Taoism" (Stanford University Press, Stanford, CA, 1969).

Kee et al. 65

H. C. Kee, F. W. Young, and K. Froehlich, "Understanding the New Testament" (Prentice-Hall, Inc., Englewood Cliffs, NJ, 1965).

Keith 74

A. B. Keith, "Buddhist Philosophy in India and Ceylon" (Gordon Press, New York, 1974).

Mann 55

T. Mann, "The Magic Mountain," translator H. T. Lowe-Porter (Alfred Knopf, Inc., New York, 1955).

Moody 76

R. A. Moody, "Life after Life" (Bantam Books, New York, 1976).

Moody 77

R. A. Moody, "Reflections on Life After Life" (Bantam Books, New York, 1977).

CHAPTER 15

Augustine 61

St. Augustine, "Confessions," R. S. Pine-Coffin, translator (Penguin Books, Baltimore, 1961).

Kierkegaard 57

S. Kierkegaard, "The Concept of Dread," W. Lowrie, translator (Princeton University Press, Princeton, 1957).

Kummel 81

F. Kummel, "Time as Succession and the Problem of Duration," in "The Voices of Time," editor J. T. Fraser (University of Massachusetts Press, Amherst, 1981).

Peirce 75

C. S. Peirce, "What Pragmatism is," in C. Sherover, "The Human Experience of Time," (New York University Press, New York, 1975).

Santayana 75

G. Santayana, "The Realm of Matter," in C. Sherover, "The Human Experience of Time," (New York University Press, New York, 1975).

Sherover 75

C. Sherover, "The Human Experience of Time," (New York University Press, New York, 1975).

CHAPTER 16

Barbour 74

I. G. Barbour, "Myths, Models, and Paradigms," (Harper and Row, New York, 1974).

Capra 77

F. Capra, "The Tao of Physics," (Bantam Books, New York, 1977).

Denbigh 81

K. G. Denbigh, "Three Concepts of Time," (Springer-Verlag, New York, 1981).

Eliade 71

M. Eliade, "The Myth of the Eternal Return," (Princeton University Press, 1971).

Levi 84

Prof. G. Levi, Department of Psychology, University of Chicago, private communication, 1984.

McTaggart 27

J. M. E. McTaggart, "The Nature of Existence," (Cambridge University Press, Cambridge, 1927).

Park 80

D. Park, "Image of Eternity," (University of Massachusetts Press, Amherst, 1980).

Sherover 89

C. M. Sherover, "Concept of Time in Western Thought," Smithsonian Lecture, June, 1989.

CHAPTER 17

Alverson 92

H. Alverson, "Cross-Language Universals in the Experience/Expression of Time," lecture, conference of International Society for the Study of Time on "Time and Life," Cerisy-la-Salle, France, 1992.

Alverson 94

H. Alverson, "Semantics and Experience: Universal Metaphors of Time in English, Mandarin, Hindi, and Sesotho" (Johns Hopkins University Press, Baltimore, 1994).

Eddington 29

A. S. Eddington, "The Nature of the Physical World," (Macmillan Inc., New York, 1929).

Fagg 85

L. W. Fagg, "Two Faces of Time," (Quest Books, Theosophical Publishing House, Wheaton, IL, 1985).

Rosen 91

J. Rosen, "The Capricious Cosmos," (Macmillan Inc., New York, 1991).

Schweitzer 53   A. Schweitzer, "Out of My Life and Thought," Mentor Books, New York, 1953).

Sherover 75   C. Sherover, "The Human Experience of Time," (New York University Press, New York, 1975).

Whitrow 80   G. J. Whitrow, "The Natural Philosophy of Time," (Clarendon Press, Oxford, 1980).

Index

Lawrence W. Fagg is a Research Professor in Nuclear Physics at the Catholic University of America. He holds a master's degree in religion and is a Fellow of the American Physical Society, an Academic Fellow and former vice president of the Institute on Religion in an Age of Science, and a member of the International Society for the Study of Time. Professor Fagg is the author of *Two Faces of Time* and *Electromagnetism and the Sacred*, as well as many articles on time in science and religion.

Library of Congress Cataloging-in-Publication Data
Fagg, Lawrence W.
The becoming of time: integrating physical and religious time /
by Lawrence W. Fagg.   p. cm.
Originally published: Atlanta, Ga. : Scholars Press, ©1995.
Includes bibliographical references and index.
ISBN 0-8223-3144-6 (pbk. : alk. paper)
1. Time 2. Time—Religious aspects. I. Title.
BD638.F33 2002   115—dc21